)E

Across a slip of ocean lies South Carolina, but for the handful of families of Yamacraw Island, America is a world away. For years the people of this haunting, beautiful island lived proudly from the sea, but the waste from industry threatens their very existence unless, somehow, they can learn a new life. But they will learn nothing without someone to teach them, and their school has no teacher. This is based on the inspirational story of Pat Conroy's year teaching the children of an impoverished island off the South Carolina coast.

THE WATER IS WIDE

Pat Conroy

EAGLE LARGE PRINT
Curley Publishing Inc.

Library of Congress Cataloging-in-Publication Data

Conroy, Pat.
  The water is wide / Pat Conroy.
    p. cm.—(Eagle large print)
  ISBN 0–7927–0815–6 (lg. print).—ISBN 0–7927–0816–4 (pbk. :lg. print)
  1. Yamacraw Elementary School.   2. Afro-Americans—Education
  (Elementary)—South Carolina.   3. Large type books.   I. Title.
  II. Series.
  LC2852.Y3C6   1992   91–20701
  372.9'757—dc20   CIP

Published in Large Print by arrangement with Houghton Mifflin Company in the United States and territories and Canada.

Distributed in the United States and Canada by Curley Publishing, Inc.

Printed in Great Britain

This book is dedicated to my wife
Barbara Bolling Conroy

The water is wide,
I cannot get o'er,
Neither have I wings to fly.
Get me a boat that can carry two,
And both shall cross,
My true love and I.

British folk song

The river is deep, the river is wide,
Milk and honey on the other side.

'Michael, Row the Boat Ashore'

ACKNOWLEDGMENTS

To Peg and Don Conroy, Carol, Mike, Kathy, Jim, Tim, and Tom for their dedication under fire. Also Margaret Stanton, my grandmother, and my daughters, Jessica, Melissa, and Megan.

To my following friends in Beaufort: Tut, Sarah Ellen, Bruce, and Melinda Harper; John, Ruby Ellis, Dale, Jan, Danner, and Betty Hryharrow; Papa and Mama Wall; Bucky Wall; Connie and Larry Rowland; John and Nip Cook; Freddie and Lindsay Trask; George and Connie Trask; the Scheins; Tim and Diane Belk; George and Jane Garbade; Lucy and Ridge Hall; Mike and Beth Jones; Herbert, Harriet, Billy, and Paul Keyserling; Richie and Aldie Matta; Ev and Ann Cooper; Jeff Greene; Henry Burke; Millen Ellis; Charles and Juanita Washington; Courtney and Elizabeth Siceloff; John Gadsden; Roy and Rose Lee; Mike McEachern; Frenchie Dawes; Miracyl Damon; Grady Lights; Pat Youngblood; Jet Ragsdale; the Ficklings; the Combses; the Delgados; the Dowlings; Marian Etheridge; Shep Trask.

Also thanks to Bernie and Martha Schein, Bill Dufford, Gene Norris, Betsy Geddes, George and Miriam Sklar; Jim and Vivian Strand; Jim and Annie Roe; Nugent and Elizabeth Courvoisie; Luke and Mary Brown; John and Clarissa Doyle; Linda Williams; K. Z. Chavis; Roy Bohon and Dot Routh; Susan Cooler; Jan and Ted Nichols; Bruce and Carol Fader; Stanley Kravit; Betsy Fancher; Joe Cumming; Carl and Nancy Turner; Herman Blake; Jim Ford; Joe Sanfort; Chuck Haffly; Allen Carlson; Frank Smith; John Rickford; Tim Biancalana; Dave

Morrison; Ed Flaherty; Jeff Hershey; Jeff Pomerantz; Dave Cannon; Allen Minor; Beau and Julie Bridges; Beppie and Marschall Smith; Dick and Carol Larsen; Dick and Marie Caristi.

Ernest Hollings, Henry Chambers, the Colquhouns; the Samses; the Aimars; Ann and Rick Pollitzer; the Hendricks brothers; the Becks; the Parkers; the Randels; the Zachowskis; George Westerfield; Harrison Drinkwater; Joe Golden; Joe and Jean Jones.

Julian Bach, Wendy Weil, Shannon Purves, Anne Barrett, Anita McClellan.

The Southern Regional Council; The N. E. A. DuShane Fund, and the Leadership Development Program of the Ford Foundation.

Special thanks to Richie Matta, Zack Sklar, Bob and Emma Lee Criddle, and the people and children of the island.

CHAPTER ONE

The southern school superintendent is a kind of remote deity who breathes the purer air of Mount Parnassus. The teachers see him only on those august occasions when they need to be reminded of the nobility of their calling. The powers of a superintendent are considerable. He hires and fires, manipulates the board of education, handles a staggering amount of money, and maintains the precarious existence of the status quo. Beaufort, South Carolina's superintendent Dr. Henry Piedmont, had been in Beaufort for only a year when I went to see him. He had a reputation of being tough, capable, and honest. A friend told me that Piedmont took crap from no man.

I walked into his office, introduced myself, chatted briefly, then told him I wanted to teach on Yamacraw Island. He gave me a hard stare and said, 'Son, you are a godsend.' I sat in the chair rigidly analyzing my new status. 'I have prayed at night,' he continued, 'for an answer to the problems confronting Yamacraw Island. I have worried myself almost sick. And to think you would walk right into my office and offer to teach those poor colored children on that island. It just goes to show you that God works in mysterious ways.'

'I don't know if God had anything to do with it, Doctor. I applied for the Peace Corps and haven't heard. Yamacraw seemed like a viable alternative.'

'Son, you can do more good at Yamacraw than you could ever do in the Peace Corps. And you would be helping Americans, Pat. And I, for one, think it's very important to help Americans.'

'So do I, Doctor.'

We chatted on about the problems of the island. Then he said, 'You mentioned that God had nothing to do with your decision to go to Yamacraw, Pat. You remind me of myself when I was your age. Of course, I came up the hard way. My folks worked in a mill. Good people, both of them. Simple people, but God-fearing. My mother was a saint. A saint on earth. I worked in the mill, too. Even after I graduated from college, I went back to the mill in a supervisory capacity. But I wasn't happy, Pat. Something was missing. One night I was working late at the mill. I stepped outside the mill and looked up at the stars. I went toward the edge of the forest and fell to my knees. I prayed to Jesus and asked him what he wanted me to do in my life. And do you know what?'

'No, sir, what?'

Then Dr. Piedmont leaned forward in his seat, his eyes transformed with spiritual intensity.

'He told me what to do that very night. He told me, "Henry, leave the mill. Go into education and help boys to go to college. Help them to be something. Go back to school, Henry, and get an advanced degree.' So I went to Columbia University, one of the great universities of the world. I emerged with a doctorate. I was the first boy from my town who was ever called Doctor.'

I added wittily, 'That's nice, Doctor.'

'You remind me of that boy I was, Pat. Do you know why you came to me today?'

'Yes, sir, I want to teach at Yamacraw.'

'No, son. Do you know the real reason?'

'No, sir, I guess I don't.'

2

'Jesus,' he said, as if he just found out the stone had been rolled back from the tomb. 'You're too young to realize it now, but Jesus made you come to me today.'

I left his office soon afterward. He had been impressive. He was a powerful figure, very controlled, almost arrogantly confident in his abilities. He stared at me during our entire conversation. From experience I knew his breed. The mill-town kid who scratched his way to the top. Horatio Alger, who knew how to floor a man with a quick chop to the gonads. He was a product of the upcountry of South Carolina, the Bible Belt, sand-lot baseball, knife fights under the bleachers. His pride in his doctorate was almost religious. It was the badge that told the world that he was no longer a common man. Intellectually, he was a thoroughbred. Financially, he was secure. And Jesus was his backer. Jesus, with the grits-and-gravy voice, the shortstop on the mill team, liked ol' Henry Piedmont.

*   *   *

Yamacraw is an island off the South Carolina mainland not far from Savannah, Georgia. The island is fringed with the green, undulating marshes of the southern coast; shrimp boats ply the waters around her and fishermen cast their lines along her bountiful shores. Deer cut through her forests in small silent herds. The great southern oaks stand broodingly on her banks. The island and the waters around her teem with life. There is something eternal and indestructible about the tide-eroded shores and the dark, threatening silences of the swamps in the heart of the island. Yamacraw is beautiful because man has not yet had time to destroy this beauty.

The twentieth century has basically ignored the presence of Yamacraw. The island is populated with black people who depend on the sea and their small farms for a living. Several white families live on the island in a paternalistic, but in many ways symbiotic, relationship with their neighbors. Only one white family actively participates in island life to any perceptible degree. The other three couples have come to the island to enjoy their retirement in the obscurity of the island's remotest corners. Thus far, no bridge connects the island with the mainland, and anyone who sets foot on the island comes by water. The roads of the island are unpaved and rutted by the passage of ox carts, still a major form of transportation. The hand pump serves up questionable water to the black residents who live in their small familiar houses. Sears, Roebuck catalogues perform their classic function in the crudely built privies, which sit, half-hidden, in the tall grasses behind the shacks. Electricity came to the island several years ago. There is something unquestionably moving about the line of utility poles coming across the marsh, moving perhaps because electricity is a bringer of miracles and the journey of the faceless utility poles is such a long one—and such a humane one. But there are no telephones (electricity is enough of a miracle for one century). To call the island you must go to the Beaufort Sheriff's Office and talk to the man who works the radio. Otherwise, Yamacraw remains aloof and apart from the world beyond the river.

It is not a large island, nor an important one, but

4

it represents an era and a segment of history that is rapidly dying in America. The people of the island have changed very little since the Emancipation Proclamation. Indeed, many of them have never heard of this proclamation. They love their island with genuine affection but have watched the young people move to the city, to the lands far away and far removed from Yamacraw. The island is dying, and the people know it.

In the parable of Yamacraw there was a time when the black people supported themselves well, worked hard, and lived up to the sacred tenets laid down in the Protestant ethic. Each morning the strong young men would take to their bateaux and search the shores and inlets for the large clusters of oysters, which the women and old men in the factory shucked into large jars. Yamacraw oysters were world famous. An island legend claims that a czar of Russia once ordered Yamacraw oysters for an imperial banquet. The white people propagate this rumor. The blacks, for the most part, would not know a czar from a fiddler crab, but the oysters were good, and the oyster factories operating on the island provided a substantial living for all the people. Everyone worked and everyone made money. Then a villain appeared. It was an industrial factory situated on a knoll above the Savannah River many miles away from Yamacraw. The villain spewed its excrement into the river, infected the creeks, and as silently as the pull of the tides, the filth crept to the shores of Yamacraw. As every good health inspector knows, the unfortunate consumer who lets an infected oyster slide down his throat is flirting with hepatitis. Someone took samples of the water around Yamacraw, analyzed

5

them under a microscope, and reported the results to the proper officials. Soon after this, little white signs were placed by the oyster banks forbidding anyone to gather the oysters. Ten thousand oysters were now as worthless as grains of sand. No czar would order Yamacraw oysters again. The muddy creatures that had provided the people of the island with a way to keep their families alive were placed under permanent quarantine.

Since a factory is soulless and faceless, it could not be moved to understand the destruction its coming had wrought. When the oysters became contaminated, the island's only industry folded almost immediately. The great migration began. A steady flow of people faced with starvation moved toward the cities. They left in search of jobs. Few cities had any intemperate demand for professional oyster-shuckers, but the people were somehow assimilated. The population of the island diminished considerably. Houses surrendered their tenants to the city and signs of sudden departure were rife in the interiors of deserted homes. Over 300 people left the island. They left reluctantly, but left permanently and returned only on sporadic visits to pay homage to the relatives too old or too stubborn to leave. As the oysters died, so did the people.

*　　　*　　　*

My neck has lightened several shades since former times, or at least I like to think it has. My early years, darkened by the shadows and regional superstitions of a bona fide cracker boy, act as a sobering agent during the execrable periods of self-righteousness that I inflict on those around me. Sometimes it is good for me to reflect on the Neanderthal period of my youth, when I rode in the backseat of a '57 Chevrolet along a night-blackened Carolina road hunting for blacks to hit with rotten watermelons tossed from the window of the speeding car, as they walked the shoulder of thin backroads. We called this intrepid form of entertainment 'nigger-knocking,' and it was great fun during the carnival of blind hatred I participated joyfully in during my first couple of years in high school.

Those were the years when the word *nigger* felt good to my tongue, for my mother raised her children to say *colored* and to bow our heads at the spoken name of Jesus. My mother taught that only white trash used the more explosive, more satisfying epithet to describe black people. *Nigger* possessed the mystery and lure of forbidden fruit and I overused it in the snickering clusters of white friends who helped my growing up.

The early years were nomadic ones. Dad's pursuit of greatness in the Marine Corps carried us into some of the more notable swamplands of the East Coast. I attended Catholic schools with mystical names like the Infant of Prague and the Annunciation, as Dad transferred from Marine base to desolate Marine base, or when we retired to my mother's family home in Atlanta when the nation called my father to war. Mom's people hailed originally from the northeast mountains of Alabama, while Dad's greased the railroad cars in Chicago, but attitudinally they could have used the same sheet at a Klan rally.

I loved the smooth-watered fifties, when I

7

worried about the top-ten tunes and the homecoming queen, when I looked to Elvis for salvation, when the sharp dichotomy between black and white lay fallow and unchallenged, and when the World Series still was the most critical event of the year. The sixties brought this spindly-legged dream to its knees and the fall of the dream buried the joy of that blue-eyed youth forever.

Yet there were days that haunted the decade and presaged the tumultuous changes of the later sixties. By some miracle of chance, I was playing a high school basketball game in Greensboro, North Carolina, on the day that black students entered a dime store for the first nationally significant sit-in demonstration. I was walking past the store on the way to my hotel when I heard the drone of the angry white crowd. Word spread along the street that the niggers were up to something, and a crowd started milling around the store. With rolled-up sleeves and the Brylcreem look of the period, the mob soon became a ludicrous caricature of an entire society. The women had sharp, aquiline noses. I remember that. Everyone was surprised and enraged by the usurpation of this inalienable Caucasian right to park one's ass on a leather stool and drink a Coke. I moved quickly out of the area, following a Conroy law of survival that says that restless mobs have a way of drawing trouble and cops—although the cops would not have bothered me on this day, I realized later. It would be nice to report that this event transformed me into a crusader for civil rights, but it did not. It did very little for me.

I moved to Beaufort, South Carolina, in the early sixties, a town fed by warm salt tides and cooled by mild winds from the sea; a somnolent town built on a high bluff where a river snaked fortuitously. I was tired of moving every year, of changing home and environment with every new set of orders, of uprooting simply because my father was a nomad traveling under a different name and occupation. So we came to Beaufort, a town I grew to love with passion and without apology for its serenity, for its splendidly languid pace, and for its profound and infinite beauty. It was a place of hushed, fragrant gardens, silent streets, and large ante-bellum houses. My father flew jets in its skies and I went to the local segregated high school, courted the daughter of the Baptist minister, and tried to master the fast break and the quick jump shot. I lived in the security of a town founded in the sixteenth century, but in the world beyond it walked John F. Kennedy, the inexorable movement of black people coming up the road in search of the promised American grail, the television performances of Bull Connor, the snarling dogs, the fire hoses, the smoking names of Montgomery, Columbus, Monroe, and Birmingham.

Having cast my lot with Beaufort, I migrated to college seventy miles up the road. I entered The Citadel, the military college of South Carolina, where for four years I marched to breakfast, saluted my superiors, was awakened by buglers, and continued my worship of the jock, the basketball, and the school fight song, 'Dixie.' For four years I did not think about the world outside the gates. Myopic and color blind, I could not be a flashy, ascotted pilot like my father, so I opted for teaching and Beaufort. At graduation I headed back down Highway 17 to begin my life teaching in the same

9

high school that had spewed me forth several years before. But there was a difference this time: the purity of the student body was forever tainted. Thanks to the dastardly progression of law, black students now peppered the snow-white Elysium that once had harbored me.

I loved teaching in high school. I dwelt amidst the fascists and the flag-wavers in relative obscurity and I liked the students, who daily trooped into my class chewing gum and popping pimples. Painfully aware of my youth, I tried to belie my twenty-one years by acting mature and seasoned by experience. My act held up, until one horrid day when I asked a government class what was causing the peculiar smell that hovered in the room. A sharp-eyed pupil pointed out that I had stepped in a pile of dog crap and had tracked it around the room. Thus died maturity. I reveled in class discussion and the Socratic method of drawing substance out of calcified minds untrained to think. I would argue lamely for peace in Vietnam while my students clamored for the H-bombing of Hanoi and the subsequent obliteration of Moscow and Peking. They called me a Communist for not being pro-war; they called me a coward for my failure to rise to the defense of my country in its hour of greatest peril. When I protested that I saw very little threat posed by the government of North Vietnam to the United States, they mumbled ominously that I would eat several hundred pounds of crow when swarms of fanatical reds waded ashore at San Francisco Bay. These were children of the South just as I was. They were products of homes where the flag was cherished like Veronica's veil, where the military was the pluperfect defender of honor, justice, and hymens, and where conservatism was a mandate of life, not merely a political philosophy.

Each night I joined my best friends, George Garbade, Mike Jones, and Bernie Schein, in front of the television for the evening news. The war in Vietnam ate people on film. The seven o'clock news smoked with napalm and bodies. After the news, we held disorganized, vehement debates. George hailed from Ridgeland, South Carolina, a rural community so conservative that it made Beaufort look like a hotbed of liberalism. Mike was a divinity student who had dropped out for a year to reflect upon his impending life of spirituality among the hypocritical flocks that would be assigned to him. Bernie Schein was the twenty-three-year-old principal of a tiny school in the next county. After the news the four of us argued until the late hours of night, exposing half-hidden prejudices. We mercilessly pounced on the member of the group who dared utter a belief without foundation or without rational credibility. Those gatherings were group confessions of guilt, of cynicism, of rudderless idealism, and ultimately of hope. At the end of the year, the four of us went to Europe with our new-found credo. The world was good, we said, and it only needed minor adjustment. People were basically good, we asserted with disgusting smugness.

In Germany I toured the concentration camp at Dachau and looked at the pictures of the piled bodies, starved and faceless, being shoved by bulldozers into mass burial pits. I stared at the furnace where Jews were reduced to piles of Jewish ash and felt that I stood on holy ground, a monument to the infinite inhumanity of man and

11

society gone insane, a ground washed by thousands of gallons of human blood, a ground astir with ghosts and memories, of Jews and Germans trapped in a drama so horrible and unreal that the world could never have the same purity again. The imprint of Dachau branded me indelibly and caused me to suffer the miscarriage of my hopeful philosophy. If man was good, then Dachau could never have happened. Simple as that. In a hotel in Paris George, Bernie, and Mike argued anew for the basic goodness of man, but I felt that I had extracted the essential message of Dachau and that our philosophy was simply an exercise of innocence and nothing more. Nor could all the paint and clay of the Louvre dim the memory of one photograph: of a mother leading her small children to the gas chamber.

I was getting tired of my own innocence. The year was 1968 and something had happened to me in April that also seemed to change my life. When the lone rifleman murdered Martin Luther King, Jr., in Memphis, the reaction among the students of Beaufort High School was explosive in its generation of raw, naked emotion. The white students, who composed the large majority of the student body, for the most part reacted passively to the event. Of course the village rednecks took vicious delight in calling Mrs. King a 'black widow' and otherwise celebrating the death of this symbol of civil rights. A contingent of black students went to the principal in a futile attempt to get him to lower the flag to half-mast. Fearing community reaction, he predictably refused and closed his office to any further discussion of the matter. Since the faculty was all white, the black students walked

12

the halls in silence, tears of frustration rolling down their cheeks and unspoken bitterness written on their faces in their inability to communicate their feelings to their white teachers.

On the day King was buried the blacks assembled at recess in their accustomed place on the breezeway at the side of the school. Apartheid was an unwritten law and there was very little crossing over. One of my duties as a teacher that year was to patrol that part of the campus where the black students congregated. It was in this capacity that I learned of the problems facing the blacks at the school. I talked and joked with them at recess, or at least I talked to most of them. One small, articulate group of girls eyed me with unconcealed hostility the entire year and I knew intuitively that in all their lives they would never approach a white man teacher without suspicion. I heard one of them say once that 'only stupid nigger boys talk to Conroy.'

On this momentous, hysteric day, however, these girls came for me. I was talking to some of the boys and did not immediately see the girls as they swarmed around me. The first to speak was Lily Smalls, a huge, imposing woman who the year before had beaten the hell out of a white girl who had made the mistake of calling her nigger. People still called her nigger but they made damn sure that Lily was not within earshot when they did. Lily shouted at me, 'What are you doing here, white man? You sent here by the white man to make sure we don't do anything de-structive?' Her friend Liz had inched closer to me and I felt the hot moisture of her breath on my neck. She sprayed me with spittle as she yelled, 'Why don't you get back with the rest of those honkies and let us cry in peace? We don't need you to tell us how sorry you are or how much it disturbs you to see us upset. Just get your white ass back into that school and leave us alone.'

'Wait!' another girl screamed. 'I want to hear him say how sorry he is. I want to hear it. Say it. Say it.'

I tried to say something, something redemptive or purgative, but no sound came from my throat. My vocal chords were not functioning well in this crisis. A sea of voices surrounded me, washed over me, and sucked me into a great whirlpool of sound and confusion. Bodies pressed up against me. A girl dug her nails into my arm until blood was drawn. Another girl screamed into my ear that the white bastards would kill all the black people in America. Lily's voice shouted, 'You white folks are happy to see Martin Luther King get shot, but you wait and see who takes his place. We gonna get mean, Conroy, and we ain't gonna take shit from no whitey. You can tell all of your friends that the days of nonviolence and prayin' for the white cat that beats you over the head is over. Man, they are gone, gone . . .' Then Lily wept. She stood there, almost nose to nose with me, and cried as though her soul was trying to wrench free of the prison of her body, as if all the tomorrows in the world were not worth the pain she felt right now.

But as she cried, other voices rose to fill the void of her silence. A boy pressed his mouth close to my left ear and rasped, 'We are gonna burn this town down tonight. We gonna burn every white man with it.' A voice behind me wailed in rhythmic cadences a strangely moving lamentation, 'Oh God, why can't they leave us be? Why can't they treat us right? Why can't they love us like Jesus taught? Why do they hate us? Why do they hate black

14

people?' More fingernails in my arm. Someone reached up and scratched my neck. I thought I felt strong fingers close about my throat, then release it suddenly. The entire mob was soon convulsed with raw, demonstrative sorrow. 'Martin's dead, Martin's dead, Martin's dead,' a voice cried. 'The whites eat shit,' said a boy. 'Fuck you, Conroy,' said a girl. And the bell, mercifully, rang.

At a later date I heard the black kids laughing and snickering when Lurleen Wallace died of cancer. I questioned the appropriateness of their response as compared to the response of the crackers when King died. 'She was a racist,' came the unanimous reply. So it was a little before Dachau that the mortar of cynicism was hardening. I was becoming convinced that the world was a colorful, variegated grab bag full of bastards.

But the shadow that hovered over me, white guilt, still had to be reckoned with. So in the days after King's assassination, greatly moved by the death of one I had admired so much, I lobbied for a course in black history in a school 90 per cent white. At that time, a black-history course was as common as a course in necrophilia. Now, with the times changing so rapidly, these courses have proliferated over the entire state. It seemed like big stuff then. I nursed the course through mild disapproval, coddled it through every pitfall encountered on the way up proper channels, argued with timorous authorities, wrote out a magnificent course outline, then realized I did not know a single thing about the history of black people in America. The course was mildly successful, but more as a symbol of the great flow of time than as a significant classroom experience. The year was fraught with

15

embittering experiences for me with some of my fellow teachers. One lady with the delicate sweetness of a lemon told me that her father had required her to carry a gun when she was growing up to protect herself from lecherous attacks by black men. That, she told me, was the only nigger history she knew or needed to know.

The same year the very coach that once had coached me in football relieved me of my job of junior-varsity basketball coach because he felt I favored the 'coloreds.' As a senior I had surmised that this coach had a brain the size and density of a Ping-Pong ball, so it came as no great surprise when he banished me forever from his gymnasium. But I was tired of fighting. Most of the teachers remained concerned and dedicated, and I respected them greatly for their efforts. Strange urges and a vague, restless energy made me look for something new and even adventurous. It was here that my good friend Bernie changed my life.

Bernie Schein first told me about the job-opening on Yamacraw Island. He is one year older than I am and had been principal of an elementary school for three years. His first job, when he got out of Newberry College, was as principal of Yemassee Elementary School. Yemassee is a bunion of a town not far from Beaufort. Trains stop there. That is Yemassee's singular mark of notoriety. Nothing else happens there. Bernie somehow talked the superintendent of Hampton County into letting him have the job. He had no qualifications, no experience, and no aptitude in administration, but since Bernie could talk a Baptist into burning a Bible, the superintendent had no other choice. Bernie took a room in a fly-by-night hotel, fought

16

off an army of roaches, ate hamburgers for lunch and supper, watched the late movie every night, and became a great principal. He discovered an infallible formula: choose a town so dismal that the only thing left is study and hard work. When several of his friends started teaching in Beaufort, Bernie got a job as principal of Port Royal Elementary School, right outside the city limits. He felt that it was time for him to leave Yemassee. A rumor had it that Bernie was having an affair with a fifty-year-old teacher on his staff, and several Klansmen in the community were looking at this liberal Jewish principal with cross-burning eyes.

We were inseparable from the beginning. We agreed with each other that Vietnam was intolerable, that the South had shit on the heads of the blacks, that the North was just as bad. Eugene McCarthy was an Arthurian figure elevated to knighthood in a moment of crisis; it was tough being a Jew in the South; it was tough being a Jew anywhere; we did not like Hitler, Strom Thurmond, Mendel Rivers, warm beer, or going to Atlanta for dates on the weekend. It was coming back from Atlanta that Bernie mentioned the job on Yamacraw Island. Since Bernie and I entertained delusions that we would somehow save the world, or at least a small portion of it, the idea of our own island, free from administrative supervision, appealed to us very much. Bernie told me what he knew about Yamacraw.

'The school is all black. They've had two black teachers out there who evidently hate each other's guts. The kids can't read very well. Same old story. Lack of materials, lack of motivation. Cut off from the outside world. I've never been over there, Pat,

17

but we can borrow a boat and visit the island to see if we like it.'

'Can you drive a boat, Bernie?' I asked.

'Hell, no. Can you?' he answered.

'Nope.'

'Then I'll ask someone about the job to see if we can both go over there for a year.'

The next day Bernie talked to the official hiring man of the county. When he asked about chances for getting the job on the island, several members of the administrative staff hooted him out of the office. Bernie reported back that the stupid sons of bitches did not even listen to him make his sales pitch. Screw them, we both said, and sent in our application to the Peace Corps. We had a tough time deciding whether we wanted to save Africa or Asia. We finally chose Africa. Within a month, the Peace Corps accepted Bernie for a project in Jamaica. I waited to hear. Months passed. No word from the Peace Corps. Toward the end of each school term, my draft board gets a restless desire to know of my intentions for the following year. I did not wish to return to the high school. I was through with teachers more concerned with the length of mini-skirts and hair than with education. But I certainly did not wish to join the Marine Corps, romp about the marshes of Parris Island, and emerge the product of a military system I had come to loathe. So I decided to go to the superintendent and ask about Yamacraw Island.

CHAPTER TWO

After the administration became reasonably convinced that I was seriously thinking about the job, they promised to help me in every way possible. Ezra Bennington, the elderly deputy superintendent, showed special interest in my teaching on the island. Before the consolidation of Beaufort County schools systems into one smoothly coordinated integer (at least in theory) Bennington had been in command of the Bluffton district, of which Yamacraw was a part. For over thirty years he had ruled his district like a Persian satrap. With consolidation he had had to accept the arrival of a more powerful presence in his midst and Dr. Piedmont had taken particular delight in letting his subordinates know that he was sitting with both buttocks solidly planted on the throne. Ezra had taken his fall from Eden gracefully, at least externally. But he still kept a vigilant eye on his old province of Bluffton, going over lists of new teachers, calling the principal who once worked under him to give unsolicited advice. When he learned that I was thinking about teaching on Yamacraw, he insisted that he be allowed to take me around the island.

Ezra Bennington was the perfect name for him. He had a finely chiseled, fashionably wrinkled face that suggested integrity and character. His blue eyes were liquid and innocent. A gray mane covered his head. Ezra was Everyman's grandfather. He would look good dressed in a white linen suit, rocking on a high verandah, shouting orders to

Negroes working in the garden below him. Ezra looked, talked, and acted like a huge southern cliché, a parody who was unaware that his type had been catalogued and identified over and over again. Yet it is impossible to dislike men like Ezra. I have met a hundred of them in my life and, despite myself, have liked every one of them.

Ezra agreed with the Piedmont formula that I sat on the right hand of the Father for going over to the island. He then said, 'Lord knows how I have tried to help these children, how I've fought to get them educated. As you know, Yamacraw is a problem, Mr Conroy. I have tried to solve it for years and years. I tried to talk teachers into going over there to live. But no one would do it. Mrs. Brown was the first decent teacher I could get. You'll meet her when we go out to the island.'

I asked him, 'Did you ever try to get anyone to commute to the island?'

'Oh, no. You obviously don't know about the waters around Yamacraw. They are very treacherous. During the winter it would be impossible for someone to commute. There are days when no one can get on or off the island.'

'It just seemed like a good answer to me, Mr Bennington. To have teachers commute to the island or to have a large boat to transport the children to the mainland. They have done this in other areas of the United States.'

'It's too far,' Ezra said, shaking his head remorsefully. 'It's just impossible. Just impossible.'

Bennington spoke slowly. Each word rolled off his tongue like a drop of cold honey from the lip of a jar. He was straight and dignified and, jeepers creepers, he seemed like the most sincere human that ever came under the glance of the Lord.

The county hired Andy Pappas to take Ezra and me over to Yamacraw. Andy was a short, fat Greek who ran a gas station in Bluffton. An avid fisherman, he knew the waters around the off-lying islands extremely well. He was the official boatman designated to take school personnel from the mainland to Yamacraw Island and he received twenty-five dollars every time he made the expedition. (The only thing I demanded in exchange for teaching on the island was that the school board buy me a boat for traveling to and from the island.)

During the ride over, I concentrated on learning the water route from Bluffton to Yamacraw. Many sandbars and oyster banks scar the shallows of the saltwater creeks and rivers in lower South Carolina. In high school I had hit a sandbar while water skiing, flipped wildly in the air, and landed painfully on my back. I respected the presence of these latent hazards. I also listened to Bennington. Like many old people's, his conversation constantly reverted to the past, and during the trip he reminisced about his boyhood and his career in education. He was reared, he said, on a prosperous farm in the upper part of the state. He was a southern agrarian, rooted in the rich, black soil of the Carolina midlands. He had farmed for a while, but ultimately decided to exchange the plow for the blackboard. He came to Bluffton as an agricultural teacher, then shifted to administration. An accomplished raconteur, he made Andy giggle hysterically on the trip to Yamacraw by relating stories salted with a rural flavor.

That first visit to the island told me very little

21

about the children I would be teaching. It did serve to introduce me to the leading personalities with whom I would have to deal. A man named Ted Stone met us at the dock. Ted was a powerfully built man with steel gray hair and ice blue eyes. He greeted us matter of factly with a restraint and distance that made me a bit ill at ease. He was friendly enough and courteous enough, but he was aloof and suspicious. According to Bennington, he ruled Yamacraw Island. He had expropriated every job on Yamacraw Island for himself. He was the Game Warden, the Magistrate, the Director of Economic Opportunity, Warden of the Roads, Civil Defense Director, and held countless smaller titles. His wife, Lou, held every job not claimed by her husband. Lou was in her fifties but still had dark brown hair. She was the island postmaster and school-bus driver. Bennington described her as a 'portrait of efficiency.'

We borrowed the civil defense jeep from Mr. Stone. The island had few vehicles and the Stones kept all government transportation nestled under the large shed attached to their house. We drove down the dirt road leaving the Stones' house. Trees, curtained with moss, dipped over the road. Only one car could traverse the road at a time. Andy spoke enthusiastically about hunting on the island. Deer populated the island in sizable herds. We took a left-hand turn at what could be described loosely as an intersection. Four weathered signs nailed to a pine log pointed toward the island's four claims to notoriety: BEACH, SCHOOLHOUSE, LIBRARY, and COOPER RIVER LANDING. We drove past several small shacks. They were in seemingly good repair. One man stood in a field, hoeing his garden. He looked up, waved absently, then returned to his work. Bennington delivered a homily based on this scene.

'These are good people,' he said, 'but they are suspicious of strangers. I've worked with these people for Lord knows how many years. They respect me and trust me. They have never seen you, Mr. Conroy, so they will look upon this entire expedition with suspicion. For all they know you might be a revenuer coming to check on their stills.'

Since I had never entered any community where strangers were greeted as affably as old friends, this information did not disturb me to any perceptible degree.

'Do they bootleg?' I asked.

'They used to,' he replied. 'In fact they used to make right good corn likker, isn't that right, Andy?'

'Damn right,' said Andy. 'No likker ever tasted as good to me as Yamacraw likker. They made the stuff with copper tubing, too. You didn't get your ass blinded if you drank the stuff. 'Course, the revenuers have put most of them out of business.'

'It sounds like a good industry,' I said.

'Yeh, it was,' answered Andy. 'Of course, they did a little drinking themselves. Ain't nobody get drunk as a nigger. 'Specially on Saturday night.'

A pack of skeletal hounds intercepted us at the next house, snapped at the wheels of the jeep, then retreated to their shady refuge under the house. A woman appeared at the door. A small, dark woman. But only for a moment. She did not wave. Bennington then repeated the stranger formula verbatim.

I am not certain what I expected the school to

23

look like. It was a very attractive and simply constructed white frame building. It looked more like a house than a school. The trees around the purlieus of the schoolyard were massive, imposing guardians whose mass added security or mystery (depending on the looker's point of view), to a scene rapidly becoming uncommon in the American South. Bennington gestured to a house on our right, across from the schoolhouse, and said conspiratorially, 'Iris Glover lives there. She has been teaching for thirty-nine years on this island. The people are scared to death of her. She's the island witch doctor. She's liable to put a spell on you if you take the job.'

'I thought she quit the job. I didn't know I'd be taking anyone's place,' I answered.

'Oh, she's retiring. At least the county is retiring her. She's passed the mandatory age. Should have been fired forty years ago.'

Miss Glover's house was immaculately white with bright blue trim on her shutters and door. The blue paint was the universal symbol of recognition of the voodoo people. The paint discouraged demons and spirits from entering a house. Blue paint was to the voodoo people what garlic was to the villagers of Transylvania or what holy water was to the early Christians. The voodoo was a leftover from the African culture of the island blacks. Its modern form is much diluted and infected by Christianity but still has sincere adherents among some blacks in the lowcountry. Without being aware of it, I subconsciously identified Miss Glover as being a prime enemy on the island. This proved to be a false impression.

Bennington glowed like a Christmas bulb when

he spoke of the other teacher. She was his personal discovery. He had championed her arrival on the island. Mrs. Brown appeared at the door of the schoolhouse and welcomed us to Yamacraw Elementory School. A large woman, she had great pendulous bosoms and huge sinewy arms and a handsome, expressive face. She was light-skinned and laughed a great deal. Everything about her seemed exaggerated and blown out of proportion. She treated Mr. Bennington like a nun would treat a visiting bishop. Mrs. Brown greeted me cordially and welcomed me 'overseas.' She told me, 'Things are tough overseas, Mr. Conroy. I'm a missionary over here helping these poor people. Only Jesus and I know how much they need help...' She spoke without a dialect and obviously was not from the island. When I asked her about this, she confided that she was from Georgia but was educated in a very fine private school where the cruder forms of black dialects were frowned upon by the Presbyterian educators who presided over the school. She was not from the island, she assured me. She had come to the island at the insistence of Mr. Bennington.

'Mr. Bennington is the only one who understands the problems of Yamacraw Island. He knows what's wrong,' she said, 'and he knows what to do about them.' She spoke in rhythms. Her speech was exaggerated, going up and down like a piano scale. It almost scanned conversations in iambic pentameter; the words rolled off her tongue in poems.

I tried to talk to some of the children, but they simply gazed at me with shy amusement, then buried their faces in their hands. The children were

25

subdued, passive, and exceedingly polite. They had risen in unison when we walked into the room. They chanted 'good morning' on cue from Mrs. Brown. They folded their hands and sat up straight at their desks. In an effort to achieve the common touch, Bennington walked among the children and cracked a few jokes. They looked at Mrs. Brown, saw that she was laughing, then laughed like hell themselves. Bennington then put his hand on one small boy's head and whispered something in his ear. The boy smiled. Bennington was a fish in water.

It was a yes-sir, no-sir world I had entered. Math and spelling papers hung from the bulletin boards. Everything was Mickey-Mouse neat and virgin clean in the classroom. A map of the world, contributed by a Savannah bank, hung on one wall. Near it was a poster which read: EDUCATION IS THE KEY TO SUCCESS. A picture of a large key drove the point home. On Mrs. Brown's desk was an item that caught and held my eye. It was a leather strap, smooth and very thick. It lay beneath a reading book.

The relationship between Brown and Bennington intrigued me. Bennington represented a dying part of the South: the venerable, hoary-maned administrator who tended his district with the same care and paternalism the master once rendered to his plantation. As I watched him perform his classroom routine, I also observed Mrs. Brown's reaction, a black teacher who nodded her head in agreement every time he opened his mouth to utter some memorable profundity. I could not tell if this was a role she was playing or if she actually believed that Bennington was the word made flesh. Anyway, they went well together. Both of them hated Miss Glover. For some undisclosed reason, Miss Glover was not at school on that day. Bennington and Brown cornered me and proceeded to blame the educational inadequacies of the children on Miss Glover.

'She had been here forty years and the children didn't even know how to use a fork,' said Mrs. Brown.

'Well, Ruth,' Bennington intoned slowly, 'that's why I sent you out here. I knew you could lift these people up.'

'I try, Mr. Bennington. You know I try. But these people don't want to better themselves. Why, Mr. Conroy,' she said, turning to me, 'the parents stay likkered up down there at the club and take the children with them when they do it. Satan smiles at all the sinnin' going on at that club.'

We soon departed. On the trip back I tried to gather my impressions together and come out with a final decision about teaching on the island. Andy handed out encomiums to several productive fishing holes we passed and indicated an osprey's nest on top of a utility pole. Bennington talked about farming. I sat in the back of the boat and decided once and for all to take the job. Yamacraw was a universe of its own. The lushness of the island pleased me and the remarkable isolation of the school appealed to the do-gooder in me. Only a thoroughbred do-gooder can appreciate the feeling, the roseate, dawnlike, and nauseating glow that enveloped me on the return trip that day. I had found a place to absorb my wildest do-gooding tendency. Unhappy do-gooders populate the world because they have not found a Yamacraw all their

27

own. All my apprehensive feelings disappeared. I had made a decision. The last statement I remember that day came from Mr. Bennington.

'Did you notice how well I got along with those children?' he asked.

'Yes,' I answered.

'I've always been able to get along with colored people. They've always loved me.'

★　　★　　★

My first night on Yamacraw Island was spent in a sleeping bag on the schoolroom floor. The forest outside the perimeter of the schoolyard was insane with insect voices and the dark seemed darker than any place I had been before. No streetlamps, no traffic lights, no squeal of brakes, nor any other evidence of city life presented itself that night. Darkness in strange places is always fearful and, lying on the floor that night, sweating from the armpits to the metatarsals from the heat, I felt the fear that comes from being alone in a new environment. When I did get to sleep, I was later awakened by a thunderstorm. Lightning flashed around the island; thunder played its favorite game of scaring the crap out of all the shivering mortals on the earth below. Overall, the night seemed to augur strange things.

But the morning was a time of renewal. The first morning was incredibly bright and tranquil. I awoke, shaved without a mirror, lost several pints of blood, and awaited the arrival of Mrs. Brown and the school bus. Mrs. Brown came first:

'Welcome overseas,' she greeted me.

'Thank you, ma'am. It is great to be here.'

28

'Ho, ho, ho. Don't speak too quick. You are in a snake pit, son. And them snakes are gonna start snappin' at your toes. You're overseas now.'

She then delivered a rather ferocious homily about the handling of colored children by a teacher so obviously white.

'You've got to treat them stern. Tough, you know. You got the older babies. Grades five through eight. Keep them busy with work all the time or they'll run you right out of that there door,' she said. 'I know colored people better than you do. That's because I am one myself. You have to keep your foot on them all the time. Step on them. Step on them every day and keep steppin' on them when they gets out of line. If you have any trouble, Mama Brown will be right next door. We got lots of trees outside, and every tree gets lots of switches. I got some in that cabinet right over there.'

'Thank you,' I said.

The kids arrived at 8 A.M. and swarmed into the class, each of them pausing to murmur a dutiful good-morning. One small fry climbed into a seat only to be accosted by a larger girl who said that he was sitting in her seat. He said something unintelligible (to me). She cuffed his head, he swung a fist, then she drifted into another seat while I watched the whole scene. I think I said something profound like 'now, now.' After this everyone sat erect in his seat appraising me with indirect glances, looking around at one another, then giggling and looking back at me. I felt ludicrously white.

I gave them a little pep talk—one of the rah-rah varieties that is a universal choice of teachers all over the world on the first day of school. It was dull, rambling, and full of those go-go-get-'em-get-'em epigrams concerning the critical need for every human being to live up to his highest potential and to squeeze every possible morsel of knowledge from the textbook. They expected it and nodded their heads in solemn, collective assent.

Not one of them knew my name, but all of them had prior knowledge that a white teacher would preside over them for the year. I printed my name PAT CONROY on the board. I then said my name aloud. When I said 'Conroy' they laughed like hell. Since I saw nothing intrinsically humorous in my last name, I asked them what was so damn funny. This seemed to increase their laughter by several octaves. Several of the kids were trying to pronounce my name. One girl got 'Mr. Corning' out of it, and this was the nearest approximation I heard.

Mama Brown ended my ruminations over the last-name syndrome by trooping her first-through-fourth graders in for the first-day assembly. They marched in single file like a well-drilled squad of soldiers. When all were in their seats, Mama Brown delivered the memorable opening-day address.

'Good morning, babies.'

A few hesitant good-mornings answered her.

'Well, now, babies, that isn't much of an answer for the first day of school. Let's try it again. Good morning, babies.'

'Good morning,' came the still timorous reply.

'Now, babies, I know your voices didn't dry up like ole fruit over the summertime. Let's use them vocal chords. Let me hear you say good morning like you mean it.'

'Good morning!' they shouted loudly. The revival of the educational spirit buried in the inertia of summer had begun, at least for Mama Brown. She took a solid position behind the podium, which was placed somewhat pretentiously in the front of the room for the occasion. She then opened up with a fire-and-brimstone judgment-day sermon like an old circuit preacher who knew well the wrath of an angry God. She exhorted the kids to study hard and keep quiet or face the possibility of incurring the disfavor of the teacher who ruled them.

'Most of you are slow,' she said. 'All of us know that. But there are two of you, Frank and Mary, who could take a test right now and move up a grade or two. That's because you got good brains and use them. The rest of you can't think as good. We know that you know that. Your brains are just slow. But you can learn if you work. You are just lazy, lazy, and lazy people just can't get ahead in life. Of course some of you are even retarded, and that is even worse than being lazy. But we know you can't help being retarded. That just means you have to work even harder than the lazy ones. Now those of you who are retarded know who you are. I don't have to tell you. But retarded people need to be pushed and whipped harder than anyone.'

Here she paused and eyeballed the entire congregation. She then turned to me with an ingratiating smile. 'I now have the privilege of introducing Mr. Patroy to the class. Mr. Patroy will be our new principal this year. He will teach the upper grades in the basics of language co-mmunication and the new math. Mr. Patroy is so good to come over here this year and we are thankful that the Lord brought Mr. Patroy to us. Now I am going to let Mr. Patroy speak to us. Now I am going to let Mr. Patroy get the floor and tell you babies what he has planned.'

I walked up to the podium and gave a brief self-conscious talk about the joys of scholarship, then quickly relinquished the speaker's platform back to Mrs. Brown.

Mrs. Brown turned solemn. 'We are now going to recite the Lord's Prayer,' she said. 'Now the Soo-preme Court said we couldn't pray on Yamacraw, but I feel if the Lord ain't on our side, then who is. If the Lord ain't with us, then who's gonna be for us. If the Lord decides to forget us, then there ain't much use in livin'. Don't you agree, Mr. Patroy?'

Mr. Patroy nodded his head in solemn agreement.

We said the Lord's Prayer, vilified the Soo-preme Court once more, then broke up the meeting.

After the room had cleared of the underclasses, I put Plan Number 1 into immediate effect. I asked the kids to write a paper briefly describing themselves, telling me everything about themselves and what they didn't like. This seemed like a fairly reasonable request to me but most of the kids stared at me as if I had ordered them to translate hieroglyphs from a pyramid wall. I repeated the instructions and insisted that they make some attempt to follow them. So they began.

As I walked around my new fiefdom, the kids earnestly applying themselves to the task at hand, I had my first moment of panic. Some of them could barely write. Half of them were incapable of expressing even the simplest thought on paper. Three quarters of them could barely spell even the most elementary words. Three of them could not write their names. Sweet little Jesus, I thought, as I weaved between the desks, these kids don't know crap. Most of them hid their papers as I came by, ashamed for me to see they had written nothing. By not being able to tell me anything about themselves, they were telling me everything.

Next I read them a story, a very simple story, I thought, about a judge and a U.S. marshal in the Wild West. The story contained a murder, a treacherous friend, and a happy ending. I asked the eighth graders and the other kids who appeared the least bit literate to retell the story in their own words on paper. Frank, the eighth grader and the boy Mrs. Brown had introduced as the intellectual torch of the Yamacraw School, wrote the following: 'Jim was a ranch. Jim had horse thef. Mike father was short in his back, Mike said Jim had shile his father.' A sixth grader wrote, 'There was a cowboy named Jim and Mike had a ranch when Mike father got shoot in his barn. Mike did not no ho shoot him fadher one he found out h.' This was Cindy Lou, who proudly produced this composition after fifteen minutes of laborious effort.

Oh, I thought, we have no accomplished essayists in the class, so let us continue into other fields of endeavor. Perhaps some latent Demosthenes was sitting before me awaiting the coming of some twentieth-century Macedonia. I asked each child to tell me about his summer, what he did, what he enjoyed the most, or what he disliked about it. Since there was an obvious dearth of volunteers, I called on a diminutive boy named Saul, a seventh grader who looked no older than six.

'Tell me about the summer, Saul, me hearty lad,' I said, desperately trying to inject some life in the deadpan atmosphere of the room.

33

Saul arose with paramount dignity, tugged on his belt, and spoke with a musical prepubic voice. 'I slop de hog. I feed de cow. I feed two dog. I go to Savannah on the boat.'

The next orator arose and said, 'I slop de hog. I feed de cow. I feed three dog. I feed two cat. I go to Savannah in the boat.'

The next brilliant innovator arose and said, quite surprisingly, 'I feed the hog. I feed the cow. I feed the horse. I feed seven dogs. I go to Savannah in the boat.'

Every other child in the class stood up and without a trace of expression or self-consciousness repeated Saul's original speech verbatim. A boy named Prophet gave the only variation of the theme when he confided to the class with a grin that 'I help poppa fick the poppa hog.' The class roared.

After this failure to learn something about each of my new students, I pulled an old trick of the trade out of the hat, one of those tricks you find in a box in the middle of an elementary teacher's magazine under the heading *What to Do on That First Day*. A girl I had been dating in Beaufort, herself an elementary teacher, suggested this to me. She promised that the kids would enjoy it and that I would find it extremely informative. I told the class to draw a portrait of me. They looked at me incredulously, jaws agape, as if I had asked them to draw a picture of horse genitals.

'No lip, gang. No questions. Just draw a picture of this handsome devil you see before you.'

'Humph, Conrack think he look good,' someone whispered.

'Conrack don't think he look good, honey,' I shouted. 'Conrack know he look good. Now you

34

just draw how good he looks.'

'Conrack look bad,' one of the twins whispered.

'Hey, twin. Conrack has big fist which says he looks good. Otherwise, fist crumples into little jaw of little twin and makes blood come out of face,' I said menacingly, as I put my clenched fist up against his face.

'Conrack still look bad,' the other twin said, halfway across the room.

'Good, then make me look bad.'

Everyone then became serious about art. Oscar, a seventh grader and the biggest boy in the class, gazed at my face with the intensity of a Parisian artist studying the contours of a nude. They all scratched and erased, hooted and squealed, and imprinted my image on their lined pieces of notebook paper. My pug nose caught hell. So did my sideburns. One girl, Ethel, was really very good. As I pinned them up on the bulletin board, I couldn't help but notice there was some correlation between those who could not draw and those who could not write.

They then drew a picture of themselves. I had no particular reason for doing this. The thought impulsively struck me that it might be interesting to compare the drawings they made of themselves with the ones they made of me. I was very glad I did this when I saw the results. Most of the boys drew themselves to look exactly as they had drawn me. Several boys had made what looked like duplicate copies. The girls saved themselves from exact reproduction by the fact they had included long hair and dresses in their self-portraits. No one had darkened his face or gave any indication that he or she might be black.

Just before the arrival of the bus, we had an impromptu geography lesson. A map of the world hung near the door. I asked for a volunteer to come up and pinpoint the location of Yamacraw Island on the map. Eight hands immediately shot up. This surprised me somewhat and for a moment I thought I had expected too little from these kids, that they were more advanced than I had given them credit for. I called on Mary, the eldest, tallest, and supposedly the brightest girl in class. She strode confidently to the map and without hesitation and without faltering an instant, she placed her finger on a spot in the northeast corner of Outer Mongolia. When I told her this wasn't quite right, the rest of the class cackled and taunted Mary all the way back to her seat. Fred prodded Mary's arm with his finger and laughed like hell, until Mary swung a thin, long, graceful hand against the side of Fred's face. A kid who identified himself as Big C walked up to the map and immediately chose a place near Bombay, India; nor did Top Cat neglect the portion of Russia that borders the Bering Sea.

Then the bus arrived. The kids filed out.

'Good-bye, Mr. Conrack,' they said.

'Good-bye, gang, see you tomorrow.'

Then Mrs. Brown poked her head in the door and asked me how it went. 'Crappy,' I answered, and she chuckled. 'You're overseas now.'

She then gave me about five hundred tons of paper, which I would need as principal of Yamacraw Elementary.

'No one told me I was supposed to be principal, Mrs. Brown. I thought you were the principal. In fact, I was told that you were the principal.'

'Oh no, Mr. Patroy. You are the principal. Of

course you're the principal.' A month and a half later Dr. Piedmont sent word over to the island that Mrs. Brown was indeed the principal.

She laid the papers on my desk, then went back to her room. It suddenly struck me that she took it for granted I was principal simply because I was white.

*   *   *

Just as the first day of school was spent getting to know the individual children in the class, the second day was spent in an honest effort to find out what they knew. No one on the mainland could tell me exactly what problems I would encounter. Everyone seemed to agree it was bad, yet no one knew what diagnostic techniques to recommend. Several administrators intimated that whatever I taught the Yamacraw children, it would be infinitely superior to what they had learned before, regardless of what methods I employed. Yamacraw was an enigma to the minions who gathered under Piedmont's protective wing. Bennington knew more than anyone, but his major preoccupation was to erase his own trail of incompetence and his contribution toward actually shoving the true portrait of the Yamacraw School before my eyes was negligible. After the second day of school, however, Bennington, Piedmont, and all the other king's horses could come to me for information about the quality and condition of education on the island. It stunk.

It is important to realize that I had never taught in an elementary school, that my experience had only been with high school students. I had not the

37

vaguest notion what body of knowledge a sixth or seventh grader possessed. Nor did I really know what I was expected to teach them. So the night after the first day of school, I prepared a list of questions, questions that seemed to be the most basic units of information I could devise. I also pulled eighteen books out of the two bookshelves that passed for the library. These books ranged from the simplest I could find to one with a relatively complex vocabulary.

In the morning the yellow school bus came into the yard at promptly eight o'clock. The kids filed in, each one of them giving me an obsequious good-morning as he passed through the front door. I swatted each one of the boys on the shoulder as he entered, called him 'chicken,' and dared any of them to summon up the courage to fight back. Big C crept up behind me and booted me in the rump. The class squealed and laughed approvingly. I chased Big C into a corner and commenced to wrestle him to the schoolroom floor. By this time the noise level had risen to an insect pitch. I was about to put Big C into a full Nelson, when a funereal silence descended on the room; I saw Mama Brown's huge head staring disapprovingly into the window. She beckoned me to the door with her finger. Her finger was the size of a small blackjack. I went.

'Mr. Patroy,' she said, 'you have already lost the respect of these children. You have lowered yourself in their eyes. They need discipline, not fun time. This school isn't any fun time, you know.'

'Yes, ma'am,' I mumbled, embarrassed as hell.

'Remember what I told you about colored children. They need the whip. They understand the whip. O.K. Do you understand me?'

'Yes, ma'am.'

'O.K., that's good. Now, this is the day we hand out books. In exactly one hour, I want you to send a child you trust to my room. The state requires us to hand out these textbooks as soon as possible.'

'Can the kids read these books?' I asked.

'They are supposed to read them. The state department requires them to read them.'

'What if they can't?'

'Then we must make them read them. Of course, some of them are retarded and can't read anything. You got to remember that we are overseas, Mr. Patroy, and things are tough overseas.'

'I'll remember.'

I returned to the classroom a chastened man. No more half-Nelsons on that particular day. I winked at Big C. Then I began the interrogation.

'O.K., gang, loosen up. Shake those hands and feet. We are going to dust the cobwebs off those sweet little brains of ours. Prophet, you are going to have the opportunity to prove that you are a genius before all the world today. Carolina, you are going to shine like the sun. Everybody is going to look good.'

One of the questionable themes developed in two years of teaching was the necessity to put students at complete ease. It worked well in Beaufort, but the Yamacraw kids looked at me as though I were a mentally deficient clown.

'What country do we live in, gang? Everybody tell me at once,' I exhorted.

No one said a word. Several of the kids looked at one another and shrugged their shoulders.

'Gang,' I continued, 'what is the name of this

grand old, red, white, and blue country of ours? The place where we live. The land of the free and the home of the brave.'

Still there was silence.

I was struggling for the right words to simplify the question ever further. 'Does anyone know what country we live in?' I asked again.

No one answered. Each child sat before me with a pained and embarrassed look.

'Have you ever heard of the United States of America?' I asked.

'Oh, yeh,' Mary, one of the eighth-grade girls said. 'I heared it. I heared it in I pledge a legent to the flag of United States of America.'

'The Pledge of Allegiance. Good, Mary. Then you knew what country you live in.'

'No, just know pledge a legent.'

'All right, gang. Now the first golden nugget of information we are going to learn this year is that all of us live in the United States of America. Now the next thing I want someone to tell me is this: who is President of the United States in this year of 1969?' Again there was silence.

'Does anyone know?' I asked.

Everyone shook his head. Frank raised his hand. 'John F. Kennedy,' he said.

'Yeh,' the whole class answered, looking to me for approval.

'Yeh,' I responded. 'That's great, Frank. Why did you say Kennedy?'

'He good to colored man,' answered Frank.

'Yeh,' the class answered.

'Yeh,' I agreed.

'Can anyone tell me who the first President of the United States was?'

40

Silence again.

'Ever hear of George Washington?' I asked.

Only a couple of students nodded their heads affirmatively. The rest had not.

'Who can tell me who Willie Mays is?'

No one could.

'All right, gang, relax. We are going to get off these goofy people for a while. I am sick and tired of talking about people. Let's talk about water. Who can name me an ocean?'

Fred looked at Top Cat and Top Cat looked at Fred, who was staring intently at me. None of them had ever heard of any ocean.

'I'm going to give you a hint,' I said, 'one of the oceans washes up against the shore of Yamacraw Island.'

Cindy Lou lit up and shouted. 'Oh, he mean the beach.'

'That's right, Cindy. Now what is the name of the beach?'

'The beach, man,' she answered indignantly.

'No, I mean the name given to that whole ocean.'

'I tole you it was the beach,' she said angrily.

'O.K. It's the beach,' I agreed. 'But it also is called the Atlantic Ocean. Have any of you ever heard it called that?'

All heads shook sadly and mournfully.

'Well, don't worry about it,' I continued. 'That kind of stuff is easy to learn. Just by talking about it, without even thinking real hard, you have learned what ocean is by Yamacraw. Mary, if I were a stranger on this island and I met you on the beach and asked you what body of water this was I was walking next to, what would you tell me?'

'Body?' she asked in a tone intimating that she

41

had incriminating evidence against my sanity.

'Yeh, body of water.'

'I don't know about no bodies,' she insisted.

'Forget about body. What ocean would you tell me I was walking by?'

'Lantic Ocean.'

'Atlantic.'

'Atlantic,' she repeated.

'What ocean, everybody?'

'Atlantic Ocean,' they shouted in unison.

'Are you sure it's the Atlantic Ocean?'

'Yeh,' they answered.

'Well, it's not.'

They looked at me again like they had been placed under the jurisdiction of a functioning cretin.

'The real name of the ocean is the Conroy Ocean.'

'No,' they said.

'Yeh,' I said.

'No,' they said.

'Yeh, it's the truth. My great-great grandfather was Ferdinand Conroy, a Spanish soldier of fortune, who swam from Europe to North America, a distance of fifteen million miles. Because of this singular and extraordinary feat, they named this huge expanse of water after him.'

'What you say?' one of the twins asked me.

'He didn't say nothen,' Cindy Lou said.

'Anyway,' I continued undaunted, 'from that day forward, it has been called Conroy Ocean.'

'No,' George said.

'How do you know?' I challenged.

'Just ain't. You said it is Atlantic.'

'I'm a liar.'

42

'You's a teacher.'

'Teachers lie all the time.'

'Oh Gawd,' Lincoln said. I had been noticing whenever Lincoln was surprised or ecstatic he would use the phrase *Oh Gawd*.

So the day continued and with each question I got closer and closer to the children. With each question I asked I got madder and madder at the people responsible for the condition of these kids. At the end of the day I had compiled an impressive ledger of achievement. Seven of my students could not recite the alphabet. Three children could not spell their names. Eighteen children thought Savannah, Georgia, was the largest city in the world. Savannah was the only city any of the kids could name. Eighteen children had never seen a hill—eighteen children had never heard the words *integration* and *segregation*. Four children could not add two plus two. Eighteen children did not know we were fighting a war in Southeast Asia. Of course, eighteen children never had heard of Asia. One child was positive that John Kennedy was the first President of the United States. Seventeen children agreed with that child. Eighteen children concurred with the pre-Copernican Theory that the earth was the center of the universe. Two children did not know how old they were. Five children did not know their birth dates. Four children could not count to ten. The four oldest thought the Civil War was fought between the Germans and the Japs.

Each question I asked opened up a new lesion of ignorance or misinformation. A stunned embarrassment gripped the class, as if I had broken some unwritten law by prying into areas where I had no business, or exposing linen of a very

43

personal nature. No one would look me in the eye. Nor would anyone talk to me. I had stumbled into another century. The job I had taken to assuage the demon of do-gooderism was a bit more titanic than anticipated. All around the room sat human beings of various sizes and hues who were not aware that a world surrounded them, a world they would be forced to enter, and enter soon.

I now knew the score of the ball game. Or at least thought I did. The kids did not know crap.

I walked up to Prophet. I put up six fingers and asked him how many fingers I had raised.

'Eight,' he answered.

'You only missed it by two, Prophet. Try it again,' I said.

'Two,' he whispered.

'No, Prophet. Now start at this first finger and count to the last one.'

'Five,' he whispered again. By this time his eyes were begging me to cease the interrogation. His classmates laughed at him each time he gave a wrong answer. I had humiliated him and his eyes carried the message.

'Don't worry about it, Prophet, we are going to bust the hell out of those old numbers before this is over. O.K.?' He nodded.

Prophet gave the general appearance that a thought never entered his head, that his brain had never suffered from the painful malady of an idea. Samuel and Sidney, the twins, by their appearance alone made Prophet look like a candidate for the 'College Bowl.' They were pitifully skinny, unanimated, dull-eyed, and seemingly retarded. Whenever I got the other children laughing by performing some insane act or saying some outrageous thing, Sam and Sidney would laugh several seconds after the other kids, as if they depended on the reaction of their peers for the proper responses. The twins seemed hopeless. Prophet smiled often enough, with his bell-ringer grin, to give me some faith that he was not completely oblivious to the world about him.

This second day proved a hypothesis formulated quickly and haphazardly on the first day. A huge, almost unbridgeable communication gap existed in the room. When the kids were conversing normally, there was not a tinker's chance in hell that I could understand them. The island blacks of South Carolina are famous among linguists for their Gullah dialect. Experts have studied this patois for years and they have written several books on the subject. It is a combination of an African dialect and English; some even claim that remnants of Elizabethan English survive among the Gullah people. Whatever the origin of the speech, I could not decipher the ordinary conversation of any of the children in the class. They spoke like machine guns, rapidly or in short, explosive spurts. Whenever I would stand off and listen to a group of them conversing, it became impossible for me to follow what they said. I could not grasp the syntax, nor could I follow any logical sentence pattern, nor could I participate in their discussions by piecing together words I did catch accidentally when one of them was sprinting through his version of a story.

To make matters even more serious, none of them could understand me. Among the peoples of the world I am not universally admired for the bell-like clarity of my diction. Words slide out of my mouth like fat fish. Having lived my life in various parts of Georgia, Virginia, and the Carolinas and having been sired by a gruff-talking Marine from Chicago and a grits-and-gravy honey from Rome, Georgia, what has remained is an indefinable nonspeech, flavored subtly with a nonaccent, and decipherable to no one, black or white, on the American continent. I am embarrassed to talk on telephones for the simple reason that operators cannot understand me. So the situation in the classroom was desperate in more ways than one. I knew the kids didn't know very much and I knew that I could teach them a hell of a lot, but I could not understand a word they were saying, nor could they understand a word I was saying. With the help of Mary a compromise was reached. Mary seemed to understand almost everything I said, and on occasion I could understand some of what she said. I designated her as grand interpreter with illimitable powers of life and death over all. When Prophet said something known only to God, Mary would tell me what he said. Sometimes the whole class would help Mary out, and seventeen voices would rise slowly in an unintelligible gibberish, grow louder as each voice tried to be heard, and finally reach a deafening crescendo à la Babel.

'Enough of this,' I'd yell. Then Mary would proudly explain to me that Prophet wanted to take a piss.

That night I fired off a rather angry, self-righteous letter to Dr. Piedmont telling him that his cute little schoolhouse on Yamacraw was not worth a pound of cow dung. Looking back, I scoff at the bug-eyed believer in the system I was then. There I sat in a small schoolroom, with a sleeping bag unrolled on the floor beside me, a

46

dinner of beef stew and Gatorade digesting in my stomach, the smell of chalk dust and old textbooks in my nostrils, the wild insect sounds of night rampant in the forest around me, writing a brimstone letter to a man I had met only once, but whom I trusted implicitly to understand, to sympathize, and to act. Because the situation was so much worse than I anticipated, I was less diplomatic than I might have been. I wanted to shock Piedmont as I had been shocked and wanted to shake the plodding bureaucrats who plowed around the heavily carpeted county office building into awareness of the disastrous education they were giving kids. Yeh, I was a tough bastard in those early days. Piedmont learned that he had not sent me to Yamacraw to preside over an intellectual wasteland with all due acknowledgments to T. S. Eliot. The letter was written in a fit of Conroy passion, the tiny bellicose Irishman residing in my genes and collective unconscious urging me on and whispering to me that a great injustice was being perpetrated and that it was up to me to expose this condition to the person with the ability and training to do something about it.

The letter was written the second day of the school year. From that day forward, no one in the educational hierarchy of the county could plead ignorance concerning the school on the island. I had told them.

On the third day I despaired. Each time I broached a new subject, it revealed some astonishing gap in the kids' knowledge. The realm of their experience was not only limited, it often seemed nonexistent. Some of them vaguely remembered having heard of Vietnam but were not

47

aware that the United States was at war in that country. When I asked whom we were fighting there, Oscar's hand shot up and he quickly said, 'The Germans and the Japs.' The whole class solemnly agreed that we had to beat those Germans and Japs. Yamacraw Island was the largest of the nine planets. When I asked who was the greatest man that ever lived, Mary answered, 'Jesus.' Everyone, of course, fervently agreed. When I asked who was the second greatest man who ever lived, her brother Lincoln answered, 'Jesus Christ.' Once again the entire class unanimously consented to this second choice.

I could understand the class not knowing Richard Nixon, Napoleon, Julius Caesar, or Alexander the Great, but I could not see how black children living in the latter half of the twentieth century could fail to know Sidney Poitier, Wilt Chamberlain, or Willie Mays. They had never heard of Shakespeare or Aesop. They had never heard of England or India. They had never been to a movie, theater or to a ball game. They had never heard of democracy, governors or senators, capitals of states, or any oceans, or famous actors, or artists, or newspapers, or kinds of automobiles. They had never been to a museum, never looked at a work of art, never read a piece of good literature, never ridden a city bus, never taken a trip, never seen a hill, never seen a swift stream, never seen a super-highway, never learned to swim, and never done a thousand things that children of a similar age took for granted.

I learned all this on the third day. I had pulled up a chair in the middle of the class and all the kids had drawn up their desks in a semicircle around me. And we just talked. We spent the whole day talking. I told them about myself, about my mother and father, about my four brothers and two sisters, about teaching in Beaufort, about going to Europe, and about my coming to Yamacraw. They were thrilled to learn that my father flew jet planes. I also told them I drove a small yellow car called a Volkswagen when I was on the mainland. The car was manufactured in a country called Germany on a continent called Europe. I showed them the country and the continent on the map. They asked me about places I had been, and what New York looked like, and had I ever been on an airplane.

They then told me about hunting on the island, and the boys became extremely animated describing the number of squirrels to be found deep in the woods and how you had to be a great shot to pick out the gray tuft of fur high in the black oaks and bring it down with one shot of the .22. The further you went in the woods, they told me, the more tame the squirrels became, the closer they would come, and the easier they were to kill. The girls then told me in elaborate detail how to clean the squirrels. They called the process 'scrinching.' You slit open the belly with a sharp knife, peeled the squirrel's pelt off like the skin of a grape, then scraped the squirrel's skin until it was white and smooth. Ethel said, 'A lady in Savannah won't eat squirrel 'cause she say after a squirrel been scrinched it look like little white baby.'

'How many in here like to eat squirrel?' I asked. Everyone loved squirrel, although there was one purist faction in the class that liked squirrel meat without any other embellishments and another who preferred their squirrel with a thick gravy and a heavy stew.

49

'I would have to be starving to death before I ate a squirrel,' I told the class. 'A squirrel looks like a big hairy rat to me and since I would not eat a rat, I most probably would not eat a squirrel either.'

Lincoln asked incredulously, 'You ain't never eaten squirrel?'

I answered negatively.

'Gawd, that man never eaten squirrel,' said Cindy Lou.

'Squirrel ain't no rat,' Saul said.

'You eat rat,' Lincoln said to Saul.

'No, I don't eat rat. You eat crow.' The whole class roared when the puny Saul accused Lincoln of eating crow. Evidently, crow-eating had connotations on the island which were literal as well as metaphorical.

'You know what you eat, Saul. You eat buzzard.' The class laughed wildly again.

'Fat man, you know what you eat.'

'What I eat, little man?'

'You know what you eat,' Saul answered menacingly, his tiny frame rigid with anger.

'Little man, better tell me what I eat.'

'Fat man eats shee-it.'

'Oh Gawd,' half the class exclaimed simultaneously. Someone shouted, 'Little man told big man he eat shee-it. He curse. He curse. Lawd, Mr. Conrack gonna do some beating now.'

Saul had slumped into his seat after he had uttered the forbidden word and hidden his face in his hands, awaiting whatever punishment I would impose upon him. Why I had let the situation totally escape me, I did not know. I had been so interested in the downward progression of gourmet foods according to the island connoisseurs that I

50

was totally unprepared for the final plunge to unpackaged feces. Lincoln, enraged at being called a shee-it eater, huffed and puffed triumphantly and waited impatiently for me to yank Saul from his seat and beat hell out of him. Meanwhile Saul had started to cry.

'Saul,' I intoned, trying to sound like a miniature Yahweh.

'Oh Gawd,' said Lincoln.

Saul looked up still sobbing. 'Saul, do you know how I used to punish students who were bad when I taught high school?'

'No,' he answered.

'I used to scrinch 'em, son. I used to take a knife and cut open their bellies. Then I'd scrape their skin until they were ready for the pot.'

'No,' the whole class said.

'Yeah,' I, the wild-eyed scrincher, answered.

'Then I'd try to sell them for people to eat, but no one would eat them because them scrinched students looked too much like baby squirrels.'

'White man crazy,' someone whispered.

'Now everyone shut up. 'Cause I am about to scrinch Saul.'

'No,' the class shouted.

'Yeah,' I shouted back. 'But I am going to give him a chance. Now if I was Saul I would say, "Teacher, I said that stinking word and I made a mistake. If you give me another chance, I promise I won't do it again."'

'Teacher,' Saul said rather quickly, 'give me a chance and I won't do nothin' again.'

'O.K. Fair enough. Now, Lincoln, is it true the stuff I hear about you?'

'What, man?'

51

'Is it true that you eat skunk?'

'Yeah, he eat skunk,' the rest of the class shouted.

*   *   *

It was strange how I marveled about their lack of knowledge concerning history and geography. On the third day, though despairing, I wondered if they felt any pity for me for not having feasted on squirrel stew or enjoyed the simple pleasures of scrinching. The boys were hunters; the girls were expert in the preparation of the spoils of the hunt. Oscar, the tallest and the blackest kid in class, told me he had shot a deer the year before. Lincoln then told me that Frank had shot Oscar the year before. With this statement the class lapsed into a profound, but uncertain silence. Frank looked at Lincoln with eyes that danced with rage and fury. Oscar looked as if he was sucking on a lemon. Finally Saul spoke up.

'Frank shot Oscar through the arm.'

'Where was this?' I asked.

'Down on Bloody Point on other side of island. They hunt bird.'

Lincoln said, 'Frank no have any guard on his trigger. Walking along, Frank trip over root. Trigger catch in his sleeve and put hole in Oscar's arm.'

'Oscar bleed like hog,' Sidney, one of the twins, said. It was obvious that Frank and Oscar still carried scars from that particular day in the woods—Oscar impulsively holding his left arm, Frank staring at his pencil, both of them thinking about the blood and pain.

'That boy nearly bleed to death, Mr. Conrack,' Ethel said.

'They walk to Mr. Stone's house and a man take him to the doctor in Savannah. Say he almost die on the way.'

'Shut up, girl,' Oscar said.

'Yeah, man. Let's everyone be quiet.' The bus was pulling up into the yard. 'Tomorrow return and we will continue to derive great pleasure from the joy of learning.'

'Oh Gawd, Conrack.'

When Friday afternoon came and the bus sucked the kids out of the school door and they bade farewell to Mr. Conrack for the weekend, it was a matter of minutes before I was untying the boat at Stone's dock and heading for Bluffton, where Bernie was meeting me. We drove to his apartment in Beaufort, where I took my first shower in a week. I luxuriated in the flow of hot water. All the crud of the island fell off me like a skin. Then I turned my attention to the mosquito bites, which were legion over the length and breadth of my body. Pouring alcohol into cotton balls, I dabbed the red swellings until they stung and glowed. One particular bite merited more detailed attention. Under careful scrutiny, I saw that it was a tick. It was just sitting there beneath my armpit, growing fat by sucking my lifeblood. He was in there deep; his snout drilled far into my flesh enjoying the refreshment of the plasma coursing through my veins. I grabbed him by his tiny behind and yanked. He split in half. His straw still remained in me, sucking away. Bernie got a match and after applying four first-degree burns to my arm, the tick shriveled and came out easily. A spot check revealed that I was

53

covered with the ravenous fellows. They preferred the warmth and obscurity of the pubic region, where they could hide and suck without detection. They were forest creatures and to the forests they retreated, hiding like guerrillas in the dense foliage of arse and scrotum. Taking a pair of tweezers, I extracted nine ticks from my body.

'An occupational hazard, son,' Bernie sang.

CHAPTER THREE

The school library would have been funny if it had not been such a tragic commentary on administrative inefficiency and stupidity. Each day we had a half-hour reading period during which the kids could read anything they liked. Since a lot of them couldn't read at all, the period had become a time when I simply tried to get them interested in books. Cindy Lou chose a book called *Tommy the Telephone* as her personal favorite. Each time Cindy read to me about Tommy, the irony struck me: a girl reading about telephones who has never used a telephone. Other books with negligible relationship to life on the island populated the shelves. There were books on Eskimos, Scandinavians, dairy farms in Wisconsin, and the Japanese pearl divers, but I could find no books or information on rural blacks in the Yamacraw school library. I brought a Sears, Roebuck catalogue to school and it proved to be one of the most popular books. The girls perused the fashions, while the boys lusted after the hunting and sports equipment. My group of rock-hard nonreaders flipped through the encyclopedias, looking at the pictures and asking me innumerable questions.

'What this here, Conrack?' Sidney would ask.

'That's a pyramid, Sid. They used to bury kings in those things thousands of years ago in a country called Egypt.'

'No.'

'Yeah,' I answered.

'Who this?' Prophet would ask then, thumbing through another encyclopedia. 'That's Babe Ruth. One of the greatest baseball players that ever lived. He used to play for the New York Yankees. He hit 714 home runs in his career, more than anyone else in the history of baseball.'

'He play now?' asked Richard.

'He's dead,' I said.

'Yeah, stupid, he daid.' Sid grinned as he punched Richard.

'That man dead?' Prophet asked again.

'Richard think that man 'live,' Sid continued. Richard slugged Sid and the discussion of the Sultan of Swat ended.

One day as the guys pored over the musty tomes, which they came to consider their personal property during the reading period, Jasper stumbled on the section dealing with snakes. The whole class ran over to look at the snakes.

'Snake bad,' Oscar said sagaciously.

'Yeah, bad,' everyone agreed.

'Snake good,' I interjected. 'Gang, snakes eat rats and other rodents which are pests around the yard.'

'Snake eat you, too,' Lincoln said. The class howled.

'Just poisonous snakes will hurt you,' I said defensively. Since Yamacraw contained some of the

55

largest diamondback rattlesnakes to be found anywhere, I could understand their fear of snakes, but as an amateur herpetologist, I felt that I had to make an impassioned defense of snakedom. 'And snakes will not bother you unless you bother them.'

'Lord, Mr. C'roy, you just don't know snakes,' Ethel said. 'We got a snake here on this island that wrap himself around you and whip you to death.'

'Yeah,' everyone agreed.

'Bullcrap,' I said.

'He cuss,' Sam whispered.

'That is nonsense. That is what we call a myth. Something that is not true. How many in here have ever seen a snake whipping a man to death?'

Naturally, every hand in the room flew up.

'Who was the man you actually saw getting the hell beat out of him by a snake?'

'He cuss one more time.' Old Sam was keeping tabs.

'His name was Jacob Hudson, used to live here on the island,' Ethel said.

'Did the snake kill him?' I asked.

'No. He run away. Have marks on his body, though,' continued Ethel.

'Yeah. Have marks on his body.' The others agreed.

'Did you actually see this man being whipped?'

'No.'

'Then you do not know if the snake really whipped the man.'

'Yeah. He have marks,' said Mary.

'Ever see a snake milk a cow, Mr. C'roy?' Big C asked.

'Oh, crap.'

'Yeah, he milk cow dry.'

56

'That is simply not true. These are all snake myths,' I pleaded to an unconvinced audience. By the expressions on their faces, I could tell they thought I was nuts.

'I seen plenty of snakes milk cows,' Big C said.

'Do they put the milk in bottles?' I now resorted to my last weapon, ridicule.

'No, they suck it up.'

'Mr. Conroy, ever see how snake eat egg?' Lincoln asked.

'No, Lincoln, but I'm afraid to ask.'

'He swallow the egg whole. Then he climb up tree, jump off branch, land on ground, and pop egg in belly.'

'That's how I eat eggs, too, Lincoln.'

I returned to the serpent mythology on numerous occasions during the year, exhorting the students to look truth in the eye and to understand that the things we learn in our youth are not always literally correct. With brilliant logic they argued that what I had learned in the city about snakes was not any better than what they learned while living on the island. They had lived with snakes all their lives; I had merely read about them.

In one remote corner of the room, the dustiest and most spider-controlled corner, sat several boxes full of books. A church had donated the books in order to rid the island of illiteracy. Give them books and they shall read. Earnest ladies and pious men had scurried around attics and unused libraries in search of books for the unread natives of Yamacraw Island. Their minister sometimes came to Yamacraw on Sundays to preach to the blacks on the island, to exhort them to quit their evil likker-drinking ways. He was enormously proud of the fact that he could summon up enough Christianity to preach to the niggers, since he made it no secret on the mainland that he did not think much of niggers. If a black had entered his church, the church would have closed down automatically. That was the plan of the hallowed vestrymen should a black foot cross the threshold. Christ must do a lot of puking when he reflects upon the good works done in his name.

Anyway, the church gathered books in cardboard boxes and shipped them to the island for use in the school. Looking at the books, I saw little possibility of handing my students *The Power of Positive Thinking* by Norman Vincent Peale. Nor did I think they could relish *Gone with the Wind*. Several books on Christian doctrine seemed equally inappropriate. A nice gesture and a good idea, but none of the books were on a level the kids could handle.

By far the greatest travesty was the public library established on the island by a concerned group of citizens who thought it deplorable that the island did not have a library of its own. It was deplorable and unthinkable that an island had no place to which a man could retire to mull over his thoughts, to write great novels, to generate lofty ideas, or to lose himself in scholarly pursuits. To solve this problem, the county decided to establish a library to serve the intellectual needs of the islanders, most of whom could neither read nor write. So the county transported 2000 books out to the island, put them in the community center, and hired a part-time librarian as custodian of the books. The books, of course, reflected the great trends of literature; the selection was vast and represented all the eminent authors. Here an old oyster-shucker could find *Look Homeward, Angel* by Thomas Wolfe, *The Sound and the Fury* by William Faulkner, *For Whom the Bell Tolls* by Ernest Hemingway. Or, if he preferred the nineteenth century, this same ox-cart driver could select *Moby Dick* by Herman Melville or *The Scarlet Letter* by Nathaniel Hawthorne. All of these books were available. When no one checked out a book in three years, officials were noticeably chagrined. 'Stupid niggers. You bust your ass to help them, and they don't even check out a book.' Good intentions flourish on Yamacraw Island. The projects of concerned white folks are evident everywhere. Supply books and by a miraculous process of osmosis, the oyster-pickers will become Shakespearean scholars. All dem nigras need is books and a little tad of education.

*　　*　　*

James Brown is the Yahweh substitute on the island. The kids tingle every time his name is mentioned; they have memorized his songs as though they were the Gospel according to Luke. Top Cat, numero uno dispenser of good poop on Mr. Dynamite and his Famous Flames, shook and gyrated his way around the room when he thought I was not looking. The contorting moves he put his body through defy description and he is acknowledged by his peers as being the finest dancer on the island. 'That Top Cat, crazy. Watch Top Cat shake that thing,' they say with profound respect. Once in a while he felt the fire within him rage and, at that exact moment, strutted and jerked up to my desk and asked to sing James Brown's

59

latest song. We turned on the tape recorder (discovered in a corner in Mrs. Brown's room) and Top Cat lost himself in his art. The kids loved it. Of course, Mrs. Brown hated it and delivered an impassioned lecture against wasting valuable school time and ignoring the sacred laws of the state government.

One day in late September Top Cat was studying the covers of some long-playing albums beside my record player. Since I had not yet moved into my house, all my earthly possessions stood in one corner of the schoolroom. The record album that came under the most careful study by Top Cat was a gift from my mother back in those ancient days when mom thought her family should develop some familiarity with the arts. She invested a considerable sum of money in the *Reader's Digest* series of records and books designed to give cultural dimwits at least a surface knowledge of the world's finer things. Somehow I had confiscated the 'Fifty Favorites,' a collection that included brief but famous fragments of the great composers. Top Cat asked me if James Brown, Mr. Dynamite and his Famous Flames, sang any 'tough' songs on this here record.

'Top Cat, James Brown and his Famous Flames were not good enough to make this record. They tried but they just couldn't make it. The *Reader's Digest* put this thing out. Ever heard of the *Reader's Digest*?'

'Nope.'

'Anybody ever heard of the *Reader's Digest*?'

Nobody had ever heard of it. Being an American and not knowing the *Reader's Digest* is like being English and not knowing the queen.

60

'This little magazine put out this little record you see here in my hands. This record is a treasure, an absolute delight. A collection of greatness. Now the first great tune I am going to play for you was written by a long-haired cat named Beethoven. Who was that?'

'Bay Cloven.'

'Close enough. Now old Bay Cloven loved music, and he could write some pretty mean songs. He was the James Brown of Germany. What continent is Germany in [pointing to the map]?'

'Europe.'

'Good. Now one of Beethoven's most famous songs was written about death. Death knocking at the door. Death, that grim, grim reaper coming to the house and rapping at the door. Does death come to everybody's door sometime?'

'Yeah, death come knocking at Dooney's door last year,' Big C said.

'Well, Beethoven thought a little bit about death, then decided that if death were really knocking at the door, he would sound something like this: da-da-da-*da*. Now I am going to place this little needle on this valuable record and we are going to hear death knocking at Bay Cloven's door.'

The first notes ripped out. Ol' death, that son of a bitch.

'Do you hear that rotten death?' I yelled.

'Don't hear nuttin',' said Prophet.

'Sound like music,' said Lincoln.

'Shut up and listen for that bloodsucker death,' I yelled again.

'Yeah, I hear 'im,' Mary said.

'Me, too,' a couple of the others agreed.

Finally, everyone was hearing old death rapping

61

at the door. Once we labeled death and identified him for all time, I switched to the Triumphal March from *Aida*. Rhapsodically explaining the glorious entry into Rome, swelling with pride over the victories in the Egypt-Ethiopian campaigns, I described Verdi's panoramic vision of the coming home from the wars. I impressed no one with the performance and discovered to my unconcealed chagrin that I had played the Emperor Waltz instead.

'We want to hear Bay Cloven.'

'Shut up. You will listen to Verdi.'

'We want death,' Fred said.

'Then death you get.' Bay Cloven was definitely the top tune of the day. When I played Brahms's Lullaby, I whisked Sam out of his seat, cuddled him like an infant, and rocked him asleep. He reacted brilliantly, as only a natural performer could, throwing his head back in a ludicrous imitation of sleep, his mouth open, his eyes closed.

The class also reacted well to 'The Flight of the Bumblebee' by Rimsky-Korsakov.

'You hear them bees?' I asked.

'Just like a honey tree,' Frank answered.

'Any honey trees on Yamacraw?'

'Yeah, they honey trees. Honey bees too.'

'Bee sting,' Prophet added.

'Bee sting bad,' someone else said.

'Who wrote this song?'

'Rinkey horsecup,' Jimmie Sue said authoritatively.

'Gang, we are going to learn all the songs on this record,' I said. 'And I just thought of a good reason for doing it. Because you are going to look like geniuses when you know these songs. People are going to come to this island to revel in stupidity and poverty. I am going to switch on the record player and you are going to look at these people and exclaim with British accents, "Pahdon me, suh. Are you perchance familiar with Rimsky-Korsakov?" We can knock their behinds off. Now, an important question: do you guys and gals think you can learn these songs and who wrote them? You already know three of them. You know Beethoven's Fifth, 'The Flight of the Bumblebee' by Rimsky-Korsakov, and Brahms's Lullaby. You learned three of them without even trying. Can you learn a whole mess of them?'

'Yeah,' everyone shouted.

'I believe you.'

So we did it. That night I chose twenty of the most impressive titles written by the most impressive composers. For the next two months a portion of each day was set aside for the consumption, memorization, and enjoyment of this top twenty. On a weekend I purchased a huge poster of Beethoven, and hung his shaggy-maned visage on the bulletin board. It tickled me to think of Big B's reaction to his celebration on an island as remote as Yamacraw. In a short time he became 'Bay-Toven the Fifth' and no matter how earnestly I tried to explain that the fifth was not an addendum to his name, so it remained. It gave an incredible feeling to put the needle down, to hear Tchaikovsky swell into the room, then watch the hands shoot up, or to hear voices excitedly identify the piece without bothering with the raised-hand crap.

Soon we derived a game out of it. I would skip all over the record, trying to fool them into guessing wrong. When it was apparent that most of them had developed an almost infallible expertise in the big twenty, I told them that they were the most advanced scholars in classical music functioning in the elementary schools of Beaufort County. Bay Cloven would be proud, I told them, and so would James Brown. I then told them that they had to look upon themselves in a different light, that they had to be convinced of their basic worth, and that they could learn just as fast as anybody else. If they didn't believe it, they could get the hell out of my class.

The music eventually proved a great ego-inflater. When I started bringing an influx of visitors in the spring, curious people who heard about the island and who came basically to pity, to commiserate, and to poke around, it gave me and the kids almost Satanic pleasure to flip on the record player, challenge an unsuspecting guest to a contest in classical music, then let the well-drilled students maul them. Oh, the joy. To see the misty-eyed whites who had flagellated themselves with visions of worm-eaten cretins and deprived idiots trounced in a head-on collision of wits was a banquet to be savored again and again. On the way home, riding through the green marshes, I would explain to the shell-shocked visitor that the children felt that Strauss was overrated, you know, old chap, a little too mawkish and sugary. On the other hand, they felt Brahms was not getting his due with the general public. He had written some fine stuff that had remained unknown to the common run of listeners. Those were such good and satisfying days.

And the kids seemed genuinely to like the stuff. One morning Top Cat leapt off the bus, ran into the classroom, and informed me that 'The Flight of the Bumblebee' was played on the 'Andy Williams Show.' Later in the year Lincoln and Mary reported that they heard 'The Dance of the Sugar Plum Fairy.'

When I brought Leonard Bernstein's Children's Concert to the school, Leonard was a mild, if not overwhelming, success. His orchestra played several of the movements we had memorized and when they played these pieces, the kids would hoot and slap each other, then say, 'That's old Shy-Koski.'

Every single film on music I could find in the county film library and every one I could order from the state department made its way into the classroom. We learned the instruments in the orchestra, then promptly forgot them. We were cocky about our music. Me, the gang, Bay Cloven, Shy-Koski, and the boys.

Each morning, as my students filed into the class, flipping me a dutiful, lachrymose good-morning, I would turn on the radio to catch the latest news. They showed great interest in the morning news.

'Oh Gawd,' Lincoln would lament, 'here come de mornin' news again.'

'That man talk every mornin' about nothin',' Oscar would add.

'Ah, the joys of learning,' I would pipe in, 'the tremendous interest you show in the happenings around the world is gratifying to see. The world is out there.' I gesticulated rather dramatically. 'Wars are being fought, people are being killed, famines are wiping out nations, and rulers are being assassinated. We can hear it all, right here on the morning news.'

My pre-Yamacraw theory of teaching held several sacred tenets, among these being that the teacher must always maintain an air of insanity, or of eccentricity out of control, if he is to catch and hold the attention of his students. The teacher must always be on the attack, looking for new ideas, changing worn-out tactics, and never, ever falling into patterns that lead to student ennui. Bernie and I both believed in teacher dramatics, gross posturings and frenzied excesses to get a rise out of dead-head, thought-killed students, who daily sat before us like shoed mushrooms. The master of clowns, Bernie could twist his face into a thousand contortions to get kids to laugh with or at him. Bernie would tell me, 'Boy, keep them laughing. Make them laugh so damn hard and so damn loud that they don't realize they are learning.'

My tactics were different. I concentrated on variety as the primary method. Sweet talk, Shakespearean monologues, Marine Corps brutality, prayers—anything that could possibly inflame the imagination, even momentarily, of someone imprisoned in my classroom all day.

'We don't like the news,' one child whispered.

'Tough crap, we are going to listen to the news whether you like it or not. Let's take a vote. Who does not want to listen to the news?' Every hand in the room shot up.

'I am going to break every arm that is raised in the air after we take the next vote. Who does not want to listen to the news?'

No one raised a single hand.

'Ah, excellent. Then it is unanimous, and I must say it is extremely gratifying that my students are sharing such a great concern for the rest of mankind.'

I put the news on, as I would for the next four months. As the announcer listed the deliriously happy events which occurred on the preceding day, I would stand by the map of the world and pinpoint the countries mentioned. Every time he named a country, a new dimension or a new frame of reference was added to my class's growing repertoire. They were geographically illiterate. The world map, pinned on the same spot probably for several years, could have been an anatomical chart of an earthworm for all they knew. When the announcer told the world that terrorists had abducted the American ambassador to Brazil, I put my finger on a big yellow blotch on the map and whispered, 'This hunk of yellow on the map is the country of Brazil.' Tracing Brazil with my finger as the announcer gave the details, I told them that Brazil produced most of the world's coffee. Then we learned of the latest border skirmishes between Egypt and Israel; Everett Dirksen dying in Illinois; Korean students rioting in Seoul. After the news, I showed them each country, gave them some juicy little fact about some of that country, and informed them that they would know something about that country from that time forward under pain of death.

'Now what bright young scholar can tell me what product we drink from Brazil?'

No one answered, naturally.

'Some people drink it black. Some people drink it with cream. Some people drink it with sugar. And some people don't drink it at all.'

'Coke,' Richard yelled.

'No,' I answered.

'Coffee!' some of them shouted.

'What is it?' I shouted back.

'Coffee,' all of them shouted.

'Where do they produce coffee?'

'Brazil,' some of them answered.

'Where is it?' I asked again.

'Brazil,' they shouted together.

And it was in this way that the pep-rally method of education began on Yamacraw Island. For the next several weeks a certain part of the morning was set aside for a daily chant or incantation to the gods of basic knowledge. Eleven of the students displayed an interest in learning little morsels or fragments of information for no other reason than just to know them. I talked about rivers, the one that flowed by Yamacraw, rivers I had seen in Europe, and then told them of the three great rivers of the world, the Nile, the Amazon, and the Mississippi. I listed the continents, the planets, and the oceans. I also gave them a brief outline of American history: Columbus stumbling upon America, Magellan's trip around the world, Balboa seeing the great Pacific, George Washington and the boys giving the British hell. Strange terms like the Constitution, the Declaration of Independence (which one of the kids kept calling the Decoration of Indianapolis), the Revolutionary War, the Civil War, and the Emancipation Proclamation.

None of these subjects did I touch in depth; I only gave a very general explanation of each one and tried to get the kids to look at history as a flow of events that somehow affects every person on earth. We used no books. It was oral history and oral geography. Nothing was written down. We talked and learned by talking and, soon enough for me, our pep rallies had evolved into wild chaotic exchanges of rote memory. I teased and cajoled them and expected them to fire back, to take no crap from me, just as I took no crap from them.

'All right, young cats. We are about to embark on a journey of knowledge. Now, I am convinced I am going to ask certain questions today so hard that you will not be able to answer any of them right.'

'No,' everyone murmured. They still thought I was a madman.

'What is the longest stinking river in the whole wide world?'

'The Nile,' all of them shouted, poking each other with their fingers and exulting in the breadth of their education.

'What continent is it on?'

'Africa.'

'Who comes from Africa?'

'Black people.'

'I came from Africa.'

'No!'

'Yeh! I came from Africa because I am white with blue eyes. Ireland is a country in Africa.'

'No. You lie. That ain't right. He crazy,' they retorted.

'James Brown came from Ireland.'

'No.'

'What's the largest planet in the universe?'

'Jupiter.'

'Second largest?'

'Saturn.'

'Nearest star?'

'The sun.'

'Largest country in the world?'

'Russia.'

'Country with the most people?'

'China.'

'James Brown comes from China.'

'No.'

'Who was the first President?'

'George Washington.'

'Second President was D. P. Conroy.'

'He crazy,' Sherman said.

'What country do we live in?'

'The United States of America.'

'What state do we live in?'

'South Carolina.'

'Are you sure?'

'Yeh, we sure.'

'What ocean washes up against this island?'

'Atlantic.'

'Where are we fighting a war?'

'Vietnam.'

'Who is the President of North Vietnam?'

'Ho Chi Minh.'

'What is James Brown's greatest song?'

'"Say it Loud, 'I'm Black and I'm Proud.'"'

'No, it's not,' I would say on cue. 'His greatest song is "Say It Loud, 'I'm White and I'm Proud.'"'

'No, man. He's colored,' Big C answered.

'No. White man crazy,' Prophet added.

'What state is below South Carolina?'

'Georgia.'

And on it went. Whenever we learned something new, it became part of the pep rally. I would often go to the map and point to a country, or a continent, or a river or ocean, and ask them to identify it. The map itself became a center of class activity—the map, a symbol of the world, where

Yamacraw was not even a pinprick, not even represented by a molecular dot when compared to the incomprehensible vastness of the world.

'Here is Asia and here is Yamacraw,' I would chant, moving my finger along the map. 'Here is California and here is Yamacraw. Here is China and here is Yamacraw. Gang, do you realize the neat things that are happening out there? The millions and millions of people swarming all over the earth? We are going to learn great stuff this year. We are going to stuff our brains with facts and ideas, and we are going to become sharp as razors.'

It should be noted that seven of the students got very little out of the pep rallies. But they shouted when everybody else was shouting, and even though they were not saying anything, they loved being a part of the successful whole. When I asked a question, they shouted a grunted reply. Flushed by success, their whoops grew louder and louder. Our pep rallies invariably ended when Mrs. Brown's large head would peer into the window and flash disapproving, desultory glances at me and the kids. The kids reacted as if a death's-head was in the window. After school Mrs. Brown would lecture me about the 'proper way to conduct yourself around colored children.' She repeated her offer to buy me a leather strap. I thanked her and told her that I was looking at a bullwhip in Savannah.

Complete illiteracy was an animal I had never encountered before. While teaching at the high school I came across some students who were not the brightest flames on the academic horizon, but none of them could compare with the seven students who formed a kind of know-nothing

71

fraternity at the Yamacraw School. Of these seven, five were unbelievable. Richard, Prophet, Jasper and the twins not only were untouched by the twenty-six letters of the alphabet, they were appallingly lacking in other skills too.

'How many fingers on one hand, Prophet?' I asked one day.

'Two,' he answered.

'Try it, Samuel.'

'Three.'

I put out the five fingers of my hand. 'Count the fingers, Sidney.'

'One,' said Sidney.

'How many fingers, Richard?'

'Four.'

'Sweet Jesus,' I said, regretting it instantly when I saw the four very embarrassed faces. The other students, supposedly working on their own projects, were giggling.

'Shut up, punks. We are in the process of education and so do not have time to be disturbed.'

Then I carefully explained the five-fingered hand. They could not count to ten. They could not add one and one, two and two, or anything else. Mrs. Brown told me they were retarded and not to waste my time on them. Someone obviously had not wasted a great deal of time trying to educate them. If I held up basic-word cards for them, they stared at the cards with blank, vacuous faces. The sum total of their education seemed to be nothing. The word *the* was as foreign to them as the word *elephant*. I found no area where they were remotely proficient.

Jasper tried like hell. He was nominally a sixth grader. His lips moved subconsciously, fighting hard to piece the proper sounds together. No sound emerged. Richard, his brother, reigned as master of the nonsense guess. I held up the word *rat* and Richard said, 'Tree.' The other four nodded their heads seriously to show their commitment and faith in Richard's judgment. I held up the word *cat* and Richard said, 'Bread.' 'Yep,' the others agreed, 'it bread, O.K.' The twins, Samuel and Sidney, sat there unruffled by my efforts to get them to respond. They seemed to like me, probably because I did not beat them. Whenever Mrs. Brown was beating one of her students and the screams and the sound of leather on flesh drifted into the room, the twins lifted their heads, their mouths slightly open, and listened until the screams turned to sobs and the song of the belt was ended. I would bet my ass they had known Mrs. Brown's calling card.

Prophet, one of the five, could look like a clown and a tragic character at the same time. His speech was absolutely unintelligible. He did not have a speech impediment; he had five impediments. If he said anything to me, one of the other kids had to translate it. He could neither talk, read, nor write, yet he was as likable and affable as anyone in the class. His smile was infectious, crafted by some supernatural mischief-maker. He played and frolicked as a profession, not a hobby, and I was important in his life only because I was constantly interfering in his fun-filled, puckish life. Every time I asked Prophet a question, he answered me with an approximation of 'yes, ma'am.' No one ever told Prophet that teachers could be male and that the phrase *yes, ma'am* is applied only to women. To Prophet *yes, ma'am* was what you said to teachers. Perhaps it was just as well, for many of the other children hit me constantly with the odious *yassuh*. And no matter how diligently I tried to eradicate the phrase from their vocabulary, they continued to use it.

After one month of anguish and labor all of them could present a reasonable facsimile of the alphabet upon request, depending on their mood and level of inspiration. They had also mastered the first ten numbers. They also recognized with varying degrees of success approximately thirty words. Sometimes we would have spelling tests to see how well the words had actually found permanent soil. I liked to give spelling tests to this group for no other reason than to watch the magnificent cheating which invariably took place. Samuel and Sidney, whose tiny heads scanned the horizon constantly for real or imagined enemies, cheated with real passion. They were inured to failure and to school. And though they were cheaters of the first magnitude, neither of them had developed any technique to avoid detection. In the middle of the spelling test Samuel's head would be practically lying on Richard's paper, while Sidney would simply move Jasper's arm aside to get an unencumbered view of his paper. The challenge of suppressing cheaters who performed their dastardly deeds so openly and disingenuously and with so much intellectual relish was immense. In fact I enjoyed the performances greatly.

A game I begged from an administrator in the county office proved very helpful with the five. It helped rescue them from total boredom in the classroom. It's called Play and Talk. It resembles a poor man's Parcheesi board, has a spinner, and the usual collection of rules. The game forces the player

74

to spell a word using the letter of the alphabet on which he lands. When I first introduced the game, Sidney started first. He landed on the letter D. 'What sound does that letter make, Sid,' I asked.

'Duh,' he answered correctly.

'Very good. Now spell a word that starts with the letter D.'

'Dog,' he said hesitantly. 'D-O-D.'

Hands shot up all around him. Samuel, his twin, giggled like hell. Sidney leaned over and socked Samuel. Samuel leaned over and socked Sidney. I leaped between them and demanded that they halt this nonsense immediately. Sid leaned around my left and yanked Samuel's ear. Samuel screamed and told me that if Sid touched him one more time he was going to kick his butt. Eventually I restored a semblance of peace and the game continued.

As I watched them play on that day and on succeeding days, it was apparent that this group played for blood and not for fun. If someone missed a word the others screamed and fought to answer it correctly. So intense was the competition that I could rarely drift too far away in another part of the room without a pitched battle arising. One occasion, I looked over to find Jasper and Richard sitting nose to nose, glaring virulently at each other, saying nothing, pinching each other's arms. Their faces were twisted in anger. Jasper pinched Richard. Then Richard pinched Jasper. And so on. When the great two-hundred-pound mediator stumbled over to intervene, I was told, 'Richard cheats,' by Jasper and then, 'Jasper cheats,' by Richard. Both of them proved their cases conclusively. Indeed, both of them undeniably had cheated. When Prophet said that he had seen it all and that both were wrong, I nodded my head sagaciously, delivered an impromptu sermon on the need for honesty, and left them to continue the game in peace. When I looked around again, Richard and Jasper were pinching Prophet.

Yet nothing bothered Prophet. He was the clown at war with a frowning world. When he found out that corporal punishment was not my trump card, he spent his whole life improvising irritations to test my self-control. He would walk up to me and make these ludicrous faces. Sticking out his tongue or rolling his eyes, he followed me around making faces or stealing my wallet from my back pocket. He loved games and this was why he adapted so well to the Play and Talk game.

It was during a session of this game that Prophet electrified the class and held it unwittingly in the palm of his hand for several staggering moments. He spun the dial and landed on the letter F. He properly identified the letter and its sound. But naming a word that started with F proved a considerable challenge. Finally, after long and tortured deliberation, he came out with a word.

'Fuck,' he said rather smugly. The class and the teacher of the class were stunned. Prophet grinned.

'What did you say, Prophet?' I asked inanely.

'Fuck,' he repeated, with bell-like clarity for Prophet.

'Would you please spell that word, prophet?' I asked, praying for deliverance.

'F-U-X,' he spelled.

'Do you mean "fox," Prophet?'

'Yas'm. Look like dawg.'

The class erupted. Prophet smiled broadly, amazed and pleased by his ability to evoke laughter

76

from the elder section of Yamacraw scholars.

CHAPTER FOUR

Each day when school was over, it became my habit to set off in a new direction on the island, exploring, walking, singing to myself, and generally enjoying the isolation and silences of Yamacraw's forests. These daily expeditions took me all over the island. And though I enjoyed these walks, several characteristics of the island made them uncomfortable and even painful.

The island swarmed with mosquitoes. Whenever a human being left the front door of his house, legions of mosquitoes with their hypodermic snouts would cover the wretch from head to foot. It is difficult to know whether I am exaggerating or not, but I do know for certain that they made life on the island extremely uncomfortable and that no matter how extensive one's precautions against them were, no matter how much repellent one applied to his body, the mosquitoes still managed to get in their licks. They buzzed around my head in squadrons during all my walks. One day Frank showed me an island trick to keep them at their distance. He tore a leafy branch from a small tree and waved it back and forth across his back. 'You hear 'em, you swat 'em,' he told me. So armed with this surrogate cow's tail and covered with enough insect repellent to kill a dinosaur, I would troop out toward the beach road, glistening like a Polynesian fresh from a coconut bath.

The beach road began about a quarter of a mile

from the school. It cut through a black-water swamp where the deer and the moccasins played. It was a dark and brooding part of the island, very wild and uninhabited. Purple and yellow wild-flowers grew in profusion. The first time I walked the road I was shocked to find two odd-looking brick structures on a curve in the road. There was a sign on one of the buildings that read SILVER DEW WINERY 1953. A little further down the road was a magnificent old house with wagon wheels in the yard and the forlorn appearance assumed by all houses that have lost their people. I went up to the house and peered into the windows. The furniture was good and functional, yet cobwebs and brown spiders had claimed the walls for themselves. At the back of the house, above the back door, was a very large and tattered Confederate flag. What the flag was doing there I never found out, but it was odd how the house and the flag seemed to fit together in this silent tribute to a lost people and a forgotten cause. I have known a great many Confederate flag nuts in my life, rabid dreamers who dwell on the glory of Fort Sumter and Bull Run and repress the reality of Appomattox. The Confederate flag summons primitive emotions in these people. Recently it only disgusts me, although there was a time I revered it as religiously as Christians revere the cross. Here on Yamacraw, fastened over the door of a peeling house, mute in its testimony to a defeated cause and an expiring way of life, the flag had more dignity than I had ever noticed before. Perhaps the dignity was, in fact, that the flag was dead and the house was dead, and I was only passing by.

I passed by the house each day in the month of

September on the way to the beach, for the beach was the best single place on the island. Ten miles of beach front and not a damn person on it except me. I would come out of the swamp and race full speed past the sand and sea oats. I would hit the beach sprinting as hard as I could go. The beach breeze kept the five million mosquitoes hovering in the forest behind me. I would run until I got tired, then strip naked and swim in the surf. The water was shallow and very warm, but the salt felt good on my mosquito bites, and there is something undeniably salubrious for the soul about floating naked in the surf without another human being in sight or sound, free from the encumbrances or worries of the classroom.

After the swim, I would walk far down the beach, often to Bloody Point, where the British once drove a tribe of Indians to the end of the island and slaughtered them, men, women, and children, at the edge of the sea. I used to walk and look at the dead horseshoe crabs, strange prehistoric creatures who simply could not cope with the pollution of the Savannah River and had washed ashore at Yamacraw by the hundred. The whole beach stunk of death and decaying marine life. At the end of the island I could see the factories belching and puking into the sky. The same factories that had killed the Yamacraw oysters and the economy of the island had not spared the defenseless, clumsy, and harmless horseshoe crabs. The legacy of the factories was here on the beach.

*   *   *

After one week on the island, I knew that Ted

79

Stone was king. The reason I knew it is that Ted Stone told me so. I would go down and pick up my mail every day at five o'clock. Invariably Ted would come out to talk about the school, about the people of the island, and about his position among them. He and his wife not only cornered every job available on the island, but their home also contained the short-wave radio that was the sole means of communication with the mainland. Piss off Ted Stone and the possibility for a delay on the radio was certainly there.

Ted was also the quintessential outdoorsman. He hunted religiously, fished expertly, and shrimped the waters off Yamacraw to supplement his already sizable income. I would often come in his yard to find the carcass of a deer strung from a tree, the carnage of the hunt in evidence all around, guts littering the ground, and Ted sitting proudly on a lawn chair. He could do things with his hands very well. He could plow a field, milk a cow, gut a hog, cook a trout, clean a rifle—all the things that made us such complete opposites.

His eyes were ice blue and suspicious. He was thickly built with powerful arms and a great barrel of a chest. He was short with a remarkable mane of gray hair and a handsome, weather-beaten face. Ted was a fine-looking man. And now a few black residents of the island had stated in no uncertain terms that Ted Stone was a son of a bitch. Yet, in the early days, Ted went out of his way to be kind to me.

His wife, Lou, was an extremely proficient woman. A lover of flowers and solitude, she seemed perfectly adapted to the Spartan existence on Yamacraw. She drove the school bus as proudly and

80

as competently as Junior Johnson drives his stock cars. She delivered mail daily, depending upon the weather and her mood. The post office was located in the back of their house. It was a small clean room, which she kept securely padlocked because of the 'nigras.' She claimed to be extremely interested in the education of the poor children I was teaching. All the educational deficiencies of the children she blamed on Miss Glover, whom she—like everyone else—believed to be the voodoo woman of the island. Mrs. Brown, on the other hand, ranked in the major leagues as a savior of epic proportions; she was teaching the children manners and one thing these children needed was manners.

Both Stones worried about the morality of the nigras. 'They're savages,' Ted exclaimed over and over. 'They sleep with one another's wives and husbands. They sleep with anyone that comes along. They are filthy savages who shouldn't be allowed to have children. They drink all night long while their children are starving. They all ought to be shot.' Ted's eyes would sparkle maniacally whenever he got upset.

Lou would add, 'There are a couple of good ones. Aunt Ruth is just as sweet as she could be. And Mrs. Brown is part Indian, you know. It's the ones who are pure black who are really worthless.'

These were my kiss-ass days. I needed Ted and Lou. I kept my boat at their dock; I would be renting a house through them as soon as certain legal entanglements were straightened out; they brought my mail; they sold me fresh eggs and milk; and they provided my transportation. According to my early philosophy of survival on the island, I had to have Ted and Lou on my side. They wielded

81

enormous power—even the power of life and death. One day during the second week Lou told me a very illuminating story. Her youngest son had gone to school on the island. When I asked if Mrs. Brown or Miss Glover had taught him, she quickly explained that he did not go to school with the nigras but had gone to the white school.

'I didn't know they had a white school,' I said.

'They built one just for my son so he wouldn't have to go to school with the coloreds.'

'You're kidding?' I asked incredulously.

'They built a one-room schoolhouse, hired a teacher to come over here and live in the school, and she taught my son.'

'No one else went to the school? No other white kids?' I questioned.

'No other white kids on the island,' she replied. 'Of course we wouldn't send our child with the coloreds. George deserved as good an education as any other white child. That's what we demanded and that's what we got.'

'One teacher for one child! That's not bad,' I said.

'Mrs. Brown lives in the white schoolhouse now,' Lou said. 'My George got a good education there. A real fine education.'

Despite my objections to Ted Stone's theories of apartheid, his paranoia about my long hair, and the new morality, I enjoyed jogging down to his house, picking up my mail, and then swimming off his dock. I also found Ted to be a fascinating raconteur. The stories he told had the flavor of earth, blood, and the hunt. He had been a trapper, a professional fisherman, a hunter of some repute, and a plasterer in Fort Lauderdale, Florida. he

82

killed deer for pleasure and for food, shot rattlesnakes as a public service, and fished the waters off Yamacraw with religious regularity. He had once run a restaurant on Yamacraw. His wife had cooked and served the food; he had plied the customers with beer. The customers were fishermen from Savannah and Bluffton. According to Mr. Stone, his restaurant did a thriving business on weekends. When I asked why he didn't still run the place, he answered rather succinctly, 'Niggers wanted to get served, just like whites. Had to close it.' Of course if it hadn't been the niggers, then the hippies would probably have wanted to buy a beer under his roof, and he would not have had any of that.

Yet his life was fascinating to me, in that it was so different from my own. My father taught me how to shoot a hook shot, lead a fast break, and feed off to the open man; he also instructed me how to throw a cross-body block and how to field a ground ball skimming across a short-grassed infield. To my father life offered no finer pleasures or more consummate skills. Mr. Stone, in contrast, could skin and clean a deer in an hour, take apart a boat motor and assemble it again, milk a cow, plant a garden, fix a muffler, and drag a seine across a shallow inlet in preparation for a shrimp dinner. My life was centered around academics and sports; Stone's was concerned with the arts of survival. I depended on supermarkets and theaters; Stone frequented feed stores and garden-supply shops when he journeyed to Savannah.

So I listened to Stone and was glad to be learning. He loved to talk about himself and nothing could have been more instructive to me. On a whim, he had once traveled to Florida with a group of friends, bought the boat which Humphrey Bogart captained in the film *The African Queen*, and brought it back to Yamacraw Island, where it survived a year then rotted slowly into oblivion. It gave me an immense thrill to think that my boat docked in the same spot which once harbored the *African Queen*. It fired the Irish romanticism within me, as did Mr. Stone's accounts of the hurricane of '59 that crushed boats and docks like playthings, that uprooted oak trees as tall as towers, that incapacitated a town thirty miles from the island and made it a national disaster area. As his house creaked ominously, Ted and Lou sipped coffee and watched the gods of storm seize the wind and river for several violent hours.

Stone's powers of description were excellent. He spent two hours one day relating his war experiences. He had landed on the third wave during D-Day, fought his way across France, teamed up with a sharp-shooting Texan, who together with Stone formed a murderously competent sniping team, and eventually crossed into Germany when the armistice was signed. With eyes blue and shimmering, yet serious and fatalistic, he described a German soldier's head rising above a roof-top ledge, how he waited until he could see the German's whole head, until he could see the face was young and unlined. He aimed carefully and put a bullet between the eyes of his enemy. It was a strange story, strangely told, and Ted Stone grew uncharacteristically reflective and philosophical as he thought of the life he snuffed out somewhere in France twenty-five years before. 'Killing a man is different from killing a deer.' Yet he was intensely proud that he had killed other men in the defense of his country.

A faded American flag flew from a wooden pole in the backyard of the Stone house. This was the symbol of the post office, yet also seemed to symbolize Stone's allegiance to his country which was blind, uncompromising, unconditional, and though he would have fought me had he heard me express the thought, almost Third Reich in its fervor and rigidity.

One night at the Stones' is memorable. It was October 15, Moratorium Day, when the United States reverberated with the chants and pleadings of those discontented with the war. I wanted desperately to watch the news that night, to see how the Washington march went, and to see the reaction of people around the country to the moratorium itself. I had a pretty good idea about what Ted thought about the moratorium, but I did not realize that I would be watching the greatest show on earth in Ted's living room. As soon as the news came on, Ted began a long monologue which continued unabated till I excused myself an hour later.

'Look at those long-haired bastards. Can't tell if they're boys or girls. Worse than Germans or Japs. Look at that hippie with the flag sewed to his butt. I'd cut it off his ass with a butcher knife if I was there. Take half of his ass with it. Lice. All they are is lice. Huntley and Brinkley are lice, too. They aren't supporting our boys in Vietnam. Naw. They're lice. Just like that nigger Martin Luther King. He was a goddam Communist sure as hell. Ask J. Edgar Hoover. Now there's a man. Finest man in America. He calls a spade a spade. Look at them lice there now. Cute, ain't they? I wouldn't give them a drink of piss if they were dyin' of thirst. There are some niggers. Every time you turn on TV you see the niggers. They even got them brushin' their teeth on TV. Hippies. Goddam Communist hippies. Dirty, don't take baths. We got some hippies coming to this island now. Those California boys are just hippies that get their hair cut before they come here. All of 'em is lice. Nigger-lovin' lice. There's the White House. Where the President of the United States lives. Where the President of the United States of America leads his people. Wallace wouldn't have had it. There would have been bodies lyin' all over the streets if he had gotten in. He'd of used flame throwers and tanks.'

Stone talked and I listened. It was insane, ludicrous, and frightening. His face curled in hatred. He forgot I was in the room. He smelled blood and his whole personality was transfixed to the thought that the marchers should die en masse on Constitution Avenue. He wanted them dead, he said, 'to give America a good name in the free world.' D. P. Conroy said nothing. Stricken with fright, I saw the awesome display of weapons mounted in Stone's front room and did not wish to give Stone even the slightest reason to identify me with the Washington marchers. When I left, Stone told me to come watch the news with him anytime.

The next day I was swimming off Stone's dock after school. The water was growing colder, but its bracing chill seemed to clean out the frustrations for a little while. Stone came down to the dock and started talking. This time he talked of fishing.

'Good fishing off this dock here,' he said. 'Catch a whole string of winter trout, right now. Might even catch a sea trout or two. My son caught a

86

ten-foot shark off this dock a year ago.'

In three strokes I covered about twenty yards of water. In a flash of spray and spume and chilled blood, I stood upon the dock a scant four seconds after Stone delivered the news about the shark.

'Are there lots of sharks out there?' I asked, my voice squeaking and my knees filled with jelly.

'Oh, lots of them. They hang around the dock a lot.'

'That's great, Mr. Stone. That is really great. You mean I have been swimming in shark-infested waters all this time and you never told me!'

'You knew sharks lived in salt water.'

'I did not know they had a clubhouse under your dock, or my young ass would never have hit water. Sharks eat people, Mr. Stone.'

'Not around here. I've never heard of anyone getting eaten around here.'

'Well, I sure don't want to become a precedent.' My afternoon swims ended for all time on that day.

★　　★　　★

Several friends of mine in Beaufort warned me about forming any kind of relationship with Zeke Skimberry. Skimberry was the maintenance man of the Bluffton district and because of a decree emanating from the high echelons of the educational hierarchy, Zeke was designated as the official guardian of my boat. Skimberry aroused suspicion in many quarters because of his sycophantic allegiance to Ezra Bennington. Zeke had survived many purges of personnel and many tumultuous years in the Bluffton school system by affixing his fate to the more luminous and permanent star of Bennington. He mowed Bennington's grass, moved cumbersome early American furniture around Mrs. Bennington's plush antique shop, and acted as Bennington's chauffeur, valet, and servant when the occasion demanded it. Behind his back, people hissed that Zeke was 'Bennington's nigger' and nothing more. I found a lot more.

He was, on first meeting, one of the warmest, most genuinely friendly people I had ever met. His large blue eyes danced and flashed expressively, puckishly; a grin constantly played about his mouth. He was lean but muscled by constant exposure to physical labor and his face revealed an intelligence, an alertness, that both surprised and delighted me. Zeke was a California transplant, a divorcé who drifted out of an unhappy marriage in the West, wandered from job to job, drank good whiskey under the skies of many states, until he met and fell in love with Ida McKee, a striking young blonde hitting a cash register in a general store near Bluffton, South Carolina. Zeke drove her to Georgia after a madcap courtship, married her with the benediction of an itchy-palmed justice of the peace, and returned to Bluffton to begin the second act of his life in completely new surroundings. In fourteen years in Bluffton he had sired two sons and managed to worm his way so completely into Bennington's life and make himself so indispensable that he sometimes seemed like Bennington's third leg. When Bennington was in power, Zeke's position was enviable, but now that Bennington's career was in its eclipse, Zeke was beginning to feel the pressure of insecurity again.

My relationship with Zeke Skimberry and his

family started slowly and inauspiciously but gathered momentum and intimacy as the year passed. He was impossible to dislike. He loved to tease, to banter lightly with all who crossed his path, and to mimic the supervisors who ruled him. At our first meeting he told me, 'People over here think you are crazy for teachin' at that school.'

'People over here are exactly right,' I answered.

'Of course, all these people are crazy themselves, so there's no tellin',' he said with his eyes dancing, mischievous, and very blue. Then he said with great seriousness, 'Course, the niggers on Yamacraw have needed something for a damn long time. I sure hope you can help those little nigger kids.'

The most fascinating thing about Zeke Skimberry, however, was his irrepressible wife, Ida. She was a poetess of profanity, an oracle of epithets who could outcuss a bathroom wall. Unlike most women I have known, she placed no value on shallow pretensions or hypocritical displays of gentility. Her first words to me as I drove into her yard on a Sunday afternoon the first week in September marked her as a person to be handled gently and with caution. From the screened-in porch of her tiny house, she yelled, 'What in the hell are you looking for?'

'Ma'am, I'm looking for Zeke Skimberry, the janitor.'

'He's not a goddam janitor. He's the maintenance man. Everybody's always calling him a janitor. Well, who in the hell are you?' she asked with eyes ablazing.

'I'm Pat Conroy, ma'am. I teach over on Yamacraw Island, and I was supposed to get in touch with your husband, Mrs. Skimberry.'

'He ain't here now. Come on inside and git yourself a cup of coffee.' As I got out of the car, she startled me again by saying, 'Hot as a bitch, ain't it?'

'Yes, ma'am, it certainly is.'

In no way had my mother with her air of gentility and fine breeding prepared me for the Ida Skimberrys of the world. The coffeepot, positioned in honorable perpetuity on the stove, was the center of the tiny Skimberry universe, and over the year we consumed gallons of the steaming, hot brew as Zeke rambled on about the idiosyncracies of his work or the insecurity of his position. Or Ida would curse fluently at the lack of money, at her husband's lack of status, or at her inability to find a decent job.

During the week I parked my car in the Skimberrys' yard under Ida's vigilant eye. After my second week on the island, after Zeke had picked me up at Alljoy Landing, and after consuming three cups of coffee while describing the events of the week, I walked out to my car to discover that Ida had washed the car and cleaned out the inside during the week. She had also found a sack of dirty clothes in the backseat. She had washed and ironed all the clothes and neatly folded them in a cardboard box. I was overwhelmed by this kindness. I thanked her with genuine emotion, but all she said was, 'Shit, the goddam car needed washin' and the goddam clothes needed a good cleanin'.' Then her face, which could be hard as a callus, softened into a magnificently warm smile and she said, 'I enjoy doin' things for people.'

It did not take me long to warm to this kind of

people. And just as I had entered a new realm of experience on Yamacraw, I also walked on fresh territory each time I entered the door to Zeke and Ida's house. My background did not expose me to white people who subsisted on $4000 a year, who did not have a set of china for special meals, who did not select a pattern of silver, and who had not graduated from high school. I had never dealt directly with people who felt their lives enriched by weekly odysseys to wrestling matches. The Skimberrys were of a different social class than I and one of the year's miracles was my introduction to their way of life, to their complete and ingenuous acceptance of me as a friend, and to the perspective they gave me of society and the men on top as viewed from the bottom.

I came to love the Skimberrys devotedly, for without reason, they took me into their home, told me their dreams and disappointments, shared with me the intimate secrets and compromises of their lives. They bared their souls before me because of an elementary honesty that did not understand guile or pretense. I was part of their life and it became important to the Yamacraw story as events took place and circumstances shifted. And how many mornings or afternoons do I remember Ida's voice rasping, as I came through the door, 'Pat, you ol' son of a bitch, git you some coffee.'

★   ★   ★

I saw the town of Bluffton through the eyes of Zeke Skimberry. In the early morning, before the insect noise had died in the woods near his house, Zeke would sit in his favorite chair, sip hot coffee from a thick, cream-colored mug, and talk about the town. He was one of those men who were gifted storytellers, who could capture the spirit of a place by recounting forgotten incidents, or by digging up skeletons the town might have preferred to leave buried and untouched. Zeke knew the merchants, the cheaters, the lonely, the schizophrenic, the lusty, the insane, the religious, the hypocritical, the blacks, the rednecks, the generous. He knew them all and could sketch an accurate biography of everyone who lived in town. He knew who slept with whom, who wanted to sleep with whom, and who would sleep with whom. He could list every murder that had occurred in the past ten years, how much blood was lost, where the bullet or knife struck, and how stiff the body was when discovered by the authorities. He knew the authorities, too, with all their frailties and flaws, with all their weaknesses and pretensions. It was over coffee that I learned about Zeke and Ida and grew to love them. Their house was alive with joy, laughter, and worry over money, derision of professionals and hacks; their house was warm, good, and filled with coffee smells. And both of them loved to talk of their town.

Bluffton perched above the winding, tide-ruled May River, egrets fished its shores, and fleets of long bateaux explored the blind inlets and creeks in search of productive oyster beds. Bluffton is a town of matchless serenity, a town thick with glinting, towering magnolias, impressive oaks, sloughs glutted with wildflowers, peeling but remarkably attractive houses. A church built from cypress stands beside the river; a structure of elegant simplicity and fine lines built by slaves, and presided over by the omnipresent town pillar, the deacon of deacons, Ezra Bennington. Bluffton is sleepy, magisterially silent, and enjoys a benediction of flowers every brilliant spring. Yet it is a town that retains many of the wrinkles and arthritic cramps of the Old South.

There was the story of Thomas, a massive black man whom Zeke and I often passed in the morning on our way to gas up. Thomas would sit in the middle of a large group of animated black men on the steps of a crumbling tenement. He was incredibly large, a redwood, among the smaller pines.

'That's a damn big nigger, ain't he,' Zeke would say.

'Yep,' I would reply rurally.

'He's had a tough life, ol' Thomas. When he was just a young boy, not more'n about fifteen or sixteen, he used to help deliver ice door to door. Now those were the days when there wasn't such things as refrigerators. When you said icebox, you meant a damn box with a big hunk of ice in it. So ol' Thomas, being a big son of a bitch, could lift them hunks of ice pretty easy and carry them door to door. One day he went up to a house at Alljoy Beach and knocked on the door. A young white girl answered his knock. Well, Thomas didn't talk real good, anyway, so he got real nervous and asked this white girl if she wanted a piece, meaning a piece of ice for the icebox. Well, the girl misunderstood what Thomas was tryin' to say, you know, thought he was trying to give her a piece of his pecker. She screamed and raised hell till every white man in town was running down to her. Now you know how this town is, now. Can you imagine what those people were thinkin' then? This big ol' Thomas trying to get into a little white girl's britches. He was lucky they didn't lynch him and cut his balls off. As it was, they tried him and sent him up for twenty-somethin' years. All the time, Thomas just stood there looking kind of dumb and muttering that all he wanted was to sell her some ice. The bad thing about it, Pat, was that this girl was crazy as hell, anyway. A month after the trial she went completely nuts and spent the rest of her life in a mental hospital.'

'What a horrible, goddam story, Zeke.'

'Just goes to show you that people will shit on a nigger and never think a thing about it. People around here are just prejudiced against niggers. Want to see them all dead. Want to see them all shipped back to Africa. All these good Christian people.'

'Good Christian people' was the most cynical epithet in Zeke's repertoire. He and Ida had been very active members of the local Baptist church until the congregation voted to close the church if a nigger ever tried to attend a service. Zeke and Ida simply never went back after that.

'Can you imagine, Pat. A bunch of Christians keeping another bunch of Christians from praying. Can you see Jesus sitting at the front door of the church saying, "Hey, you shit-eatin' niggers, you can't come in this here church. Go to your own nigger church." Yeh, I can just see Jesus doing that.'

Zeke and Ida mouthed the regional prejudices against blacks constantly, and believed implicitly in almost every stereotype ever concocted against blacks in the South. Yet every black man or woman

94

I brought to their house was invited inside, offered coffee, and treated with dignity and warmth. Later, Ida would tell me, 'That was sure a nice nigger man you brought here this morning. I hope you bring him back again real soon.'

I could never place this dichotomy of attitude, could never understand it, could never be comfortable around such a casual, unself-conscious use of the word *nigger*, but ultimately came to accept it as the way Zeke and Ida were, no more and no less. They instinctively liked all people but had been conditioned to dislike and depreciate blacks. Several conversations with Ida were enough to convince me that all the sermonizing in the world could not shake the foundation of her thirty-three years in Bluffton.

I came from the river one day in the spring, and Ida said, 'Pat, I just done a terrible thing today. Little Eddie has been havin' trouble with his glands again, so I decided to call a specialist in Savannah to have a look.'

'It's best to go to a specialist when you think somethin's really the matter, Ida.'

'Yeh, that's why I called. Well, this doctor gets on the phone and tells me to bring Eddie in on Thursday morning, ten o'clock sharp.'

'Nothin' wrong with that, Ida.'

Then she lowered her voice and said, 'Pat, I do believe I called me a nigger doctor.'

'No,' I said, shrinking back in mock horror.

'It ain't funny. Wouldn't make no difference to a stupid bastard like yourself, anyhow. But goddam it, I ain't sending my young 'un to no nigger doctor.'

'Why do you think this doctor is black, Ida?'

'He talked like a nigger,' she answered. 'You know that funny way niggers talk. You can tell a nigger a mile away when he opens his mouth. And I looked at his street in the phone book, and Pat, I ain't never heard of no street by this name. Have you?'

I looked at the address and professed ignorance.

'Only a nigger doctor would have an address on a street no one's ever heard of,' she continued. 'I think the phone company should tell you who is and who isn't a nigger doctor.'

'He's probably as good as any of the white doctors, Ida.'

'Goddam it, Pat, if I don't think you're part nigger yourself sometimes. Now tell me quick what I kin do. Kin I call him down there, very polite and all, and say, "Hello, I made an appointment with you the other day, but I didn't know you were a nigger doctor. I meant no harm and I thank you for your kindness. I just feel that a person should go to his own kind." You think that'd do it?'

'That'd do it O.K., Ida. He'd probably tell you to get laid.'

'And I'd kick him in the goddam ass if he did,' she bristled.

Yet within her own family circle, Ida was considered an unregenerated liberal. Sometimes her mother, sisters, and in-laws would stop by her house to exchange gossip while I was still there. These exchanges always amazed me. The subject of race was a violent and recurrent theme.

'If one of them nigger teachers even lays a hand on my child, I'll kill her deader than hell. I'll kill her, I swear on a Bible, I'll kill her,' one of Ida's sisters would say.

'Shore you'd kill her,' someone would say.

'If one of them niggers even looks cross-eyed at my girl, she's gonna have me sittin' on her ass,' another voice of reason rang out.

'Shore you would, honey.'

In the midst of all this, Ida's youngest sister would turn to her little girl and ask softly, 'What are you, sugar?' And the little girl would reply dramatically, 'I'm a sweet little Christian girl who loves the baby Jesus.' And everybody would answer chorally, 'Sure you love Jesus, honey. We all love Jesus.' Except Ida. She would mouth the word *bullshit* and wink at me.

Then the harangue would continue on the other side of the kitchen table. 'I mean if these niggers want to teach in white schools, they can't go around knockin' white children. Otherwise, I'm gonna have to knock their goddam heads off.'

'Shore you will, honey.'

Then Ida would shock the gathering by declaring, 'Hell, I told Eddie's teacher to beat the shit out of him if he gave her any sass. She's a damn good teacher and a nice lady besides. I want her to hit my young 'un if he acts up. How else is she gonna teach 'im?'

'Why, Ida, sometimes you talk just plain trash.'

'You shore do, honey.'

'You'd let a nigger hit pore little Eddie?'

'Damn right, I would,' Ida answered.

Then, to heal the wounds opened by the argument, the youngest sister again would gaze worshipfully into the eyes of her child and say, 'What are you, sugar?' And the fat, saccharine, little cherub would reply, 'I'm a sweet little Christian girl who loves the baby Jesus.' And Ida

97

would mouth the word *bullshit* again and wink.

★ ★ ★

At the end of September, a month which had
assumed the dimensions of an eternity, I left my
corner of the schoolroom for the more spacious
quarters of the Buckner house. Taking all things in
consideration, I had hated living in the school,
shaving without a mirror with cold water, cooking
in pots big enough to hold small cows, and sleeping
on a cot sprinkled lightly with chalk dust. Chalk
dust has a way of conquering a room, and I was
faintly weary of waking up feeling like a butterfly
wing or a powdered underarm. And I was tired of
dwelling in the same place I worked. The whole
situation was becoming unbearable.

A lot of frustration had to do with me. When I
first envisioned myself on the island, a noble
creature enshrined among the illiterate masses
working in the primitive conditions that would have
warmed the cockles of Henry Thoreaus' heart, I did
not consider my compulsive need for friends and
good conversation. I love people and collect friends
like some people collect coins or exotic pipes. So
far, the people of the island had 'yassuhed' me to
death. I was the white principal, a figure of
authority, which in itself could not be trusted. The
white people, without exception, were back-to-
Africa advocates, believers in the small-brain
theory, and as suspicious a bunch as I had ever met.
To everybody I met, I flashed the toothy grin, the
hearty salutation, and the slap-happy demeanor of
someone desperately in need of friendship. But in
the space of a month I had failed to establish any

allegiances.

I had often fantasized myself as being the world's greatest undiscovered poet, living in obscurity and biding my time until the seeds of greatness germinated and I would cast poems to the world. In the first month I tried to write these poems. In fact, I tried to write many things, but my mind was so boggled by the circumstances of my students and my own life was so uncertain and without direction that I found myself writing mawkish doggerel and prose of an extraordinary purplish tinge. The month of September was a ludicrous month and I was a ludicrous person.

There was another reason I wished to leave the schoolhouse. One night, as a storm gathered over the island, and the thunder rumbled menacingly above, I was lying in bed reading. The night was coal black except for brief intervals when lightning illuminated the sky. As I was reading, my head against the pillow, my bed underneath a window that afforded me a view of the playground, I felt a sudden strange and frightening sensation. I looked up and saw the face of a grinning black man wearing a beret, staring at me through the window. His face was less than two feet away from me. I was momentarily stunned with fright and shock. My face evidently reflected my emotions, for the man turned suddenly and raced off in a sprint toward the forest. As he ran, a maniacal, animalistic howl split the darkness. The howl grew fainter the farther away he ran. Massaging my heart, trying to get it beating again, I tried to make some move appropriate to the situation. The face had startled me; the noise had terrified me. The face, framed in the window, against the backdrop of night and storm, was a metaphor of lunacy, a blank and uncomprehending face with a smile devoid of feeling.

I was completely unnerved. I turned out the lights and tried to see if the creature still lurked around the school. I grabbed a baseball bat and went from window to window trying to catch a glimpse of my unnamed visitor. Since no shades hung from the windows, I had no way of preventing eyes from peering into my room, no way to shut myself off from the outside. Had I seen this stranger again, peeking in at me with those possessed eyes and demonic smile, I am certain I would have died of fright. The baseball bat slept with me that night, an uncomfortable but comforting bed partner. I slept miserably, fearing that whoever the guy was, there was always the chance he could break into the kitchen and gain access to my room. If he did, I promised myself, he would be facing an antagonist crazed with fear, a desire to live, and carrying a baseball bat that would remove heads if the occasion required. When the dawn finally arrived—oh blessed dawn, oh holy light, oh lovely sun—and I explained to Mrs. Brown what had happened, she told me that I had met face to face with Mad Billie.

I got to know Mad Billie well after the incident. He was the resident crazy person on the island, the genuine Quasimodo who earned his living and insured his survival by being considered crazy. Everyone called him Mad Billie to his face and behind his back. He chopped wood, carried packages, and delivered messages for people on the island, white and black alike. The Stones told me authoritatively that Billie was crazy, but harmless and would not hurt a fly. Mrs. Brown ran him off the school grounds every time he came around, saying that he was 'retarded' and liable to molest the girls. Billie's guise of craziness dropped whenever he spoke to me about Mrs. Brown. He hated her guts and his most common epithet directed toward her was 'shitass.' Billie talked as if he were living a dream sequence, which perhaps he was. He cursed with gusto, smiled constantly and vacuously, talked strangely and vaguely and mostly to himself, and lived rather contentedly while playing his role of island lunatic.

Billie always seemed to know what was going on. One would find him all over the island—coming out of the woods carrying an ax, or running full speed up one of the island roads. He was rabbit fast and ran almost everywhere he went, often making the preternatural noise I heard on that stormy night. The noise was his personal trademark, a kind of calling card he carried with him. I walked with Billie to the beach one afternoon in October. He suddenly broke into a run, emitted his patented hellish whine, and disappeared into the forest. By now accustomed to Billie's personal flamboyancies, I continued toward the beach. As I walked along, Billie froze me once more by making his noise from the branch of a tree I was walking under. When he saw me jump, he threw back his head and laughed his registered crazy laugh. Ol' Billie was a weird guy.

Because of Billie I was glad to be moving out of the school, but tragedy brought me to the house I was renting. Viola Buckner, an island matriarch and an important bridge in the tenuous relationship between blacks and whites on the island, left home during the summer for an operation. She never returned to the island. When the doctors opened her stomach, they found that cancer had established complete dominion. She died several days later.

Her house was a neat, clapboard structure with a wilderness of vines and plants running over the yard and field around the house. Inside, the house was a patchwork of various woods, a gingerbread house of conflicting colors and patterns, pasteboard and tile thrown together at random. One attribute made this house a palace on Yamacraw. It possessed a shiny, glistening white commode, a treasure of inestimable value and an invention that overshadows the wheel as necessary for man's comfort and convenience. Since I had sampled several of the Yamacraw privies, the presence of the toilet delighted me. The smell of feces and urine-stained wood has never struck me as a gratifying sensual experience and my middle-class background had not prepared me for life without scented toilet paper.

This particular commode was a monument of sorts. Viola, like the other black residents of the island, used the outhouse her entire life. But Viola had had dreams. She had the toilet installed several months before she died. She had told people that if she sat on her commode only one time, it would have been worth the price to her. As I stared at Viola's toilet, I saluted her and her dream.

Some unknown hand had painted the bathroom walls a passionate pink. A calendar hung on one wall advertising Black Draught Laxative and Cardui Pills for women 'who really want help on "those certain days."' The living room was small and cramped with dark brown, squatty furniture. A picture of the risen Christ with the attendant angels swarming like pigeons around him held the place of honor above the oil heater. A great many framed photographs lined the walls. Photographs have always made me very sad. Here in Viola's house, it seemed sacrilegious to stare at old photographs of nameless blacks, many of whom had died years before. The scrubbed faces of smiling people were beautifully captured by a lens that froze a brief, escaping moment, froze it into a single, essential study; the moment having passed, those lives continued and finally snuffed out. Age had faded the photographs.

One picture particularly caught and held my eye, not only for its inappropriateness to the other memorabilia in the room but also because of its haunting relationship to my own life. It was the picture of a Corsair, a stubby black fighter plane whose vintage years were in the early 1950s. My father, a career Marine, had often flown over our house when I was a first grader, dipping his wings and otherwise making his presence known to the tiny world assembled on the front yard below him. In my youth, when I looked to planes as sources of illimitable power and freedom and looked to my father as the tamer of the great black birds he controlled, the Corsair became a symbol of the past. As a boy I worshiped the Marine Corps, her planes, and her pilots. I built model airplanes and dreamed of the day when I would pilot a black plane through the blue skies. But the 1960s and the turbulence of social change and the ominous presence of the unholy Asian war killed my dreams of flight and soldierdom. From the ashes of the Corsair rose the passionate do-gooder.

Here, on Viola's wall, in odd juxtaposition with the other artifacts of Viola's house, flew a Corsair, the dark shadow of my childhood. Why the Corsair? I would never find out.

My bedroom resembled a small cave. With the shutters closed and the lights out, I could not see my five fingers in front of my face. I was in. I was home. My depression had nothing to do with my house. It was me.

All of the people were fishermen. Good fishermen. They were good because it was necessary to be good. The river was their supermarket, their corner store, and their largest garden. In my afternoon walks I would often come upon a silent group of men and women sitting on the edge of the dock, studying the long and jointed cane poles that rested on the weathered railings. A couple of men would always be crabbing, using the skinned corpse of a possum for bait. In a tree near the river was the skeleton of an osprey who had come too near the fishermen the previous summer. It must have been a large, beautiful bird with magnificent plumage, but its skeleton, hung like a warning to other fowl, was a portentous reminder that the fishermen were also hunters who killed for pleasure as well as for food.

They fished in conjunction with the tides. They read the message of the tides as easily as commuters read newspapers. I learned this after a very short time on the island. I would sometimes go down and watch them fish, although many times I would find no one on the dock. 'The tides ain't right,' it was explained. If the tides were not right, then there would be no fish, and if there were no fish, then there would be no people. And I would sit on the dock alone with the osprey's skeleton behind me.

I tried to decipher the tides and what certain part of the cycle marked the coming of the fish. One thing I knew for certain, the people and the fish arrived together as though it had been arranged by a higher power for a long time. After watching several times it seemed that the people fished when the tide slowed somewhat and was beginning to consider a rest before the great reversal and the heavy flow of salt water in the opposite direction. When the water grew sluggish, relinquished its swiftness, rested against the marshes, and waited for the moon to assert its power again, then the people would appear with their shrimp and poles. They fished at the beginning and end of the tides, never in the middle. The fish abided by these rules.

I met many of the black islanders in this manner. They threw a thousand *yassuhs* in my direction, which made me uncomfortable, but I met some of the island's most colorful figures when I went down to talk with the fishermen.

Aunt Ruth was one. She was eighty years old, in marvelous physical condition, and possessed the face of a lost cherub. She loved conversation and enjoyed talking about her life on the island.

'I be on this island plenty long time. I the midwife over here. All these chillun on this island my chillun. I take them out of their mothers. I see 'em when they first be born. I deliver so many chillun. Over one hunnert. All those chillun you teach yonder schoolhouse. They all my chillun. My husband be the undertaker befo' he die. I bring the people into the eart'. He put 'em back in.'

She would talk about her memories of the island in the past before modern civilization had ruined it.

She remembered the first car that had driven on the island and the first plane that had flown overhead. She was a kind of repository of history and island lore. She also made potent batches of plum and blackberry wines at her house. She kept me supplied with both types during the entire year.

Quick Fella was another. I saw him pass the school one day on the way to the island church. The kids saw him at the same time and one of them shouted, 'Oh Gawd, that Quick Fella move so fast.' He moved fast indeed. His gait was a modified sprint. He walked as though possessed by demons, a jerky, mechanical walk with his head bobbing and his arms pumping to keep time with his legs. He was lanky and thin and his stride was awesome. He disappeared into the trees swiftly, an apparition, a passing thought.

'Quick Fella never slow up. He jes' keep on movin' down the road so fast,' Lincoln said.

I met Quick Fella while he was fishing one day. I introduced myself and started a conversation. I learned two things about Quick Fella during that first talk: that he spoke in a rich language that seemed almost Elizabethan and that he gave an exceptionally detailed weather report.

'So very nice. So very nice. So pleased to make your acquaintance. I am so pleased to tell you that the chillun seemed to think you are a fine gentleman. Yes, a fine gentleman. So very nice. So very pleased to make your acquaintance,' he said—very quickly, I should add. We talked a bit about the school, then I mentioned something about the thunderclouds that had rolled in from the east. 'Oh yes. I believe there will be a storm. Yes, yes. The temperature is about ninety-three degrees and slightly falling. The rel'tive humid-aty is eighty-seven per cent and rising. Scattered thundershowers late in the afternoon. Winds out of the east at fifteen miles an hour. Small boat warnings out for small boat. Big boats O.K. and don't have to worry about nothin'.'

I was listening to a Quick Fella special, his interpretation of the weather given over the Savannah radio. He often disagreed with this report and would alter the forecast according to his own studies of existing weather conditions. He was an astute observer of cloud formations and wind shifts. The people of the island generally believed in his reports and ignored those coming from Savannah. Of course, all people who live on islands become skillful at predicting the weather, but Quick Fella had transformed his skill into an art.

The other resident who provided a glimpse into island life was a powerfully muscled man called Sam. He did not tell me his name. I heard him called that by the other fishermen. He was a scowling, taciturn man who made no pretense of wishing to engage in small talk with me. He looked at me with a malevolent glance that could have melted a fishhook. Amicability was not Sam's greatest virtue. His foot was crippled. He dragged it behind him like an old anchor. It was bent, gnarled, and stuffed into a correction shoe. He liked to sit on the dock with his fishing pole and swing his feet underneath the dock, so his deformity would not show. I would make attempts to talk to him.

'How's it going today? You caught any big ones?' I would say.

He would answer me with one of his fishhook stares.

'Fish not biting today, eh? Well, some days are good. Some days are bad,' I would whine with infinite wisdom. 'You just gotta stick with it when you're fishing. Yes, sir, patience really pays off.'

Throughout this monologue, Sam has continued to stare at me. There is nothing human in his face. He is not amused or entertained by my intrusion. His crippled foot is swung out of sight under the dock. His stare is hollow, uncomprehending but hostile.

'Well, it's been great talkin' to you. I really enjoyed the conversation,' I say, as I walk away from him.

I learned about Sam from the kids at school. When he was an infant, his mother left him untended in a crib while she went to the nightclub to drink. While she was out, Sam slipped out of the crib but caught his left foot somehow in between two of the slats. The foot broke. He hung suspended from the crib for a long time screaming in agony. His mother came home finally and freed him. She never took her son to the doctor to have his foot set, and the bone healed itself at a grotesque, crooked angle that grew worse as Sam grew older. The kids said Sam didn't smile much.

But I saw him smiling once. He owned the finest horse on the island, a graceful mare with a handsome head and a sleek, somewhat spare body. I saw Sam riding this horse down the main road at full gallop, the horse straining for acceleration, the man bent over the horse's back shouting encouragement and smiling a full, evocative smile. The horse was swift and the man was intoxicated with the speed of his animal and the feel of the wind along his spine. Sam waved to me as he passed. I watched as the man and the horse grew smaller down the road and it made me glad there were horses in the world for people like Sam. When Sam was on his horse, then Sam, the cripple, sprouted wings and flew. Sam's horse was a good foot and his horse made him smile.

*   *   *

Even though I was on Yamacraw, I was not of Yamacraw. My first overtures of friendship with the people on the island, although not rebuffed, failed to win me any friends with whom I felt completely comfortable. I thought constantly of my friends in Beaufort. Consciously I began to wish for a way to extricate myself from a job and a situation I felt incapable of handling. The loneliness was beginning to shred my nerves. I became distracted with myself and my vainglorious attempt to act as a symbolic bridge between the children of the Yamacraw and the outside world. I was impatient because I had failed to turn illiterates into lovers of the great classics in the span of a single month. I had tired of measuring victories in terms of whether Prophet had learned the alphabet or Sidney could spell his name. Nor could I shake the feeling that everything I taught or achieved was a worthless, needless effort that ultimately would not affect the quality of my students' lives. What could I teach them or give them that would substantially alter the course of their lives? Nothing. Not a goddam thing. Each had come into the world imprisoned by a river and by a system which insured his destruction the moment he uttered his first cry by his mother's side.

Many of my friends drew me aside in those early

days, before I had defined myself in relation to the island, and told me they envied my opportunity for solitude, for reflection, and for time to assemble my thoughts and generate ideas. Almost every man dreams of a place where he can withdraw into himself, away from the roar of engines and squeal of tires, away from the push of crowds. Yet, by placing myself on Yamacraw, I was denying my natural gregariousness and my compulsive need for good friends. As a lover of conversation, I found myself strangely restless in the mute house, or the mute forest, or walking beside the mute ocean. I was an island within an island. And something far more profound and debilitating was occupying my mind in the month of September, long before I had conditioned myself to the isolation of the island and the frustration of the task at hand. In the midst of resolving the most traumatic adjustment I had ever made, I found myself struck with a new and foreign emotion that had not appeared in the prescribed blueprint of the year. On September 18, 1969, beknownst only to God, me, and one other person, I fell in love. On October 10, 1969, the unlikely triumvirate cooperated once again and I married Barbara Bolling Jones.

Barbara and I had been neighbors the previous year when I resided in a comfortably picturesque apartment in Beaufort. The house rested on the edge of a slough formed by the Beaufort River. It was behind one of the oldest houses in Beaufort and its many-windowed view of the river traffic of boat and fowl made the fifty dollars' rent I paid seem like the most incredible bargain in Christendom. The neighborhood went by the name of The Point, a collection of splendid old houses with fine white columns and dreams sundered by a great war and changing times. It was a genuine remnant of the Old South, with rocking chairs on high verandahs and venerable octogenarians and their aristocratic progeny carrying on the myth and legend which ended reluctantly at Appomattox Courthouse. I liked The Point for many reasons: for the quietude of its shaded, narrow streets, the courtesy and refinement of its residents, the imposing presence of its history, and for its essential apartness from the pace and hustle of the earth—its eccentric removal from all things plastic, electric, neoned, cheap, contrived, or asphalted. A visitor from the North once told me that The Point was evil because its people were prejudiced against blacks. 'Then leave,' I answered. I did not stop to explain my feelings for the place. I should have.

It was in a great yellow house on The Point, a house of exquisite proportions, that I can remember first feeling some compassion and insight into the condition of black people. I was sixteen, and in the prime of my nigger-baiting days, when I visited Gene Norris' apartment on the second story of this yellow house. Gene dwelt in Beaufort as the prophet before the storm, an intense bespectacled man who preached love for all humanity at a time when it was physically dangerous to do so. He perpetuated the great blasphemy of having his students read the *New York Times* instead of the Charleston *News and Courier*. An inveterate radical, he assigned *Catcher in the Rye* to his students before the town could mobilize its committees of repression. He reigned as the village eight-ball, the left arm, the joker in the pile, the odd number in our even-numbered world. Like many students in

111

Beaufort, I owe a great deal to Gene Norris. At any rate, one night in my junior year, he invited me and several other students to his house for dinner. The assembled group started teasing Gene about being a nigger-lover. Gene spat out a devastating reply, then asked us to listen to a record he had bought that day. He played 'We Shall Overcome' by Pete Seeger. I remember that moment with crystal clarity and I comprehend it as a turning point in my life: a moment terrible in its illumination of a toad in my soul, an ugliness so pervasive that it seemed my insides were vomit. Of course, I remained a nigger-hater for many years afterward, but the journey at least had a beginning, a point of embarkation. And the beginning had happened in an ante-bellum house on The Point.

So, The Point, bedizened with moss and the memory of slavery, symbolized to me a place, not of evil and of minds anchored to a corrupt past, but a place where change was possible, even imminent. As soon as I graduated from The Citadel, I house-hunted in The Point area and there only. Here I was to live and here I planned to die. At twenty-two I had decided that it was best to live and grow old in a small town. The call of the city failed to capture me.

Barbara lived next door to me, but the currents of our lives did not cross. I once started her car on an unseasonably chilly October morning when her profanity streamed into my bedroom window as I was shaving. I walked out and started her car. She apologized profusely when I commended her for the salt of her tongue. That was all. The first thing I noticed about her was the wedding ring on her left hand. Bachelors reflexively study a strange girl's left

112

hand. Without the formality of introducing ourselves, we parted.

I heard of her again a month later. Her husband, a Marine pilot, had been shot down and killed in Vietnam. A week later I heard through Beaufort's well-developed grapevine that Barbara was pregnant with her second child.

We had few occasions to talk after that. I would often see her in her yard as I drove to and from school. I watched the child grow within her and measured time by the changes in her condition. Her second child, Melissa, was born in April.

In May I met Barbara at a party. We talked. I went to her house for a drink after the party. Initially, I felt uncomfortable around her. Her husband had died in a war I considered immoral and unjustified. I could sympathize with her loss but could not condone or defend the cause for which he died. Teaching had preserved me from the draft and from facing the decision of fighting in an ignoble war because my country decreed it. So I steered away from talk about the war or the military. A week later she left to visit her parents-in-law in Norway for the summer.

My falling in love was simply a gradual awareness that I wanted to live with Barbara. When she returned to Beaufort in August, I was there. The idea of assuming the role of father for two young children terrified me, and the additional burden of entering a house where the shadow of a man I never knew was imprinted in every corner seemed a legitimate reason for hesitating on the brink of matrimony. And we were so different. Barbara cared not one bit for the social issues of the day that were so important to me. Her main interest in life was the ineluctable pursuit of the contented home and happy family. Hers was a life of order, of cocktails served promptly before dinner, of napkins and candlesticks, of military protocol, and attention to form. Mine was chaotic, plebian, and disjointed. She voted for Nixon, while I prayed for the elevation of McCarthy. Whatever the differences between us, none of it made much difference on October 10.

Before a small crowd of friends, we were married in St. Helena's Church in Beaufort. Bernie was there poking me in the ribs and grinning like hell. Big George Garbade towered above the guests, who were whispering occasionally that now I'd have to get off that goddam island. Gene Norris was there, a classic portrait of the tweedy English professor. Yamacraw, far away and oblivious in the October sunshine, seemed mysteriously remote and inaccessible, like a dream that lingered just beneath the surface of memory, and not part of me at all. I had invited everyone I knew on the island to my wedding: the kids, the parents, Mrs. Brown, the Stones. All said they would try to attend, and predictably, because of distance, inconvenience, and the fact that none of them knew me very well, none of them showed.

We honeymooned on Yamacraw Island. For some reason, Niagara Falls, the Virgin Islands, or any of the other meccas for the hordes of lusty young couples checking into motels did not arouse any enthusiasm in me. Since Barbara had not seen Yamacraw and since it was important she understand the problems of the island and its isolation from the rest of the world, we decided to spend our honeymoon on the island.

Zeke put the boat into the water, taunted me with the ancient jokes directed at newly anointed husbands, and watched as we headed toward Bull Creek. I drove the boat and pointed out the high spots of the trip: the osprey's nest atop the utility pole on Savage Island, the huge crescent sandbar that blocked one whole section of navigable creek at low tide on Bull Island, the thousands of brown oysters encrusted in the mud flats along the shore. A porpoise fin broke like a green shaft in the water besides us, the sun flashing off his body in brilliant knives of light. A great blue heron, disturbed by the boat, flew patiently and majestically to another spot. The boat was an intrusion. It always was.

We stayed for two days. My living quarters did not impress Barbara to a great extent, but the weather cooperated and even the mosquitoes seemed to diminish the fury of their attacks. We wandered about the island exulting in the aloneness. Barbara picked ticks from her body and took cold-water baths with Spartan determination. We had never considered her living on the island. She did not want to bring her young children to a place without doctors or telephones. I would live on the island, come home on the weekend, and during the week when I was able. Thus, our marriage was planned for the first year. Barbara would remain in Beaufort; I would live on the island.

How different my life would be had we followed this original plan. I was young and surpassingly naïve at this juncture and I saw no undue hardship resulting from this arrangement. Barbara had lived a year without a husband and an absentee husband seemed infinitely better than no husband at all. I was not about to quit my job on Yamacraw, nor was

115

she going to bring her children to live on the island. As I look back, it is surprising we both did not tell each other to go to hell and forget the whole thing.

Anyway, it was a good honeymoon. I took my bride back to Beaufort and deposited her in our Beaufort home. The house we had rented had all the character of a hamburger stand: cyclone fence, picture window, carport, and all the other accouterments of suburbia. I hated the house and the neighborhood. The Point had nothing for rent or sale, so we were forced to join the ranks of the red-brick people who drive station wagons and play bridge. I lived on a remote island during the week and next to George Babbitt on the weekend.

After October 10 I was not happy on the island. Separating myself from Barbara only seemed to heighten my loneliness on the island. I became rather irritable and impatient in dealing with the kids in class. Mrs. Brown and her tirades seemed less amusing to me. Ted Stone began to fray my nerves. I missed Barbara and wanted to be with her. I could not quit, yet I wanted to quit. I was also starting to feel guilty about the two-year-old girl, Jessica, who was now my responsibility. She thought of me simply as 'that man, Mommy' and had not realized that I was her father. Jessica needed a father, not a weekend visitor. These things preyed on my mind in the middle of October. I was a father and a teacher, yet I could not throw myself completely into either project. It was not until December that I became a daily commuter.

CHAPTER FIVE

On a reconnaissance foray into the bowels of the great closet that harbored the jetsam and flotsam washed into the schoolroom over the years, I unearthed a brand-new automatic movie projector. When I queried Mrs. Brown, she told me that films were difficult to get to and from the island; in fact, they were more trouble than they were worth. Therefore the projector sat in permanent exile. I also found an SRA Reading Kit and a fairly new record player gathering dust on one of the closet shelves.

I was ecstatic. I am a firm and uncompromising believer in the audio-visual age. The projector was gold bullion. It became my habit from that day forward to make damn sure that the room was filled with films on all subjects. I raided the film library at the county office each month. Since the difficulty of transporting films was so obvious, I was allowed to take as many films as I wanted and to keep them for as long as I wanted. Though this entailed a broken rule, the woman in charge of the films was very flexible.

The films were divided into three groups: boring films that imparted a body of knowledge I felt the gang should have partial exposure to, interesting films that I accidentally picked up with the boring films, and fun films whose sole purpose was to provide entertainment. The class generally liked films better than any other part of the day and voted to have at least one film daily. They also insisted that when a film especially appealed to them, they

117

would be allowed to view it a second time. I acquiesced to the will of the majority. A film on the Calgary Rodeo received three curtain calls. At the third showing, the Gorgonian head of Mrs. Brown peered in through the glass window, called me out into the hall, and gave me a splendid lecture.

'Every second of school time is important, Mr. Conroy,' she intoned, 'and we cannot afford to waste any time with movin' pictures. These children need the basics. The basics. If they get the basics that's all they need.'

'Yes, ma'am,' I answered.

Several times during the year Mrs. Brown attempted to sabotage the film program. She constantly derided the fact that I was wasting valuable time, when I could be drilling the class on those good ole, French-fried, batter-whipped basics. A couple of the kids watched movies as if they were partaking of a sacrament, completely enthralled and religiously attentive. Fred fidgeted through movies, but Fred would wiggle through his own interment. Lincoln chattered throughout the movie, but much of his conversation was directed toward characters on the screen. So, no matter how much the film series offended Mrs. Brown, I was determined to keep it part of my program. On one occasion, a film was the fuse for an explosion of enthusiasm for the whole class in which eighteen children momentarily forgot the prison of the classroom, forgot about the iron-clad rules of propriety, forgot about the frowning Mrs. Brown in the next room, and danced maniacally in the pure joy of group sharing and identification.

It started with Walter Cronkite. Walter, with his voice of doomsday sincerity, came on a brief visit to

Yamacraw via film. In the film library I came across *The Salem Witch Trials*, part of the old 'You Are There' programs, which Cronkite narrated. The film launched me back into a bucket of tears' worth of nostalgia and reminiscing. I cannot estimate how many times I watched the program as a child, but seeing young Walter with his unlined face and dignified thinness was like welcoming an old friend back into my life. I tried to tell the kids about the part Walter Cronkite played in my childhood, when I sat transfixed before the television set as my favorite shows flickered on and off. They seemed to understand.

The kids loved the resonant, stirring quality of the phrase *You are there*. In the film, the alleged witches swear their innocence before a noncompassionate judge. Their accusers moan and squeal in delightful overacting. Soldiers drag people off to the gallows. The kids were going wild. 'Hang the judge,' they chanted. The supernatural held a macabre fascination for the children; they discussed it frequently, and believed implicitly in the existence of witches, warlocks, ghosts, and devils.

After the film, I extracted several hokey morals to discuss the nature of justice and other such manure. The kids would have none of it. They hadn't had a good bull session about witches for a damn long time—too long, they decided; let's discuss them now.

Ethel Lee spoke first, 'I know two witches in Savannah—they mean.'

'Damn right, they mean,' Fred said to Big C, not knowing I had heard.

'They ain't as mean as the one in Bluffton,' Cindy Lou added.

119

'Meanest witch in the world right here on Yamacraw,' Frank concluded.

'How many of you ever seen a witch?' I asked. Every hand flew up. Damn right they'd seen witches.

Big C screwed his face up into his question-mark look. 'It true if you throw water on a witch, she disappear?'

Suddenly every eye in the room was riveted on me. Only the pigs grunting and rooting on the schoolyard disturbed the silence created by this single question. And there was something about the question itself, something ancient and primordial, something that disturbed the hidden and oft lost mythology of my own youth; I felt something stir as I thought about the wet witch, and knew that a feeling in my subconscious was rising like an air bubble to the surface. Then I had it.

'Big C, you've seen the *Wizard of Oz*.'

Eighteen voices shouted hosannas to the trembling faker of Oz. Cindy Lou broke off into an impromptu rendition of 'Over the Rainbow.' Others pretended they were cowardly lions. Richard stood up and walked like a scarecrow suspended from his stake. Each member of the class had memorized the movie classic, had watched it religiously each time it appeared on television and had added personal interpretations to the bizarre forces rampant in the spirit-haunted land over the rainbow. And if the Yamacraw children knew about Oz, then I was convinced a hell of a lot of other children in America knew about it, too. My jeremiads against television since my first days on the island had continued undiminished, fed with the plentiful food of my students' ignorance about

120

people, events, and the world. Now, in a single moment, I had to retract my sweeping indictment of TV: it had not failed completely, only partially. Every child in the room knew the legend of Oz by heart, the importance of the yellow-brick road, the incarnate evil of the wicked Witch of the West, and the ultimate hypocrisy of the great wizard himself. Oz, it seemed, had entered into the consciousness of American children, and not just a selected few, but almost every child in every situation. I considered Yamacraw a touchstone: if the Yamacraw children knew about it, then the chances were excellent that the vast majority of American children had been reached. The *Wizard of Oz*, through the medium of television, had become part of American mythology as important and relevant to the children of America as the Homeric legends were to the children of Athens.

So Big C's question was the catalyst for a great and memorable afternoon, one of those rare moments generated by chance, planned by no one, spontaneous and joyful, transcending the need for a teacher or a classroom, and making me once more think of education as something alive and helpful, instead of as a withered dream in need of formaldehyde. Oz took over the rest of the day. For a couple of minutes it was utter pandemonium. Fred introduced a moving argument in incomprehensible Fredese in favor of the proposition that water could evaporate witches. Prophet thought this was crap. He told Fred so. Fred told Prophet he would kick his butt if he continued to think it was crap. Mary mumbled something into her left hand about fire being better than water. Saul said that there ain't no sure way to

121

kill a witch.

Cindy Lou's voice finally broke through the general upheaval of noise and offered to recite her King James Version of the story.

'O.K.,' said I.

'There was this little girl who got blown away in a rainstorm,' she started.

'That ain't the way it was,' said Jimmy Sue.

'How was it then, you old ugly self?' Cindy Lou shot back.

'Ain't no rainstorm, sister.'

'Damn right it was a rainstorm.'

'No, girl, it was a tor-nay-do.'

'Yeah,' the class agreed, 'it was a tornado.'

'Same thing,' claimed Cindy Lou.

'No, girl. Tor-nay-do take your head clean off,' offered Mary.

'You tellin' the story, girl?' Cindy inquired menacingly of Jimmy Sue.

'No.'

'Then you keep your mout' out of it.'

'This girl got blown away by a wind and the house she was in hit a bad witch on the head and kill her dead. Then the girl and her little dog go marchin' down this yellow-brick road 'til they meet this chicken lion who try to act tough.'

'No,' a chorus of voices shouted.

'No, what?' Cindy Lou asked.

'That girl don't meet no lion,' said Samuel, in one of his first vocal contributions of the year.

'Sure she meets a lion.'

'No, girl, first she sees the scarecrow. Ain't got no brains.'

'Yeah, scarecrow first,' the class agreed, acting out the chorus in this impromptu drama.

'You tell the story, cockeye.'

'Call me cockeye and I bust your head,' Samuel shouts, clenching his fists.

'Don't call Samuel cockeye, Cindy Lou.'

'He is cockeye.'

'Yeah, he cockeye,' the chorus agrees.

'No,' I say.

'I bust your head,' Samuel warns the whole class.

'You cockeye,' the class chants.

'The scarecrow first,' says Richard. 'Let me tell the story.'

'Oh boy, Richard, give it to us.'

So Richard rendered his version of Oz. Then Oscar, then Frank, then Mary, then Sidney, each adding their own peculiar interpretations, each emphasizing a different part of the story, and each feeling perfectly free to combine incidents from the *Wizard of Oz* with incidents that occurred in other television programs. Sidney got Oz confused with an episode from 'Bonanza.' Hoss Cartwright battling the witches of the Purple Sage. According to Oscar, Oz and Disneyland were somehow related. Richard somehow got Captain Kangaroo confused with the wizard, and Mr. Greenjeans confused with the scarecrow.

Ethel, a purist in the group, strutted to the microphone and began a long, precise, but monotonous epic, which was technically unflawed and accurate except that everyone in the class believed she was making the stuff up. In the middle of her story, Top Cat got up and started singing a new song just released by swing-man James Brown. He hopped and swayed what he called a 'new jive' while the kids clapped their hands and tapped their feet until the great head of Mrs. Brown appeared in the window, flashing a look the Romans must have worn on their faces when turning thumbs down on some prostrate Christian. But even though the kids quit responding and reverted back to their classical pose of scholars erect in their desks and lusting for knowledge, Top Cat gyrated on, a grin like a jack-o'-lantern carved on his face and eyes raised in adoration of some muse deep within him.

When Top Cat finally subsided and sank back into his desk, Prophet of the unknown tongue continued the interrupted marathon of Oz, an untranslatable potpourri of grunts and monosyllables, punctuated only by Prophet's beautifully effusive smiles.

When the afternoon was over and the bus ambled into the schoolyard, and the kids had filed out of the room, I had on tape the story of Oz as it had never been told before—a new Oz, a land that Judy Garland had never entered, but one especially created on a December afternoon by children of an island ruled by a river, and possibly another wizard, with perhaps a greater claim to credibility.

*　　　*　　　*

The first two California boys arrived on the island in early October. They were part of an unusual college program emanating from Cowell College, a part of the University of California at Santa Cruz. The program had survived for a solid year. Herman Blake, a black professor at the college who had been born on a sea island further up the coast, was the mercurial, driving force behind the program; he devised it, implemented it, and was the strong shaft that supported the experiment in the early days and nurtured it past the stormy and vehement disapproval of the island troll, Ted Stone.

Mr. Stone told me about Blake, about the California boys, and about the program. 'All of them are Communists trained in Havana. If they keep comin' to the island there is bound to be trouble. One of them has already gone back to California and married a nigger girl. Another one named Zach Sklar was a Russian Jew.' Stone considered the program an insidious, corrosive threat to his domination of the island's people and politics.

'What exactly do they do, Mr. Stone?' I asked. 'You can tell me.'

He answered, 'It don't appear like they do nothing.'

It seemed improbable that two Californians would travel 3000 miles for the experience of dwelling among black people on an unbridged island solely for credit in a sociology class. Whatever the probability, I met Jim Ford and Joe Sanfort the first week in October.

With all six of the California boys I worked with during the year there was a period of aloofness, of deintoxification, before we could communicate on a serious level with each other. The prime reason was my background. I was a white southerner, a graduate of an all white male military college, a nine-year resident of Beaufort, and the first white teacher encountered in the Cowell College program. During the training sessions for their journey to Yamacraw, Blake concentrated on prepping his missionaries well in the psyche of the rural blacks, but he did not prepare them well at all for dealing with the southern whites. In their simplistic assessment, all southern whites were incorrigible racists who loved to eat grits, smell magnolias, and lynch blacks. Blake told them to handle the Stones with oily diplomacy. In fact the major command passed to them before they left the protected enclosure of their campus was not to piss anybody off, white or black. Remember the program, it must go on at all costs. So Jim and Joe approached me with extreme caution, said nothing that would ruffle the white supremacist feathers that lay directly beneath my bright red neck, and generally said nothing at all. They were the first people I had met from an infamous California college. I am positive I was the first person they had met who had worn a uniform to the latrine in his college days. From the beginning it was a merger of opposites and a meeting of two extraordinarily different worlds. After we thawed our suspicions, we became good friends and they introduced me for the first time to that land gilded with Sierras, pocked with surfers, and as strange and multifaceted as Yamacraw itself—California.

Jim and Joe explained the program one night soon after my marriage, as we drank beer and killed mosquitoes in the gloom of early evening in my house. Each quarter Blake selected two people for the Yamacraw Island Project. The twosome spent an entire quarter living among the people of the island, talking to them, helping them in whatever service that they could provide, and absorbing the atmosphere and culture of the island in the process. One of the ultimate aims of the program was to get into the school and help the teachers with the children. Thus far, Mrs. Brown had proved to be the major obstacle. Jim and Joe ran a recreation program every day after school. More aptly, they stood in the middle of a great surge of children racing wildly about them, engaged in some unidentifiable game that had been brought to the island as football and corrupted over the years.

Jim's personality was such that he desired to see order emerge from the chaos, form to somehow overpower the void, rules to tame and dignify the surface appearance of his program. In fact, beneath his long hair and mustache, Jim Ford was the quintessential organization man who was not happy unless a football game spread across the playground with Lombardian precision. To Jim a recreation program, or at least his recreation program, was something sacred and if he had any say in the matter, his program on Yamacraw would be a model for sea islands everywhere. So when Jim would clap his hands and ask for order and the dust cloud of children kicking a ball and each other would swirl past him oblivious to his command, and when he would clap his hands again, this time louder and more peremptory, and the great cloud would nearly trample him as it passed his spot again, I could only smile and thank God that I had taught awhile and knew where I stood in the great chain of being among the children of Yamacraw School. I knew Jim wanted to have a program he could be proud of when he returned to California. Therefore, my heart saluted him when I saw him standing alone, a sentinel waving frantically beneath the stand of oaks beside the school, asking for quiet, for attention, for anything that would let him assume command and control of a situation that he could not control.

Joe, on the other hand, cared little for

organization, for achievements to boast upon, or anything else. Joe's cynicism appealed to me greatly; he would sit alone on the seesaw, deprecating the fact that a black man would send two blue-eyed white boys bursting with bullshit and idealism to an island that needed them like it needed two escalators. Every once in a while guilt would cause Joe to make an attempt to organize a softball game or a kickball game, but after his efforts had melted into mere remembrances of things past, he returned to his seesaw and ruminated upon the folly of the recreation program.

Of course, Mrs. Brown would watch the entire spectacle shaking her head disgustedly, screaming at every child who raced past her that this was no way to run a recreation program, that whoever was running this recreation program sure didn't know what in the hell they were doing, and if she were running the program it would certainly be organized better. Jim would hustle over to her side, they would huddle together in great seriousness, Jim would then break from the huddle like a center from the Green Bay Packers, trot to the middle of the playground, clap his hands, shout hopelessly to the mass of kids racing in every conceivable direction, and the entire cycle would begin anew.

God, did I sympathize with both Jim and Joe. About the third recess at Yamacraw, I became momentarily inspired to teach the boys the finer nuances of football. They knew nothing. They could not pass; they could not block or kick the ball or line up in a semblance of a formation. Their version of the game was pure, unsullied madness. Whoever held the ball at any time was simply murdered by every other player on the field.

Sometimes Top Cat and Oscar, the two largest, would team up together while the frail youngsters tried vainly to drag them to the ground. I had never seen such ferocity on the field. Sam and Sidney, emaciated and puny, would fly into the churning legs of Top Cat without losing a bit of momentum. Top Cat would shake them off as if they were made from butterfly wings, then face Richard's seventy-pound charge into his stomach. Everyone growled, foamed, and grunted appropriately. When someone hit the ground, all participants felt duty bound to leap on the fallen prey; fists would pound heads, feet would kick any and every exposed leg, thigh, or head. Curses flew from the pile in dangling, disjointed clusters. I'd never seen anything so brutal, so dangerous, so insane in my whole life.

So I decided to teach them rules, fair play, and sportsmanship: the essence of the noble game, the proper manner in which gentlemen and athletes conduct themselves on a field of honor. I taught them huddles, the stance for blocking, the way to pass a spiral, the science of plays, the beauty of the stiff arm. This took two whole recesses. After I was convinced that I had given them enough theory, that they were well grounded in the basics of the game, I flipped the ball to Lincoln and told him to kick off. He was immedlately buried under an avalanche of bodies kicking, gouging, biting, and hitting at the unfortunate Lincoln, who howled at the bottom of the pile. This was one of my last attempts to organize the time-honored version of football on the island.

Jim and Joe were in a strange position on the island. They were there conceivably to serve the people. If there was a fence to be mended, a privy to be built, an errand to be run, or an itch to be scratched, the islanders knew that all they had to do was ask the California boys. It did not take long for the more savvy islanders to take more than full advantage of this miraculous labor force from across the continent. Nor did it become unusual for someone to see healthy black men sitting in the shade sipping Scotch and watching Joe and Jim sweating in the broiling sun over a collection of nails and boards that would soon be a new privy. I identified with Joe and Jim and saw that they were merely putting their burning liberalism to the test of the sword. Joe and Jim, archetypes of white, middle-class America, could come to the thickets and backwaters of the Carolinas and master the art of shit-house building. Dear Mom, Sallie May Toomer now craps in elegance and style, so my life has not been in vain.

I once asked Mrs. Brown if the California boys could come into the schoolhouse and work with some of the kids on remedial reading. It seemed natural that two juniors in college would be moderately qualified to help out in the scholarly environs of Yamacraw School. Not that I disparaged their field work, for they were becoming so proficient in shit-house building that they completed these structures with remarkable speed. But both of them felt that they could accomplish far more if they could help the children in school. I agreed. It was funny how we thought education to be the great gilded key which would solve all problems, eliminate all poverty and disease, eradicate differences between social classes, and bring the children of okra-planters up to par with

130

the children of emperors. A trinity of white-toothed white boys, Joe, Jim, and I, entered into the stream of Yamacraw life-style and felt all that was needed was a meteoric reading level, a couple of shots of new math, and a high score on the college entrance exams. So the guys wanted me to approach the unapproachable Mrs. Brown to see if she would put her approval on their apprenticeship within the schoolhouse walls.

'Mr. Conroy, do you realise that these boys have no credentials? The state requires all of its teachers to have the proper credentials. What if the man from the state department comes walkin' into this here school, carrying his badge, and askin' to see everybody's credentials? Now what we gonna do with these California boys? Hide 'em in the ladies' room? No, Mr. Conroy, we must abide by the rules of the state.'

'Mrs. Brown, all these guys want to do is come in during the day and help us out. Nothing else. It cannot hurt a single thing.'

'It will hurt the reputation and cree-dentials of this school.'

'This ain't Harvard, Mrs. Brown.'

'Rules are rules, Mr. Conroy. The state makes the rules.'

'There are no rules which say these guys cannot come and help us every day.'

'I am the principal.'

'Yes, ma'am.'

So Joe and Jim remained the grand officiators of the recreation program. I explained to them that I was relatively powerless to cope with Mrs. Brown when she so adamantly refused to listen to reason. White guilt, that nasty little creature who rested on my left shoulder, prevented me from challenging Mrs. Brown on this or any other point. At this time of my life a black man could probably have handed me a bucket of cow piss, commanded me to drink it in order that I might rid my soul of the stench of racism, and I would have only asked for a straw. Blacks who have gone through the civil rights struggle have met a hundred white boys and girls who would dive head first in a septic tank to prove their liberation from the sins of their fathers. I thought Mrs. Brown was wrong, but did not have the moral courage to tell her so. In the fantasy of the races conceived in my mind, all blacks were noble people who had struggled against a repressive social order for years and who were finally reaping the tangible rewards of this struggle. All whites, especially myself, were guilty of heinous, extraordinarily brutal crimes against humanity. It dawned on me that I came to Yamacraw for a fallacious reason: I needed to be cleansed, born again, resurrected by good works and suffering, purified of the dark cankers that grew like toadstools in my past. I was on the island for expiation, and I think I liked to watch Joe and Jim struggle so patiently because I saw in them a reflection of myself.

The word had passed. The California boys were banned from the classroom. I thought credentials constituted the primary reason why they were not allowed to enter the school. Then one day Mrs. Brown told me conspiratorially, 'We can't let white boys and colored girls rub elbows too much. Them boys are young bulls with no cows on this island 'cept them colored cows. We can't afford to have no half-breed cows on this island.'

*　　　*　　　*

I had borrowed a tape recorder from Mrs. Brown that I had noticed sitting in a corner of her room, virginal and unused. She let me have it reluctantly, telling me some crap that it was too valuable a piece of equipment to use with my 'babies' around. I swore by the whiskers of Jehovah that I would treat the priceless machine as I would a tiara from Tiffany's. Then I carried it into my room. Tape recorders are great instruments, I knew this intuitively, though I had never used one in a classroom environment and had no idea, at that particular moment, how exactly I would utilize one in this class.

Since I am a virtual idiot when it comes to machines of any kind, it took a good fifteen minutes to figure out how to operate this box full of hidden levers and submerged screws. Finally, after incredible fumbling on my part, the tape recorder whirred proudly and efficiently into action.

Mary told me the machine had sat idle the year before and that Mrs. Brown had not played it at all. 'Fine,' I said, 'we are going to play the hell out of it.'

I told everyone to come up to the tape recorder and give name, address, and grade. Big C was first. He rolled his eyes, lowered his head, then mumbled, 'My name Charles Graves. I am in the seventh grade. I live on Yamacraw.'

Then I replayed his performance. When Big C's voice came back into the room, I think I gained some insight into a magician's feeling of power when he pulls a rabbit from his hat before a roomful of children. Lincoln yelled, 'God Almighty. Good gracious.' Whoops and giggles spread around the room as each succeeding voice came stuttering magically from the tape. Poor Prophet caught hell from the rest of the class when his own version of the language rolled incomprehensibly forth, and his brother Fred was so self-conscious about his inability to articulate that he merely grunted into the microphone. Oscar, however, the completion of the Simmons trinity, was so proud of the sound of his voice that he volunteered to tell the story of the book he had just finished reading. So he launched into a lengthy monologue about Moolak, an Eskimo salmon fisherman. Since Oscar was not a proponent of brevity, he described in intricate detail how Moolak caught what seemed to be a few million salmon. But while Oscar was droning on, a burst of noise arose spontaneously around Top Cat.

'Top Cat gonna sing,' Mary trilled.

'That right. He sound better than Brother James Brown,' Saul added.

Top Cat strutted and shimmied to the center of the room as if possessed by an orchestra of demons. His whole body danced and shook, and the class deferred to his assumption of an inalienable right to the microphone. Something had moved Top Cat.

'Do you need any music, Top Cat?' I asked.

'All I need is that there mike,' he said, his eyes closed and his lips already moving.

I gave him that there mike and sat down to enjoy the show. Top Cat was a great showman. He threw his head back, threw out his arms, wrinkled his face like an old raisin, and burst into a classic Otis Redding number, 'Sittin' on the Dock of the Bay.' The kid I had thought nearly illiterate had

134

memorized the words of a fairly complicated song and developed a diction and sense of timing that was almost perfect. The class sat respectfully silent while Top Cat performed. When he finished, they applauded vigorously. Then came the flood.

Richard who I knew damn well was illiterate, who could not string the twenty-six letters of the alphabet together, who could not add two and two, and who could not write his name, came striding manfully to the microphone. Richard was terribly bashful in class and would hide his face in his hands if I even looked in his direction. He also had developed an infallible escape mechanism; if it looked as though I was going to involve him in some class activity, Richard would raise his hand and ask to go to the bathroom. On one day he had gone to the land of pee eleven times. I followed him into the bathroom the last time and watched as Richard looked out the window at the forest surrounding the school. He almost hemorrhaged when he saw me looking at him. So Richard, striding to the microphone, smiling shyly and mumbling incoherently to himself, was kind of a big thing. And old Richard could sing like hell. His voice was high and clear, almost bell-like. He sang a spiritual with style and emotion.

'Will the circle
Be unbroken?
By and by, Lord,
By and by.'

His brother Jasper grabbed the microphone from Richard as soon as possible and launched into a song notable primarily for its epic length. It was called 'Alabama Moonshine.' The song went on and on, an endless song not enhanced or flattered by Jasper's flat, monotonic voice or his uninspired delivery. He sang it like a Trappist chant without life or humor, just a long, long ballad with piles and piles of verses—like Moolak with piles and piles of salmon.

Lincoln quit crapping around long enough to sing 'The Birds and the Bees.' He was awful, but he enjoyed singing so much I remained silent and appreciative. The class unanimously declared him to be a lousy singer.

'Lincoln, you so bad,' shouted Big C.

'He sound like shee-t,' Saul said in a whisper, but of course, every time Saul whispered, everyone within three miles heard it.

'Saul cuss,' said Ethel.

'Shut up, girl,' Saul said murderously.

'I pinch your head, little man,' Ethel said back.

'Don't you call me little man,' Saul warned.

'I call you little man, little man,' she answered.

Saul started to cry. He was extremely sensitive about his height and any mention of it would make him cry. Naturally, his classmates taunted him unmercifully and with unrestrained cruelty.

'Little man crying.'

'Cry, little man.'

'Shut up, punks,' I yelled.

'You a punk, big man,' Samuel told me.

'Sam, I am going to pinch your head like a pimple.' Sam talking was such a rare event that I would almost have let him tell me to lunch on manure.

'Sam call Conrack a punk,' someone yelled.

'Sam die now.'

'Sam no die. Sam live,' said Sam, for some reason. Meanwhile, Lincoln had not skipped a note and was finishing up his mauled rendition of 'The Birds and the Bees.'

'Want me sing 'nother one, Conrack?'

'No, Lincoln, I can take only so much pure pleasure in one day.'

'Pretty good, huh?'

'Great stuff, kid.'

Top Cat then gyrated to the center of the room again and belted out another one called 'Cloud Nine.' When he sat down, Ethel and Anna teamed up for what was probably the worst duet in history. It was so bad, and they knew it was so bad, that I did not even replay it when they were finished. Then back to Richard, who sang eight brief words, then forgot the rest of the song he was singing.

'You sing, Conrack?' Lincoln said.

'Doggone right, I sing. I'm a great singer. I once worked my way through college dancing in a go-go cage and singing rock and roll.'

'No,' the class yelled.

'Yeh,' I yelled back. 'I'm such a good singer, in fact, that I only sing for money.'

'How much?' Oscar asked.

'How much you got?' I answered.

'Three nickels,' he said.

'That ain't enough, son. I'm used to singing for hundreds of dollars.'

'You lie.'

'Darn right I lie.' I have a voice that sounds like a flushing commode, and it is only under optimum circumstances that I allow myself to be pilloried by the world for my lousy voice.

After school, Mrs. Brown rushed to my room and

delivered a long sermon.

'Singing is a waste of time, Mr. Conroy. Just a waste of good school time. Those children love to sing. Lord, they'd sing all day if you'd let them. They need readin', writin', and arithmetic. The state requires it. If some big man from the state department comes over here and finds your class singing, they gonna run you clean off this island. They got textbooks. Otherwise, nobody in your room can be promoted. Lord knows. Singing! Next thing, they'll be dancin' and cuttin' up and drinking wine in school just like their parents. They gonna be just like their parents if you don't watch out. Drinkin' and singin' and sinnin' on Saturday night. Not going to visit the Lord on Sunday morning. We run this school here for education's sake. Give them seat work. Keep them busy. We not here to have fun. We're here to educate. We got rules to follow.'

*   *   *

A major theme of mine during the year resulted from observing the manner in which my students treated their pets and animals in general. I was labeled squeamish when I found a toad minus his two back legs crawling painfully along the front steps. One of the twins had removed his back legs with two quick strokes of a knife before he entered the school after recess. The portrait of the toad, trailing blood behind him on the gritty steps, crawling off to die under the schoolhouse, made me mad as hell.

'What d'you do that for, Sam?' I yelled.

'Kill 'im dead. Hee, hee, hee,' Sam replied.

138

'How'd you feel if I ripped your legs off?'

'I shoot you dead. Hee, hee, hee.'

'Man, you guys treat animals like crap. I have never seen a bunch of people treat animals any worse in my whole life. I swear I wouldn't give you kids a dead flounder for a pet. You kick your dogs around, you starve your cats, you torture squirrels, shoot songbirds, and maim turtles. You treat animals with kindness or leave them the hell alone. If you kill them to eat them that is fine. Killing an animal for fun is not right and if I see it again there's gonna be a fist fight.'

'Jes' an ol' frog,' someone mumbled.

'You are jes' an ol' person,' I shouted back.

'Frog ain't good for nuttin'.'

'They're good for eating insects,' I said. 'All animals are good for something.'

'Oscar shoot my pet dog daid,' Saul whispered suddenly.

'No, boy. You lie.'

'No, you shoot 'im.'

'You shaddup, boy.'

'Oscar get his gun and put hole in that ol' dog's haid.'

'That one nasty ol' dog.'

'Dog daid now.'

'That my dog,' cried Saul.

'That dog daid now. Ain't nobody's dog,' Lincoln cackled.

'Oscar, that is a rotten, lousy thing to do. Shoot someone's dog.'

'Dog bad. He try to bite me.'

'I wish he'd bitten you on the throat.'

'Someone shoot all Oscar's dogs too,' Ethel said.

'Yeh. Two man dogs. One woman dog,' Prophet

139

piped up. 'One dog, red dog. That my dog.'

'Who shot them, Prophet?'

'Someone shot 'im daid in the head. Dog rot up in the woods when Poppa find 'im. Ain't got no dogs now.'

'And you shot Saul's dog after someone shot your dog, Oscar. That's terrible.'

Oscar was feeling persecuted, refused to discuss the subject further, and lowered his head as a sign that he had ended his participation in the discussion. But this was not the only conversation I had with the kids about their treatment of animals. Their overall treatment of animals was deplorable or worse. Big C once picked up a large, bloated toad and smashed it against the schoolhouse wall. One day some of the smaller kids in Mrs. Brown's class scoured the entire playground for insects. Whenever they found a beetle or captured a dragonfly or grasshopper, they tore its wings off and watched it buzz convulsively and helplessly on the ground.

I would launch into long-winded diatribes condemning senseless violence perpetrated against helpless creatures while the class nodded in solemn agreement. Then they would go home, chastened by the sharp barbs of my logic, and kick the hell out of their dogs. The dogs of Yamacraw were a special breed. Without question, they were the gauntest, mangiest, slinkiest and most oppressed group I had ever laid eyes on. They had bred and interbred time and again and the net result was an animal so lacking in character or nobility that a possum looked like a racehorse in comparison. At some houses the dogs were so drained of energy that they would bark at strangers without lifting their heads. They were emaciated, undernourished, and listless refuse who were alternately loved and abused by their masters. Only Edna Graves' dogs showed signs of enthusiasm and that was when the pack decided to rend an unsuspecting visitor to shreds.

'You have to take better care of your dogs, gang. Most of your dogs look like walking skeletons. You gotta fatten them up. Make them happy. Make these miserable, wretched dogs proud and healthy.'

'My dog look a lot better than your dog, that ol' ugly Beau,' Cindy Lou said indignantly. 'Gawd, that a funny-lookin' dog.' She was referring to my pet dachshund I had brought to school for a visit.

'Beau is a beautiful beast of great nobility, Cindy,' I retorted.

'Gawd, Mr. Conrack, that dawg so skinny and long. That dawg make me sick.'

'Beau is supposed to be skinny and long. Beau is a dachshund.'

'I don't know what that dawg is but he shore is ugly.'

'You look like a dawg,' Jasper yelled at Cindy Lou.

'Watch what you say, boy.'

'She look like dawg.' Sidney giggled.

'Watch yo' mout', boy.'

'Who you tell to watch yo' mout', girl.'

'I tell you, that's who, boy. You ain't deef.'

'Children, children, children. We must show love, compassion, and understanding for each other,' I intoned.

'What that man say,' said Big C.

My be-kind-to-mongrel addresses usually degenerated into these backbiting arguments with

141

Cindy Lou making deprecating remarks about the much-maligned Beau. I never could quite convince her that Beau was supposed to look the way he did and was not a victim of abuse or starvation. It was Zeke Skimberry who finally provided the means for me to carry out an experiment in the proper treatment of pets. Two of his dogs gave birth almost simultaneously and Zeke suddenly found himself the proud owner of not four, but sixteen dogs. He asked me if any of my students would be interested in acquiring a new pet. I told him I would check the following day.

'All right, gang. Very important news to give you. Zeke Skimberry's beloved dog Lady has sired ten lovely little puppies who are whimpering for a good home. Now I told Zeke that none of you like dogs or knew how to take care of them.'

'No. That not right. No, Conrack,' the cry rose.

'I've seen the way you take care of dogs. Man, I'd never give you a dog of mine.'

'No, I take good care of dawg,' shouted Lincoln.

'Me too,' shouted Oscar.

'Since Saul's dog was shot,' I said, 'I'm going to bring him the best dog in the litter to make up for the one he lost. Now how many in here would take real good care of a dog if I brought him one?' The air was full of uplifted, frantic arms. I spent another twenty minutes defining what I meant by the proper care of dogs. Then Mary made a list of who wanted dogs and what sex they preferred.

Oscar said, 'Bring me a man dog.'

'Me too,' said Lincoln, 'I want a little man dog.'

'Don't bring me no woman dog,' Jasper said, 'I need me a good man dawg to take huntin'.'

'What if I bring you a woman dog, Jasper?' I

asked.

'Den I shoot 'im,' he replied.

'That's the wrong damn attitude, Jasper. That's exactly what I don't want you to say.'

The next day I loaded seven man dogs and one woman dog into a large cardboard box and delivered them to their new owners. All the recipients seemed to take proper care of their animals and love them passionately, and gave me progress reports from time to time. I felt that by introducing these hardy, durable Skimberry hounds into the island strain, some healthy, Darwinic principle would be served. Many months later I went by a house and stopped to admire one of the dogs I had transported to the island. He had acquired all the negative characteristics of his peers and his listlessness and general appearance caused me to regret my condemning these dogs to such a life. But, before my melancholy could reach epic proportions, the dog, in a flash of former glory, shot out of his resting place under the house and bit me on the boot.

CHAPTER SIX

On a Friday afternoon just before three o'clock and the arrival of the bus, I stood in the middle of the room having a bull session with the class. Top Cat was telling me about Saturday night on Yamacraw, when all the black people gathered in the boxlike building on the West River, danced to the music of James Brown and his Famous Flames, jumping a new type of jive until early in the morning. 'It's so much fun, Mr. Conrack.' I promised to make it one Saturday night, but that my new wife would not approve of my absence on a weekend just yet. Anna, the small, delicately featured sister of Saul who rarely spoke but who possessed one of the brightest, most inquisitive minds in the class, was copying a witch out of a book. The witch, of course, instantly summoned up visions of Halloween and those lost nights from my childhood when I would leave my house sporting the casual work clothes of a ghost or Frankenstein monster. I was curious about the traditions of Halloween on the island, and especially what modifications or exaggerations had evolved over the years. Since the kids believed as fervently in ghosts or witches as I believed in Chrysler motors, I imagined that Halloween was a much more macabre and meaningful night to them than it was to me. Imagine wandering out into the Yamacraw night, with the spirits and graveyards astir with disinterred fury, and the witches congregating in wicked clusters around the funeral sites of souls long dead and resurrected for a single night. God, I was fired up to hear about Halloween on Yamacraw.

'What are you cats gonna be doin' on October thirty-first?' I asked satanically.

'Nuttin',' Prophet answered without flinching.

'C'mon, man. There is something going on October thirty-first. A holiday where we go from door to door with bags in our grubby little hands. Well. What holiday am I talking about?'

They all simply stared at me with their inscrutable expressions that collectively said that they were in the hands of a madman who asked

144

impossible questions.

I became more animated. Every time they did not respond to some obvious question I handed them, I always thought that it was simply because I was not explaining it adequately or that I was not elaborating properly on the given theme. Articulation was not a personal forte, and I often had to backtrack, slow down, or repeat something again and again before they caught the gist of what I said. Since it was inconceivable to me that Halloween was not as much a part of their vocabulary as it was of mine, I felt that I had obfuscated the high festival of witchcraft with a combination of too much talk and too much bull. Finally I said, 'What are you going to do on Halloween?'

'Nuttin',' said Prophet.

'Nuttin',' said everyone else.

'What do you usually do on Halloween?'

'Nuttin',' came the answer again.

'Wait a minute. You mean to tell me you have never dressed up as a ghost and gone out trick-or-treating?'

'Man crazy,' Frank said.

'Triggertricking?' someone asked.

'I ain't dress up no ghost clothes,' said Cindy Lou.

'You have never gone out with a bag, dressed up in a costume, knocked at people's doors, said "trick or treat," and had them give you candy?'

'Naw,' Top Cat replied.

'That is ridiculous.' I was amazed. 'That is un-American and is completely ridiculous. Halloween is one of the truly great parts of being a kid. Running around a neighborhood, soaping up people's windows, collecting big bags of candy. Those are great memories.'

'What he say?' Ethel questioned Cindy Lou.

'He didn't say nuttin',' Cindy Lou answered.

'Well, I'll have to check into this stuff. No life is complete without a little trick-or-treating in it.'

When I arrived home that evening, Bernie was sitting in the living room talking with Barbara. Three teachers together, by definition, means that the talk centers around events in the classroom and at school. I told them that I had just learned that none of my students had participated in that great celebration of life and after-life, Halloween.

'Why don't you bring them over to Beaufort for Halloween?' Barbara asked.

'Bring them over and they can come to the Halloween party we're having at my school. Hell, bring them over early and they can go to the carnival, then ride on a float in the parade.' Bernie's voice grew louder.

'Where will they stay?' I asked.

'I'll get them places to stay. My PTA is coming along fine this year. They are ready to go. To do something. The kids can stay in the houses of the parents.'

'Bernie, you are not living in Harlem. You are living in Port Royal, South Carolina, an area where white people historically have, shall we say, looked down upon black people.'

'You forget one thing, my boy. They love me. They think that Bernie Schein is a genius. And do you know what, Conroy?' Here he whispered low, intimately: 'They are absolutely correct. I am a genius.'

'You are an asshole,' I whispered back, 'but you

have a great idea, my lad.'

On Monday, I unveiled the master plan to the kids. I told them we would dress up in costumes, get bags with pictures of pumpkins on them, and hit every house in Beaufort for candy. I related my own personal Halloween history for them: two years as Casper, the friendly ghost, two years as a hobo, one year as Frankenstein. I did not tell them that one year my best friend and I put soot on our faces and went disguised as black minstrels.

Then I recounted the houses of the truly generous people of the world who prepared for Halloween with a joyful spirit and vastness of heart. When I lived in Florida, when Dad was shipped to the Mediterranean, there were two elderly women with tiny hands and wrinkled faces who inhabited a great white house with a shrub-choked garden. On Halloween, they made candy apples and gave them out to children who came to their door. A man in Virginia, who lived alone, gave out all-day suckers every Halloween—round, multiflavored suckers. Halloween was a time of candy corn, jack-o'-lanterns, candy kisses, peanut-butter cups, bubble gum, Fig Newtons, soapy windows. I tried to tell about Halloween and what it represented to me—a great ritual of childhood when the world for a single night opened its doors and its coffers of candy and fun and happiness.

'Can you go to Beaufort for Halloween? It is this Friday, and we are going to have to work fast.'

'Yeah.' Everyone could go. There was no problem.

'O.K. Everybody is going to have to get a note from his parents that says, "I give my permission for so and so to go to Beaufort for Halloween." The big shots demand that I get this note in case any of you die at the shock of being under the Big Lights in Beaufort. Bring your notes in tomorrow so we will be ready to go.'

'What boat you take us out?' Frank asked.

'I don't have a boat yet. I am leaving the island this afternoon to find a boat.'

'How big?'

'Look, gang, it ain't going to be no aircraft carrier or battleship.'

Later I went in and told Mrs. Brown about this superb brainstorm. I expected her to praise me profusely, tell me what an outstanding job I was doing, and offer to help me in any way possible. I would blush modestly, shuffle my right foot back and forth over an imaginary mark on the floor, lower my head, and say, 'Aw, shucks,' or something as appropriate.

'No, you cannot go,' she said simply.

'Why the hell not?' I asked incredulously.

'These children don't need trips. They need fundamentals. They need drill and more drill.'

'Mrs. Brown, that is what *you* think they need. It is not what I think they need. It is not what I think they need and since those eighteen children are my responsibility and since it is up to me to decide how best to educate them, I am going to take them to Beaufort for Halloween.'

'I am the principal.'

'I was the principal for a while in this school. And did you notice, Mrs. Brown, that I did not interfere with the way you conducted your classes or how you treated your kids? I did not constantly remind you, "I am the principal." I acted as if neither of us was in charge, but as if we were equals

148

trying to get a job done under very trying circumstances. I admire you very much for having taught on this God-forsaken island, but I am going to give these kids the experience of spending Halloween the way the rest of the kids in America spend it. If you want to file a complaint, then file it. We are heading off this island Friday. If you want to come along and chaperone this trip, then that is just dandy. If not, then that's dandy too.'

'I am the principal and I am in charge of this school.'

'Sweet Jesus.'

That afternoon I left the island by boat. I had told Zeke to meet me at four o'clock. I also told him to wrack his brain to figure out where I could find a boat large enough to transport twenty people off Yamacraw. Had the government boat been functional, no problem would have existed for me. But since it was going on the second month in drydock, it did not look as though Yamacraw was to have daily transportation for several more weeks.

When I reached Alljoy Landing, Zeke awaited me with his truck and the boat trailer. On the way to his house, he told me that Ed Samuels, a black man who headed up the local Office of Economic Opportunity, owned a boat large enough for my purposes. I drove to Beaufort, talked with Mr. Samuels, begged for charity and cooperation, got the boat after only a little bit of cajolery, then went to see Bernie.

'How are you doing with the parents?'

'Two ladies have already offered to house four of the kids. There are three more solid possibilities. Leave it to Bernie Schein, my good man. I also called an assembly of all the kids in the school, told

149

them about the island, its problems, and then informed them that the Yamacraw kids are coming for Halloween.'

'Good man, Bernie. Did you mention to the parents the minor fact that these kids are black?'

'No, I do that tomorrow.'

'Bernie, you are an idiot.'

'Of course I told them they're black. That was the first thing I told them. Then I shot them the bill of goods, the patented sales pitch that once made me the "Top Tiger" salesman of the Southeast when I sold sewing machines one summer. I just remembered what the district manager of Singer sewing machines used to tell me: "Bernie, throw enough shit against the wall and some of it's bound to stick." Well, it stuck today when I talked to those ladies.'

'So you think housing is no problem?'

'None whatsoever. Did you get the boat?'

'It's picking the kids up at eight o'clock in the morning this Friday. Can you arrange for people to pick them up?'

'Already done. A group of VISTA workers are going to meet them.'

'Great. Now, Bernie, if anything goes wrong I'm going to be forced to become physically violent with you.'

'You won't lift a finger, because you know I can whip your ass.'

All was proceeding well. The major problems seemed solved by Tuesday morning. I walked into class, a jubilant and triumphant conqueror of obstacles.

'We got houses to stay in and we got a boat to ride in,' I shouted, as I walked in the front door.

150

'We are heading for the big city on Friday for a weekend of witchcraft and candy-chomping. Now, everybody, hand in your permission slips from your parents.'

Naturally no one moved.

'If you forgot your permission slips, I am going to strangle every damn one of you.'

All eyes turned downward. No one looked at me, no one smiled at me, and no one hinted that they might be moved to talk to me.

'What is wrong, gang? Before I start beating heads, I want to know what's wrong.'

'Ain't goin',' said Frank.

'What do you mean, "ain't goin'?" Of course you're goin'. We are all goin'. We are going to have fun and learn things and it's just goin' to be great.'

'Not goin' nowhere,' Mary said.

'Be right here,' Cindy Lou mourned.

'All right, gang. Listen up.' Here, they at least raised their eyes a little bit. 'As you know I am not used to the way things work around this goofy island. Right?' They nodded. 'Yesterday everyone was keyed up to stash up on candy in Beaufort. I mean, you were going wild, going absolutely ape-crap about going to town, about spending the night off the island. Now everyone looks like they buried their mother last night. What happened?'

'Can't go,' Sallie Ann finally said.

'Can't go,' Saul said.

'Can't go,' Cindy Lou said.

'What in the hell do you mean "can't go"? Of course you can go. We are going. You mean to tell me that none of your parents are going to let you go trick-or-treating? I just think that's crap.'

'Conrack curse,' Sidney said.

'My grandma just laugh when I say we goin',' Frank said.

'My momma just say no,' Saul said.

'Your momma is the cook, Saul. She likes me. I wash dishes for her.'

Like an avenging angel, I dashed for the kitchen and confronted Mrs. Wyler with the accusation that she was holding back the relentless pace of education; that it was criminal for her to prevent Saul and Anna from benefiting from the fruits of travel and experience.

'Yassuh,' she said, 'they can go.'

'Please don't call me yassuh, Mrs. Wyler. Call me Pat.'

'Yassuh, Mr. Pat.'

'Jesus, Mrs. Wyler. Just Pat.'

'O.K., Pat.'

I ran back to tell Saul and Anna that I had won permission from their mother.

'No,' said Saul. 'She just tell you that. She not let us go.'

'She just told me you could go.'

'She tell you that so you not bodder her.'

I zipped back to the kitchen again, breathing like a dragon, unable to fathom the game I was playing, unable to figure out what exactly was happening.

'Mrs. Wyler, Saul just told me that you agreed to let him go just to get me off your back. Is that true?'

'Yassuh.'

'Pat, Mrs. Wyler, please. Can Saul and Anna come with me to Beaufort?'

'No, suh.'

'Of course they can come to Beaufort. They'll have a ball. It'll be good for them. There is no

152

reason on earth why they can't go.'

'They can't go because I say they can't go.'

'A good reason,' I agreed. I paused, trying to approach the argument from a different perspective. 'What if I told you, Mrs. Wyler, that I was going to kick the hell out of you if you didn't let them go?'

'Then my husband shoot you dead.'

'Ah! An excellent response. Then you can be assured I will not lay a single pinky on you. Let me just ask you one question, Mrs. Wyler. What can I say to you or how can I convince you to let your children cross the river for Halloween?'

'Nothin'. They ain't goin'. None of the chillun on the island goin'.'

'I am going to hound the hell out of you people, Mrs. Wyler. I am going to get those kids off this island. We are going to Beaufort for Halloween.'

Angry and frustrated, I went back to the classroom and told Saul that he was going to go home, sit in the middle of the kitchen, beat his fists against the floor, scream, rant, and weep hysterically until his mother granted permission for him to go to Beaufort. I told every child who sat before me that one plan and one plan only was in effect: they were going to make the lives of their parents so miserable and unbearable that the parents would throw them on the boat on Friday in utter desperation.

'Your parents might beat you to bloody pulps,' I raved. 'They may stomp on you and swat you with hickory sticks. They may put you outside with the chickens and the hogs, but we are going to Beaufort for Halloween. Now, Mary, tell me what you're gonna do when you bust in your door tonight.'

'Ain't gonna do nothin',' she answered.

'My momma kill me if I say sumpin',' Jasper said.

'You tell 'em, Conrack. Not me tell nothin',' said Ethel.

'O.K. I will tell them. At lunch time I am going to every house on this island and talking to every parent on this island.'

Then I paused and reflected on what Ted Stone and Mrs. Brown had told me about the people. Mrs. Brown had pictured the people as a savage, blood-thirsty leftover from African tribes. Ted put his distrust of the island blacks into an epigram: 'Can't trust a nigger when your back's turned.' I did not put much stock in either source, but both of them had had far more extensive dealings with the people than I had. In fact, I had met very few of the parents, much to my discredit. I do not have genuine self-confidence in walking up to a stranger and carrying on a conversation. And every time I attempted to make a friend among the adult blacks, I was put off by an unassailable barrage of the unremitting *yassuhs*.

I asked, 'Now, gang. If I go running up to your house real fast . . . No, let me say it differently. If I walk to your home unannounced and uninvited . . . No. There ain't no chance that I am going to get shot, is there?'

'No, Conrack,' Frank said with mild disgust. 'My grandma shoot Brown dead. But she no shoot you.'

'No,' the class agreed.

'O.K. I believe you. But if I end up picking buckshot out of my behind, I may have to whip some fanny.'

154

At twelve the kids rushed out to the playground. I informed Mrs. Brown as gently as possible that I needed to see a few of the parents during recess.

'Do you have written permission from the superintendent of schools?' she asked majestically.

'No, ma'am.'

'You are being paid by the state of South Carolina for recess time and class time. You are required to be present on the school grounds at all times.'

'Yes, ma'am. I would hate to jeopardize that big salary I'm getting, but I really have to see some of the parents.'

She shook her head negatively and kept repeating over and over that she could not grant authority for me to leave the school grounds without written permission from a loftier source.

'See you, Mrs. Brown. Let's argue later.'

I went out to the car, started it up, then headed for the house where Frank, Big C, Samuel, and Sidney resided under the iron rule of their grandmother, Edna Graves. Edna's reputation went before her. I heard her grandchildren talk about her with deference, almost adoration. She was reputed to have the best garden on the island, and other residents went to her for advice about the best time for planting and harvesting. A rumor, persistent and enlightening, said that she and her husband made some of the best moonshine in the lowcountry during the bootleggers' heyday. I went to Edna first because I knew if I could sway her, I would have won half the island.

Her house was gray and neatly situated beneath a tall oak. Pigs rooted behind her house and chickens fluttered nervously as I entered the yard. I fluttered nervously as I saw a pack of foaming hounds

155

emerge from under the house to challenge my entry into the yard. There were a lot of teeth showing in that yard. I was muttering, 'Here, boy. Nice doggie. Good boy. Don't you bite me, you goddam son of a bitch.' I then started yelling at the dogs to keep away from me. A clothesline pole stood in the middle of the yard, a couple of feet away from where I stood. With a frantic bound, I leaped up on that pole and sat perched precariously as the pack closed around me, jumping and snapping at my dangling heels.

Then I heard Edna coming down the steps, swinging a broom over her head, shouting at the dogs and scattering them in six directions. She looked at me on the pole and in a voluminous voice—powerful, masculine, and incredibly loud—she bellowed, 'What'ch you doin' up on that pole, man?' Then she bent double laughing. 'Ha, ha, ha! Lord, you look funny up on that pole.'

My dignity was more than a little ruffled. I dropped from the pole and tried to assume a more professional air.

'Your dogs chased me up there,' I said with solemnity.

'Well, what you want from Edna?'

'I would like to talk to you about your grandchildren who are in my class at school.'

'Oh Gawd,' she said loudly.

'What's the matter?'

'Oh Gawd. Oh Gawd Almighty. You is Mr. Conrack.'

'My name is Pat Conroy.'

'Oh Gawd, Mr. Conrack. My grands talk about you all de time. They come home and say to me, "Mama, you know what Mr. Conrack say today."

156

Oh Gawd, my grands love Mr. Conrack. So that's who you are. The white schoolteacher.'

'Yes, ma'am.'

'Oh Gawd. O-o-o-o-h-h Gawd. I been wantin' to dress up and meet you at the schoolhouse. People say you is a wonnerful teacher. Lord, I hear some mighty nice words about you from a lot of people.'

'Thank you, Mrs. Graves. I appreciate that. I really do. But I have come to talk to you about...'

'Oh Gawd, what we doin' talkin' out here. Come into my house and I fix you some coffee whiles we talk.'

'I don't have time, Mrs. Graves.'

'Call me Edna, Mr. Conrack.'

'Call me Pat, Edna.'

'Pat is a boo-tiful name, Mr. Conrack.'

'Thank you, Mrs. Graves.'

'Now,' she said, appraising me closely, scrutinizing every feature on my face. Hers was a beautiful, strong, wrinkled face with warm, powerful eyes. 'Now, what you want, Mr. Conrack?'

'Mrs. Graves, I want to take your grandchildren to Beaufort for Halloween. I have a boat to take them over in; I have places for them to stay. Everything is set up and taken care of. The children will be well chaperoned. They will have a great time. It will be an educational experience for them that will do them a lot of good. I have the whole trip set up and now the only thing I need from the parents and grandparents is permission. If y'all don't give me permission to take the kids, it's just going to ruin everything.'

Edna continued to study me intently as I talked. Her stare was penetrating and a slight smile played

157

on her lips. She did not seem to be listening to a word I said.

Finally she spoke. 'Gawd, you is a nice-lookin' teacher.'

'What did you say?'

'You is a fine-lookin' teacher, a fine-lookin' man. Ain't you just a fine-lookin' man, now.'

'Edna, I swear this is one of the strangest moments in my life. I am askin' you about the Halloween trip.'

'Gracious, those chillun didn't tell me what a fine-lookin' white teacher. You look like a man I see on television. He come on "Love of Life," and Lawd, do I love dat man. I watch "Love of Life" ever single day, Mr. Conrack.'

'That's nice, Mrs. Graves.'

'You watch it too?'

'No, ma'am. I'm teaching then.'

'Oh Gawd. Well now, Linda had gone way from Edward. Left him clean to go with that doctor fella, Steve. Steve is so nice. Gawd, he is a nice man. Edward been drinkin' a little too much and runnin' around with Betty. Betty's man done die the year befo' in a bad wreck. Steve tried to fick him up, but he too far dead to get fick. Oh Lawd, those people all in a mess. Linda got something bad wrong with her too.'

I looked at Edna as she related the soap-bubbly plot of her favorite program and it suddenly struck me that a hell of a lot more people derived dramatic pleasure from the plight of Linda and Doctor Steve than ever derived it from Hamlet and Ophelia. The idea intrigued me so much that 'Love of Life' was the Shakespeare of the late twentieth-century masses that I lost the momentum and indignation

158

which was with me when I charged into the yard. Finally, I got her back on the subject.

'Mrs. Graves, will you just tell me why you won't let your grandchildren go to Beaufort with me?'

Her eyes hardened suddenly and she shifted her weight from one foot to the other and raised a long, callused index finger toward me.

''Cause I know the river. I lose three fam'bly in the river. They drop in the water and sink like rock to the bottom. When they come up, they swell like toadfish. I been libbin' on Yamacraw for seventy plus seven more years and I ain't gonna lose no grands to that river. You young and you don't know the river. I is old and see what it can do. Dat river can eat a man. None of my chillun goin' along wit' you.'

'I finally understand what the problem is, Mrs. Graves. And I am glad you told me. What I have to convince you of is this. Nothing is going to happen to the children. I promise you that. I give you my word that nothing is gonna happen. They will be with me and they will be my responsibility. I am going to take care of them. We are going to have the best time these children have ever had.'

'What kind of boat you got? They ain't going on your boat.'

'I've got a big boat and a shrimp-boat captain to drive it.'

'Oh Gawd, that's good.'

'Can they go?' I asked hopefully.

'No,' she said, with a certain perceptible degree of finality in her tone.

Then she smiled again, a mysterious, enigmatic smile that was full of wisdom, 'Love of Life,' and perhaps pain. 'Gawd, you is a good-lookin' teacher.'

'Don't say that, Edna. It's not true. You are just saying that.'

'You got such a nice face for a white teacher.'

'For God's sakes, Edna, please cut it out. I feel like a fool.'

'Lawd, Lawd. Well, mebbe I let the oldest go. Frank and Charles.'

'What about Sidney and Samuel?'

'No, great Lawd, no.' She stamped her foot on the floor. 'Those is bad chillun. They too bad to go on trip.'

'Why?'

'Because they is bad.'

'But Frank and Charles can go.'

'If the weather be good.'

'It will be great. Could you write a permission slip?'

'What dat you say?'

'Could you sign a piece of paper for me that I can show to Mrs. Brown?'

'That debbil woman.'

'Pardon me.'

'That damn colored woman at the schoolhouse. She the debbil herself.'

'Mrs. Brown is a pretty nice woman, Edna. You just gotta get to know her.' I was not expecting this vehement denunciation of my colleague, nor did I know exactly how to change the subject tactfully.

'You don't know that debbil woman. She know. She never set one foot in this yard 'cause she know that I'll use Betsy if I have to.' Edna had suddenly turned into a madwoman.

'Ah, who is Betsy, if I may ask?'

'Betsy my good friend, Mr. Conrack. She do a lot of talkin' when Edna get riled.'

'Well, I don't think we need Betsy, Edna. Give her my love when you see her. And think about letting the twins go. They'd really enjoy it.'

'No, they too bad. Gawd, you is a good-lookin' white man.'

This phrase was making me extremely uncomfortable, so I finally retorted with, 'Gawd, you are a good-looking woman, Edna. A real nice-lookin' woman.'

'Lawd, you is too much. You is too much, Mr. Conrack.'

The snarling pack closed in for the kill again, so Edna waded through them with broom aflying once more and cleared a path to the car.

I had taken the better part of an hour to convince Edna that she should let her grandsons, at least two of them, make the trip to Beaufort. By winning Edna, I had won the island. Every parent I talked to was hesitant, dubious, unconvinced by my protestations and plans, but all of them eventually decided that their chillun could go 'if the weather be good.'

Naturally, the weather was horrendous. On Friday morning, the last-minute preparations with Bernie completed, Zeke put me into the water just before seven in the morning. It was already drizzling slightly, the sky was overcast and foreboding, and tiny whitecaps were forming on the river surface. 'Suck,' I said to myself as the boat headed into Bull Creek. I looked toward the sky and demanded fairness from the Great Weatherman. The nearer I got to Yamacraw the worse the weather became. Barbara and I had spent the previous evening in a five-and-dime store picking out Halloween masks for my students. I

161

had worked them into a frenzy in the days preceding our exodus from the island. Halloween was going to be the greatest event in the history of the world; we were going to have more twenty-four-carat fun than any group in the long history of mankind. The masks Barbara picked out ranged from the ludicrous to the macabre. Some were vampires, others were monstermen, and still others mad scientists and ghouls. Barbara also selected eighteen heavy-duty, witch-inspected, certified Halloween bags to put the candy in. Everything was planned to perfection. As much logistics went into this trip as went into the planning of D-Day, or so I thought. As I rode over that morning, I thought the goddam weather was sabotaging me.

As I pulled in sight of the public landing, I saw the whole class huddled under an oak tree near the row of sheds where the islanders stored their fishing and shrimping paraphernalia. Joe and Jim came down to help me tie up the boat. Mrs. Brown, who relented the day before the trip by canceling her classes and declaring it a state law that the principal of the school must accompany every school-sponsored trip, stood ponderously on the bank herding the children together as if she were shepherding a flock of recalcitrant sheep. Miss Glover the crippled teacher of forty years, had asked me on Tuesday if she could come along as a chaperone. I told her I would be delighted if she would come. We were becoming very good friends despite the warnings that she would use her powers of darkness on me before the year was over. As I walked up the dock, I saw Miss Glover glowering at Mrs. Brown, her avowed and eternal enemy.

162

A few of the parents were milling around the ring of children, looking at the sky and shaking their heads negatively. The weather seemed to worsen as each moment passed. One of the parents said to his child, 'Don't think you should make this trip. Weather no good.'

'The weather is fine,' I broke in. 'The weather is going to be perfect. Listened to the weather report this morning and it said that the sun was going to break out at about ten o'clock this morning. Relative humidity about fifty-eight per cent. Temperature a very nice and satisfying seventy degrees. Looks like it is going to be perfect weather for the trip. Things clearing up already.'

I then passed out masks and bags to all the kids. Before I finished meting out the bags, Richard was poking Lincoln in the belly because Lincoln had coveted Richard's vampire mask and subsequently absconded with it. A few other minor skirmishes broke out over the masks but peace eventually reigned over all.

Only three of the kids were not present. Samuel, Sidney, and Prophet were not among the ones chosen by the elders of the island to cross the waters with me, but I could not mourn over the fate of those who remained. I was damned nervous about the boat that was to transport us to the mainland. The captain promised that his craft would be moored to the Yamacraw dock at eight o'clock.

At nine o'clock the boat puttered into sight at the edge of Ramshorn Creek. The entire congregation around me groaned when they saw the boat; it looked as if it had been designed and constructed during the Peloponnesian War. It creaked and lurched up to the dock like an arthritic old man, wheezing and coughing a diesel asthma that appeared incurable. The boat looked like part of a ghost fleet, a mothballed potpourri of poor design. The captain, whom I had not met, stared confidently down at all of us. Then he commanded that we lead the kids into the ship's hold. He made no pretense of hiding the fact that he would rather be doing other things and that this trip was an infringement on his valuable time. I led the gang quickly into the greasy, noxious hold and prayed silently that none of them would die of carbon monoxide on the trip over. Mrs. Brown shouted at them, tugged at their ears, and crammed them into the narrow passageway leading to the bowels of the boat. The hold could comfortably seat four people. Mrs. Brown crammed fifteen students into it.

'Ain't no air down here, Conrack,' Lincoln cried.

'Gonna puke, Conrack,' another shouted.

'Lord, we all gonna die,' Mary shouted.

Joe and Miss Glover went aboard. Jim and I jumped into my boat and headed for Bluffton, where Zeke Skimberry was waiting to pull the boat out of the water. I was driving a load of kids in my car and I wanted to be damn sure that the VISTA workers were at the appointed rendezvous point on Hilton Head.

So far, things were running fairly smoothly, I thought. I wanted perfection, for I knew if there was any accident or mishap connected with this voyage, then I never again would be able to convince the parents to let me take their children from the protective embrace of the island. I looked back, saw the boat leave the dock and the parents waving, and realized that I had succeeded in the first major step of the operation: my students were

164

no longer bound to the island and had begun what was perhaps the greatest adventure of their lives.

Then my great drama, directed brilliantly for a time, lapsed into farce. The first thing Zeke said to me when I got to Bluffton made me realize that the supreme allied commanders in the county office knew all about the trip.

'Bennington has a bus ready to take the kids to Beaufort. He's sending the bus down here to the landing.'

'Why is he doing that, Zeke?'

'I think Ted Stone called him up on the radio and said that you didn't have any transportation for the kids.'

'Did he think we were going to walk the thirty miles to Beaufort?' I asked.

'Don't know, Pat. Just know that old Foxy is sending a bus down here in about ten minutes.'

'We gotta stop that damn bus, Zeke.'

We loaded the boat on the trailer hurriedly. Zeke gunned the blue pickup down Alljoy Road.

'I've had 'er up to a hundred on this road before,' Zeke said matter of factly.

'That's great, Zeke.'

We skidded in front of Bluffton High School. Sure enough, a bus and a rather puzzled, nervous driver waited for instructions near the front door of the school. He was about fifteen years old and looked faintly perturbed about being pulled out of class for a project so ephemeral and disorganized. One noteworthy thing about South Carolina is the quality of school-bus drivers in the state. To qualify for a bus license one must have reached puberty and be able to recite the alphabet without stuttering. Anyway, the kid told me that 'Mr. Ezra' had called

165

his school (the black high school) and ordered the principal to have a kid out of class for the purpose of delivering the Yamacraw children to their proper destination in Beaufort. In a towering rage I told the driver to tell Bennington to stick it up his behind, to attend to his business as supervisor of instruction, and to keep his nose out of my life.

My car was parked at the Skimberrys' house. Ida fixed Jim and me a hot cup of coffee while Zeke told a few Bennington stories. Jim and I departed soon and drove rather quickly over to the marina on Hilton Head where the VISTA workers had promised to meet the boat. As I rounded the curve to the marina, I saw in one swift glance that the boat had landed precisely on schedule, that the children and chaperones were safely grounded, and that no one had been drowned, lost, or fumigated on the way over. I saw in another glance that no VISTA workers were there to meet the boat.

Mrs. Brown perceptively analyzed the situation by saying, 'We don't have no wheels on our feet, son.'

I put in a phone call to my dear, steadfast friend, Bernie Schein. In a calm, constrained, rational tone I asked Bernie a single question, 'Where the hell are those VISTA workers, you goddam son of a bitch?'

Bernie, the acknowledged master of all situations, whose coolness and vision under pressure brought him admiration from all quarters, said in a quiet, modulated tone, 'Those stupid bastards promised me they'd be there.'

Somewhere along the Atlantic seaboard, four government cars driven by idealistic young VISTAs stood in formation facing the rising tides and looking for the boat from Yamacraw Island. So in the prodigious planning and mapping out of strategy during the past week, the one breakdown of logistics came in transportation overland.

Mrs. Brown said, 'It don't look like very much planning went into this trip.'

I leaped back into the car and drove furiously back to the black high school from whence the rejected driver had come. I arrived at the high school, sprinted into the principal's office, and demanded to know why a bus was not waiting for the poor children at Yamacraw Island. No less a person than Ezra Bennington himself, the grand patriarch of Bluffton, had requested a bus to meet the boat from Yamacraw. Why, I demanded, was this bus not forthcoming?

'You sent him back,' the secretary, nonplussed, answered me.

'A monumental mistake. My fault, of course, but I have got to have that driver.'

'I will get him for you, sir.'

The secretary was flashing me one of those looks I sometimes notice I get from strangers. By nature I am high-strung and animated, but when frustration confronts me head on, I degenerate into a demoniac. It is harmless and only a little schizoid, but it often intimidates people.

When the driver, the beautiful, enchanted prince of a driver, arrived in the principal's office, I rushed him to his bus and told him to follow me. Once again I was airborne between Bluffton and Hilton Head Island. The driver, whose name was Robert, seemed to grasp the urgency of the situation and headed for the marina as quickly as his regulator would allow.

At the marina everybody mobbed my car,

shouting, chanting, wailing about something that I could not fathom amidst the gibberish. Finally, Joe Sanfort got across to me that Mary had hurt her knee by falling on the asphalt. I got out of the car and ran over to where Mary was sitting.

'Little skinned knee never hurt anybody, Mary. You just been living on that island where there ain't no cement,' I said, walking over to her. She was covering her knee with her hand, and dark, red blood oozed between her fingers. I asked her to move her hand so I could see how badly she was hurt. She moved her hand and I was jarred by the sight of Mary's blood-stained but ivory white kneecap. A flap of skin lay smashed against the right side of her bone.

'That girl just don't have any meat on her bones, that's why the cut looks so bad,' Mrs. Brown intoned. 'Lawd, if a high wind come along, we'd have to put rocks in that girl's pockets to keep her from blowin' away.'

I knew that Mary was extremely sensitive about her weight. She had grown tall quickly and her body had not filled out proportionately to her height. Almost as tall as I, she had a beautiful face and one day would be a stunning woman. A shy thirteen, she hated being teased about her weight. She gave Mrs. Brown a look that would have melted a submarine.

The bus drove up and all the kids and chaperones piled on, the kids wearing their masks and clutching their bags. I gave the driver instructions on how to get to Bernie's school. Then Mary and I lit out for the doctor's office. Her knee merited immediate treatment and it took no specialist to realize that her wound would require quite a few stitches. For the sixth time that day, I was thundering down the Bluffton road.

We headed for Dr. Wohlert's office. Mary knew and trusted him. He was the only doctor around for thirty miles. He was also the most controversial figure in South Carolina at that time. The previous year, Dr. Wohlert had publicized the fact that many of the lowcountry blacks he treated were worm-ridden and dying of malnutrition. Immediately after this announcement, national magazines came out with stories about intestinal parasites and hunger in Beaufort County. National attention was focused on Beaufort, and her white citizens smouldered in self-righteous fury as more and more statistics were made available, proving the doctor to be correct. He was vilified unmercifully by the local press and residents. I had never met the man, but many of my white friends had pictured him as a malignant tumor, demented, loco, a drug addict, an incompetent, a carpetbagger, an unregenerated liar who should have his gonads cut off and hung like two trophies in the chamber of commerce building. Therefore, with all of this Anglo-Saxon wrath directed at him from the good solid citizens of the county, who thought blacks and chimpanzees were somehow parallel in evolutionary development, there was an excellent chance that Wohlert was a damn good guy.

The blacks from Yamacraw loved him. Ted Stone called him 'a Communist trained in Havana.' Whatever he was, I found it extraordinary that he could still be functioning in a county that had done so much to torture and discredit him. The community pressure levied against him would have sent me to an asylum. There was, in fact, another

169

rumor that he was bouncing from one crazy house to another.

Dr. Wohlert's waiting room was filled not with patients but with unsmiling young men and women who reacted strangely when I broke through the door and asked if Wohlert was in. The men were long-hairs; the women were sallow-faced, with hard eyes and yellowish lips. I realized after a moment that they acted as bodyguards for the doctor; no one passed them without going through a security check.

'Who are you?' one of the guys asked me.

'Who are you?' I asked back. 'Look, man, I teach on Yamacraw Island and one of my students cracked her knee open. It needs some stitches.'

A nurse appeared from behind me, a very pleasant woman with an amicable smile.

'Bring her in. The doctor will see her in a moment.'

I went to the car and helped Mary into the office. The guards loosened up when they saw Mary's knee bone sticking out. The nurse led us to a back room, where I sat Mary on a table. I joked with Mary a little bit. She was beginning to worry me, since she had not uttered a single word since her accident.

'Mary, I have seen many cases like this before when I worked as a doctor's aide during the Punic Wars.' I stared at her wound with professional detachment.

'It is my opinion that Doctor Wohlert will have to cut your leg off.'

Mary looked horror-stricken.

'It's a joke, Mary. It's just a joke,' I quickly amended. Mary, with a majestic silence, let me know that she was not amused.

170

Presently Dr. Wohlert entered the room. He moved frenetically, eyes darting and bloodshot, hands quick and nervous, gestures sudden and unplanned. He was a small man with a birdlike fragility about him. His glasses were thick, his hair was disheveled and wildly amassed on a narrow, strikingly intelligent head. His eyes caught me. The toll of martyrdom weighed heavily on him, and the wrath of the citizenry had taken a considerable toll on his physical appearance. Without asking a single question, I could discern that the good doctor had been through hell.

He shook my hand as if I had handed him a two-week-old herring—no warmth, no firmness, a noncommittal handshake. I could see that he could not make the connection between Mary and me. As briefly as possible I explained that I was teaching on Yamacraw Island, was in the midst of an abortive field trip, and that Mary's knee bone had screwed things up by popping out of her knee. Mary, meanwhile, still looked dazed and resigned to a silent, unflinching suffering. When the doctor asked her if she was hurting, she merely nodded her head affirmatively. His office was not a model of order, but he found what he needed, pumped the knee full of Novocain, and began to tie the flesh together.

When he was almost finished, he asked me a question which I thought strange and troubling. 'Have the rednecks tried to get you yet?'

'Not yet, Doctor.'

'That's good. I hope they don't.'

I thanked him, helped Mary off the table, and walked out to the lobby, where I asked the nurse to send the bill to the Beaufort County Board of

Education. I figured they had more money than Mary's parents.

We now traveled the thirty miles from Bluffton to Port Royal in record time. The bus carrying the others had arrived a half-hour before. An air of excitement had descended over the playground beside the school. Each Yamacraw child was surrounded by five smiling, peppy white kids from Bernie's remarkable school of Port Royal.

Bernie's school was entrenched in a white neighborhood pocked with trailer parks and residents who had given George Wallace a heavy chunk of support in the 1968 presidential election, but somehow, he sold the idea of the Yamacraw expedition to the entire community. I think the good people of Port Royal were expecting the Yamacrawans to paddle over in their dug-out canoes, chanting in the unknown tongue to the wind god. Several of the Port Royal sixth graders I talked to that day were disappointed because my students did not wear bones in their noses, or carry spears to drive away enemy warriors that might attack them on their journey back to the island. Yet the year was 1969, and Bernie had mesmerized white parents sufficiently so that they were accepting fifteen black children into their homes.

Bernie emerged from a cluster of giggling girls when he saw me, raised his cigar in salute, then ran over to my car.

'You missed it, boy. You missed the greatest welcome since Caesar returned to Rome.'

'What happened, Bernard?'

'I was in class, trying to teach, and worrying that your ass would never show up. Then the bus drove up in front of the school. A kid came running into

172

my class and said, "They're here!" Well, boy, when that kid said that, every goddam kid in this school, every single child in this whole school, ran out of their classrooms, trampled down their teachers, and surrounded the bus, cheering and clapping and raising hell. They were so glad your kids made it. The Yamacraw kids peeked out their windows on the bus, looking like the world had gone crazy. I walked through the crowd, you know how I am, like a god among men, and got on the bus and gave the official welcoming speech. I escorted Mrs. Brown off the bus, then Miss Glover, got my sixth graders to lead the Yamacraw kids off and into the lunchroom. I just want to tell you one thing, son. It was the greatest, the most spontaneous demonstration of excitement I have ever seen.'

Evidently my students had been completely won over by their peers from Port Royal. I saw Oscar and Big C riding around the basketball court on brand-new bicycles. A couple of the other boys were teaching the mainland kids the island's perverted version of basketball. The girls were busy decorating the floats that would be used in Bernie's second annual Halloween parade. A spirit of good-will seemed to reign over the proceedings, a shrill, Fat Tuesday drone of voices and cries of children pierced the air. PTA mothers with soft rumps and good smiles manned carnival booths. Saul came strutting up to me carrying a yo-yo.

'I pop two b'loons to get it,' he bragged.

'You couldn't pop a paper bag, Saul.'

'Yah! I pop two b'loons with two darts.'

Lincoln breezed up with a plastic Jesus he had won by knocking milk bottles down with a baseball. Cindy Lou ran up to tell me, 'That man Bernie is crazy man. Lawd, he so crazy. He stick his ol' ugly tongue out at me.'

'Stick your ol' ugly tongue back at him.'

So there was this great carnival. Bernie had drilled his students well. They treated the Yamacraw kids like visiting royalty. I thought later that perhaps Bernie and I had concocted a shallow arena for the betterment of race relations, that what we had done was better for us (some crowning achievement we could point to and say, 'Look what we have done for the improvement of mankind') than for the people of Port Royal or the children of Yamacraw. We wanted to do so much, wanted to be small catalysts in the transformation of the disfigured sacramental body of the South, which had sired us. I was a cynic who needed desperately to believe in the salvation of mankind or at least in the potential salvation. Bernie was an optimist who needed proof that his philosophy of joy and the resurrection of the spirit was not the delusion of a grinning Pollyanna. God, we were concerned about things: war, prejudice, injustice, education. Together we were insufferable, pontifical, self-righteous voices of the Eucharist, pipelines to the Almighty. We could not be wrong, because we were young, humanistic, and full of shit.

But on this day it seemed that Bernie and I had stumbled on something that transcended our personal preoccupations. Frank, Top Cat, Jasper, Ethel, Richard, Lincoln, Jimmy Sue, and all the rest of the insular, world-protected crowd that came across the river that day were having a ball. I could see it and they told me.

When I revved up the pickup truck, decorated with red and purple streamers and with a boat

174

hooked onto the back, at the start of the Port Royal Halloween parade, every one of my students clambered all over the truck and boat, faces hidden in soggy masks, bags saturated by the light drizzle that had fallen all day, Top Cat leaning in the window saying hi to Barbara, Mrs. Conrack, the strut of majorettes, the roll of drums, the lines of spectators bracing the rain, Jessica sitting in my lap, Oscar blowing his noisemaker constantly, vigorously, and without end. All of it was surrealistic, gray-misted, a spoof of never-never land that had little to do with Yamacraw Island.

After the parade, I had a brief meeting with the gang, told them to enjoy trick-or-treating, to be kind to their hosts, to remember that I would casually kick the hell out of them if they got scratched, hurt, or injured, and that I would meet them in front of the school the following morning at nine o'clock. I also told them that each one of them would give me exactly half of the candy they collected on Halloween night.

'No, Conrack. You no get nuttin'',' said Cindy Lou.

The next morning a straight line of five cars met in front of Port Royal Elementary School. Everyone assembled rather slowly. The weather was not good. To avoid complete hyperbole and to describe with a fair amount of accuracy the kind of weather the gods saw fit to plague the sea islands with on this critical day of November the first, I would have to say that Beaufort was experiencing a mild hurricane. Torrential rains flooded the streets and driving winds swept through trees bent like old men. The weather will clear up, I told everyone.

When we arrived at the dock at Hilton Head, the

weather had gotten worse. I heard Oscar, who was riding with me, lean over to Frank and whisper, 'Shee-ut, waves so big!' The boat captain had to be roused from his house, which was near the dock. He started talking about the storm of '59 and the shrimp boat that had sunk and taken six men with it. Then he mentioned the great storm of '52, which had splintered ships of iron and littered a fifty-mile stretch of beach with debris. 'That's very nice, Captain, but can you tell me if you can get those kids back to the island safely?'

'Oh, I s'pose so,' he answered. 'Why don't we wait a little while. I do believe the weather gonna clear. Fact is, I can feel it in my bones.'

'Great. Captain, I have got to get those kids back to the island or their parents are going to kill me.'

'It gonna clear up.'

Two hours later the weather had worsened considerably. Great, high waves smashed over the dock and the whole river was boiling, savage, and unrestrained. Jesus could not have gotten across that river. Moses couldn't have opened it up. A miracle could not have calmed those raging waters soon enough to get those kids across the water to their homes.

I called Bennington, told him the situation, and asked where I could house those kids. I had to fight back an urge to ask him if we could bring the entire group over to snooze in the luxury of his walnut-paneled, many-columned house by the river. He was ingratiating on the phone and said we could sleep on mats in the Hilton Head Elementary School. He would see to it personally. I then called the sheriff and asked him to radio Ted Stone, so he could let the parents know that the children were

176

safe and would be home, hopefully, the following day.

The gang bedded down in the school. A few noisemakers sounded. Everyone ate a lot of Halloween candy. Mary sat by herself in considerable pain. I vowed to myself that this was the last transriver venture of which I would be a part. And the rain came down.

★   ★   ★

All of my doubts about parental retribution for the extra day spent away from the island were dispelled when I walked into school Monday morning. Almost every mouth in the room chomped on pieces of Double Bubble gum, candy corn, or caramel squares. The wet sounds of eating and chewing filled the air.

'Did you have a good time, Halloween?' I asked.

'Oh, Gawd. We have so much fun,' Lincoln answered first.

'That town the nicest place in de world,' Ethel added. 'All you do is knock on door and people pop their head out d' door to give you some sweets.'

'That is sho' a fine town,' said Carolina.

'People so nice. Feed us so good and treat us just fine.'

'You know what Lincoln say to the white lady we stay with?' Oscar giggled.

'You shut up, boy,' Lincoln shot back.

'Oh, Gawd, it so funny what Lincoln say,' Top Cat said.

'I bus' some head good,' answered the angry or embarrassed Lincoln. (I could not distinguish which it was.)

177

'The white lady she talk funny, kind of,' Oscar began.

'I git yo' ugly face,' said Lincoln.

'Yo' face too ugly to get my face ugly,' answered Oscar. 'White lady talk funny and say, "Lincoln, how did you enjoy the parade and carnival today at the Port Royal School?" Now ol' Lincoln's fat, ugly self was eatin' mashed potatoes and gravy when this lady do her talkin' and he don't look up no how. He just say, "Yes, ma'am, I sho' enjoy this dinner. It's a fine dinner." Lord, Mr. Conrack, I laugh myself fool when I heard that. She ask him about the parade and he tell her he sho' do like the dinner.'

The entire class giggled and pointed their fingers at Lincoln, who squirmed uncomfortably, then broke into one of his patented, high-pitched laughs. 'Oh Gawd, that lady talk so funny.'

Jasper spoke up and said, 'Saul made me laugh so hard. He walk up to this big ol' white man readin' a paper and say to him, "'Scuse me, but you gots a place I can wash my foot?" That man look at him so funny.'

'You tell lie,' yelled Saul.

'You know what I say true,' retorted Jasper.

Ethel said she wanted to tell the class what she and her group of girls saw at one particular house. 'We see this man come up to the door. Only he look like woman. He dress himself up in fish-net stockings and a girl's dress. He have a wig on his head and powder on his nose. He wear the bead and high-heel shoes.'

'That so?' said Frank.

'It so if I say it so, boy.'

'Any complaints about the weekend besides the weather?' I asked. 'Did everybody treat you all

178

right?'

'Everybody but that big fat boy at the school,' said Top Cat.

'He bad,' said Saul.

'He big and so bad. He tell us to keep away from him and his bike. I so scare,' said Top Cat.

'Did you tell Bernie about the fat boy?'

'No. I 'fraid that boy kill me if I say nuttin' to anybody.'

'That boy mean, C'roy.'

'All the other children nice,' said Carolina.

We spent the morning recounting our trip to Port Royal. I had the older children write down their impressions of the trip, then write thank-you notes to Bernie and the families who housed them. Then, to split the reverie of the mood, to shatter the spirit of exaltation over the successful crossing of the river and the return, Mrs. Brown poked her head in the doorway, saying ''Scuse me, I'd like to have a word with your babies, Mr. Conroy.'

Sensing that Mrs. Brown was preparing to launch a verbal grenade but not knowing exactly how to divert the attack, I simply shrugged my shoulders and prepared for the worse.

'Boys and girls, all of you know you are my babies, isn't that right?'

'Yes, ma'am,' came the predictable, formulated reply.

'Now you know when we slept in the elementary school the other night, one of you boys wet the wrestling mat.'

The boys lowered their eyes and tightened their lips into thin lines. Mrs. Brown did not realize it at the time, but her inquisition ended before it started, and no amount of cajolery or intimidation

179

on her part would wreak a confession or a betrayal from the brotherhood she now interrogated.

'Now, babies, everybody had got to u-rin-ate. Isn't that right?'

'Yes, ma'am,' the class replied again, dutifully but suspiciously.

'And there is nothin' wrong with a man u-rin-atin', is there?'

'No, ma'am.' The voices were getting lower, angrier.

'But a man got to know when to urinate and when not to urinate. Isn't that right, Mr. Conroy?'

'Yes, ma'am.' Spinelessly, I had joined the Greek chorus.

'Now, that somebody who wet the wrestlin' mat most prob'ly wet the bed he slept on the night before. Now mattresses in white folks' homes cost sometimes between fifty and one hunnert dollars. Sometimes one hunnert-fifty dollars and sometimes even two hunnert dollars. You can ruin a mattress by urinatin' on it. All of us know that urine is made out of acid. And you can imagine what acid can do to a two-hunnert-dollar mattress. Eat right through it. Whoever it was has no reason to be ashamed. There are plenty of weak bladders in the world. A bladder's just like a muscle. Some weak. Some strong. Lots of people wets the bed. Whoever that person is, and he knows who it is, should come up to me and say, "Mrs. Brown, I have a weak bladder and I'm very sorry." Isn't that right, class?'

Only this time silence reigned where there had once been the peremptory 'yes, ma'ams.' She grew angry and threatened to flunk the child for the year if he did not confess the dire crime of bladder weakness to her immediately. The scene was

180

unbearable. From the reaction of the children, I could tell who the acid-spiller was. All their heads and eyes were directed away from Saul. So obviously protecting him by their complete obliviousness to his presence, they were singling him out as infallibly as though everyone in the room had stood up and shouted his name to the world. Mrs. Brown was too absorbed in her anger to notice this. She had grown accustomed to a system of stool pigeons whereby she retained a godlike omniscience through her pampered, spoiled informers. Since I had forbidden anyone in my class from going to her with information that could get another classmate in trouble, her intelligence system had been crippled badly. Only one student in my class fed her hot poop with any amount of regularity, and unfortunately for Mrs. Brown, in this particular case, her most reliable informant had also been the heinous monster who had wet the white folks' two-hunnert-dollar mattress. Saul, to add to his innumerable problems, was not only Mrs. Brown's major supplier of facts concerning the strange, incomprehensible machinations of my class, he was also a bed-wetter. When she saw that no one was going to tell her what she desired to know, she huffed out of my class muttering something to the effect that I had been the ruination of discipline at Yamacraw School.

The next hour was spent attempting to stem the indignation and rage that invariably erupted after one of Mrs. Brown's visits. I thanked them for not telling Mrs. Brown that it was me who wet the wrestling mat, but even jokes failed to soothe them. I then told them that I once had a real problem with wetting the bed and that my mother had sworn that

181

I would wet the bed until I was fifty years old. I described my being afraid to accept invitations away from my house for fear of some friend waking up in the middle of the night to find that I had sprayed his leg.

This seemed to revive them a little bit. Frank asked me how old I was when I quit wetting the bed.

'I quit last night, Frank.'

'What you say?' asked Frank.

'I quit last night when Barbara told me she just bought a two-hunnert-dollar mattress. I'll tell you, gang, if you're gonna live with these white folks you gotta cut the flow of acid.'

'Hee, hee,' giggled Cindy Lou. 'Conrack so much a fool.'

I could neutralize the effect of Mrs. Brown's speeches on the surface, but I could never be sure how much damage she was inflicting under the surface, where it counted most, in the gut of one's being, in the soul. Nor could I forgive Mrs. Brown her little tirades. No man or woman has the right to humiliate children, even in the sacrosanct name of education. No one has the right to beat children with leather straps, even under the sacred auspices of all school boards in the world.

I knew that the high noon between Mrs. Brown and myself was just around the corner. The old demon, white guilt, could control me for a while, but one factor in the composition of Mrs. Brown's personality was beginning to come clear in my mind, and the more clear it became, the nearer I was to establishing a liberating, important universal truth: because a person is black does not mean that he or she thinks black or is proud to be black. She

182

wished she were white, which one could interpret as an indictment of our society. That was fine. But because the society had corroded Mrs. Brown's image of the black man, I did not feel sufficiently compelled to allow Mrs. Brown to infect my students with her malady. In her own eyes Mrs. Brown felt as though she was instilling values into the children that their likker-swilling, devil-dancing, illiterate parents could never do. In my eyes she was the unflinching, strong-armed proponent of white values, mores, and attitudes. It now was breaking down into a war of eyesight.

*   *   *

My assimilation into the mainstream of island life quickened after the Halloween trip, although I was not aware of it at that time. Even though one of the children suffered a relatively serious injury and I failed by twenty-four hours to transport the group back to the island on time, the power of the children's unanimous, animated support of the venture erased any reluctance the parents might have experienced. For days my class could talk of nothing else but Port Royal.

'I sure do like that town over yonder, Mr. Conrack,' said Jasper. 'All you do is rap the door and some man pop his head out to give you the candy.'

'I wouldn't try it every day of the year, Jasper. Especially in that neighborhood you were in.'

When the letters from the Port Royal kids started pouring in, each child who received a letter would read it in class (if he could). Carolina, Ethel, and Cindy Lou convinced me that they had won the

183

undying love and admiration of the family who had housed them.

'Lawd, those people sho' loved me, Conrack. They thought I was so fine.'

'That's because they don't know any better, Cindy.'

'That's 'cause you don't know nuttin',' she flashed back at me.

'The lady you stayed with told me that if that girl, Cindy Lou, didn't shut up soon, she was going to have to flush her down the commode.'

'That not true.'

'Cross my heart and hope to die.'

'Oh Gawd, man gonna drop dead.'

The residue of the entire trip left a good taste and it proved a pungent stimulant to class activity and awareness for many months. But I still did not really know how the parents reacted to the whole concept of field trips as an educational experience. I knew for a fact that Mrs. Brown and Miss Glover both believed that education was best served in the cramped environs of the classroom, that both of them made a vast distinction between learning and recreation, that both of them felt that education and the leather strap went together like whiskers and catfish, and that both of them thought the trip was a welcome vacation, but not an experience that could be counted as having furthered the name of education.

I was yet uncertain about my own philosophy of education as applied to the Yamacraw kids. They were not going to be candidates for a Rhodes scholarship after having served an apprenticeship under my vigilant tutelage; none of them would write significantly or make any conspicuous contribution to the arts, as far as I knew. The five illiterates who were served to me like hors d'oeuvres at the beginning of the year would still qualify for membership in that august classification. I was slowly learning to measure the importance of small victories. In fact, I was coming to the painful conclusion that all my victories would seem minuscule and trivial compared to my expectations at the beginning of the year. I was proud of Sidney and Samuel, who could now scratch their names legibly on a piece of paper, proud of Prophet, who could count to ten, proud of Richard, who could read the simplest preprimer, and proud of Saul, who had learned not to cry at every taunt thrown at him. Slowly, the awareness came to me that no matter what happened, my struggles and efforts could not eradicate the weight and inalienable supremacy of two hundred years: the children of slaves could not converse or compete with the offspring of planters, the descendants of London barristers, the progeny of sprawling, upward-climbing white America. And slavery was still a reality, considering that none of my students grew up in homes where books flourished, where ideas fluttered, and theories dwelt comfortably in dinner-table discussions.

How could I compare or relate my childhood to growing up on Yamacraw? My mother's reading to me each night was a celebration of language and tradition, a world of Mother Goose and lyric poetry, where Bobby Shaftoe goes to sea and intrepid, prepubic heroes stand on burning decks. My youth was a glut of words, a circus of ideas nurtured by parents dedicated to diplomas and the production of professionals from the tribe of children they sired.

My youth sang the glory of books, the psalms of travel, of new faces, of the universe of Disney animation, of Popsicle sticks and county fairs, of parables of war spoken by a flight-jacketed father, of parables of love and Jesus sung by a blue-eyed mother, a renegade Baptist, a converted Catholic, a soldier of the Lord. And all the memories I had of the travels: the two-lane highways connecting Marine bases through the swamps and cypress shadows, the station wagon clogged with children (and a black, mongrel dog) rolling into parochial villages past midnight, beneath the hulk of a many-columned, stern-mouthed courthouse—a traffic light, the changing gears, the hum of a restless engine, the pressure of Dad's foot on the accelerator, the children sleeping, and the radio shifting night announcers and easy songs until distance and static overcame station after station.

My past had no relationship to my present except that I saw a direct connection between the education of my parents and the education of their children, the dreams of my parents and the dreams of their children, just as there existed a link, straight and uncomplicated, between the parents of Yamacraw and their children. Everything occurred in cycles, fanged and implacable cycles. Somehow I had to interfere with the cycle or interrupt it, interject my own past into the present of my students. If I let my students leave me without altering the conditions of their existence substantially, I knew a concrete, sightless ghetto of some city without hope would devour them quickly, irretrievably, and hopelessly. I could hear some white voice coming from some collective unconscious deep within me saying, 'They don't

186

know any better. They are happy this way.' Yet all around me, in the grinning faces of my students, I could see a crime, so ugly that it could be interpreted as a condemnation of an entire society, a nation be damned, a history of wickedness—these children before me did not have a goddam chance of sharing in the incredible wealth and affluence of the country that claimed them, a country that failed them, a country that needed but did not deserve deliverance.

These were the deep, serious thoughts I sometimes had to drive from my head like flocks of pesky starlings. I was too pragmatic and impatient to let such thoughts flog me into impotence, yet I sincerely needed a working philosophy on which to hang my hat. After the Halloween trip, one began to form and crystallize without my knowledge, and when I finally acknowledged its presence, it was already a part of me: simply, that life was good, but it was hard; we would prepare to meet it head on, but we would enjoy the preparation.

CHAPTER SEVEN

That the children hated Mrs. Brown's guts with their complete power of hating was not readily apparent to me in the first two months of school. The awareness came slowly, and when it finally came, I realized they were not merely venting their frustration on a figure of authority, but that they hated with reason and justification. At first I did not take her speeches to the children seriously, whether she was telling them that they smelled bad, that

187

they were retarded, or that they would end up alcoholics or wastrels like their parents. I did not take them seriously until I realized how seriously the kids took them, how they suffered under this constant humiliation, and how powerless they felt to cope with her attacks on their basic worth and dignity. They hated her and they feared her. Because of her size she could physically overcome any challenge raised by them. She carried two leather straps with her. One of them she called Dr. Discipline; the other she called Professor Medicine. The beatings she administered were not funny.

I heard her beating her students regularly in the class next door. Mrs. Brown's major teaching technique was the extended scream. Her voice constantly yelled out commands to her charges; it would rise in tempo and volume, until finally, as an adjunct to her voice, the strap against flesh would sound, followed by the scream of the child. I heard this every day. Every time it occurred I saw my students stiffen in their seats and listen intently to the drama played in the next room.

I do not believe in corporal punishment, yet I did not feel it was my place to admonish Mrs. Brown about her corrective actions. Then through a series of events, it finally dawned on me that my students loathed the woman. It was not long before I was caught directly in the middle of this war, and it was not long before I had to choose sides.

I thought Mrs. Brown had one of the greatest natural senses of humor I had yet encountered. Her manner of phrasing and inflection often left me convulsed with laughter. I had never worked with a black teacher before, and I appreciated her view of the white man and his world. 'Gotta go by the man,' she would say. 'Gotta please the man and see him smile. Then everything rolls along just fine.' For the first sixty days we were real, if reluctant, allies. I did not like the strap, nor her dehumanizing speeches to the kids, nor her constant derision of my teaching approach. But I liked peace and I liked tranquillity to reign in a situation where only two of us had to get along. When I told her she was principal, that a misunderstanding on her part had projected me as the titular head of the school, the change which came over Mrs. Brown was as noticeable as the first freeze. She now did not make recommendations to me; she issued ultimatums. She did not give opinions; she threw out commands, orders, and laws with the signature of 'the man' on them. Most of these I could ignore by joking about them. I still refused to use a strap, race through textbooks the kids couldn't read, or give the kids hours of homework. Nor was I about to stop playing music, showing movies, or just talking things over with my students. I had a history of not responding well to lousy or pernicious administration, and though I tried to tell myself that she was the boss and I would have to obey her instructions, I would be goddamned if she was going to turn me into an overseer instead of a teacher. As she pressured me more and more, I knew that sometime during the year I would crack open like an egg. Time worked against me.

One speech she delivered to the children was so nasty that they started answering her back. She threw venom in their direction and they spit fire back at her.

'May I have a word with your class, Mr. Conroy?'

'Of course, Mrs. Brown.'

'It has come to my attention that some individuals have not been brushing their teeth. Now filthy teeth smell bad and when we don't wash our hair or our bodies either, the smell would drive a preacher out of church. Smelling bad at school will not be tolerated. I'm tired of people stinkin' in this school.'

'Better not talk so loud,' Cindy Lou said.

'What'd you say, girl?' Mrs. Brown asked menacingly.

'She say watch out,' Mary said, almost inaudibly.

'Don't whisper under your breath. Shout it out so Mr. Conroy and I can hear what's on your mind.'

'You don't wanna know what's on my mind,' someone said. They talked low and everyone kept their eyes down on their desks, so I could not tell who was talking. Nor could Mrs. Brown.

I steered Mrs. Brown toward the door, thanked her for her ingratiating speech, and promised her I would severely punish the whisperers in the class. Then I launched into a speech.

'Gang, we have been getting these talks from Mrs. Brown all year. You get too damn upset by them. Just don't listen to what she's saying. Think about something else. If she wants to be a big talker, let her talk, just don't get involved with snapping back at her.'

'She ain't talkin' to you,' Frank said. Frank's temper was volcanic, and he was hornet-mad at this latest sermon of Mrs. Brown.

'That's a good point, Frank. She isn't talking to me, but she is talking about you and it hurts me to see you get your feelings hurt. You may not believe me yet. You may not trust me yet. But you can

190

damn well believe that it pisses me off to hear Mrs. Brown talk to you like that. There might be nothing I can do about it, but I'll try to keep her out of this room.'

'She ain't got no right to say things like that,' Cindy Lou said.

'Bitch woman,' Richard said.

'Yeah! Bitch woman.' The echo passed around the room.

'I bet you call me bitch man behind my back,' I said, trying to cut through the ominous, murderous atmosphere building in the room.

'No, Conrack,' Fred said.

'I call you bitches and bastards when I get mad at you sometimes.'

'God Almighty Jesus!' Lincoln exclaimed.

'Everyone gets mad, gang. But we have to learn when not to show our anger. That could get you killed.'

'Get Brown killed,' Ethel warned.

'Get Brown killed tonight,' Sidney said.

'Get Conroy killed this afternoon,' I added.

'How?' Ethel asked.

'If Brown hears you cats talking ...' I began.

'She runs her mout' too loud,' Mary said.

Sure enough Mrs. Brown was ranting about something to her kids. This provided enough comic relief to enable me to change the subject, but that day I saw the seed of an enmity so profound that I did not realize the nature and magnitude of the beast until it was almost too late. This was the first day I decided to study Mrs. Brown, her relationship to the people of the island, and her relationship with the children.

That afternoon I asked Mrs. Brown to be less

191

abrasive when addressing the kids, to be a wee more diplomatic, and to have a greater concern about their feelings. Her answer was long, rambling, antagonistic, and evasive. She ended the barrage by saying twice, 'I am the principal. I am the principal.'

I answered her by saying sarcastically, 'Then I am the assistant principal. I am the assistant principal.'

Despite all this Mrs. Brown possessed an unflinching sense of humor that often fractured me. It was her way of saying things more than anything else. I don't know if she was conscious of being witty. If not, then she had her finer moments as the greatest natural comic I had met.

One day I walked into the boys' bathroom and found Prophet hanging from the tank which held water for the boys' urinal. The tank was eight feet above the floor. At first I just saw a single black arm suspended from this tank for no particular reason. I walked around the divider and faced Prophet. He looked at me, grinned, and remained hanging from the tank. I stared at him with my stern, ineffectual glance, not knowing what a proper response would be. Mrs. Brown passed the door, saw Prophet's arm, and ended any necessity for me to respond at all. She roared into the bathroom and jerked Prophet down from his tank. Since she thought I lacked toughness in situations like these, I could tell she was going to make an object lesson out of Prophet to help me deal with crises in the future.

'Boy, what you doin' hangin' from the urinal up there? You think we got candy hidden up there?'

'No, ma'am,' Prophet answered. He was terrified.

192

'Boy, you think we put Christmas packages in that there tank for some monkey like you to find?'

'No, ma'am.'

'Well, boy, there must be some reason for you holding on to the pot every time you tinkle, son. What's the matter, boy? Is your pinky so big that you have to hold the bowl 'cause you are afraid you might fall in?'

For a moment I thought she had asked Prophet if his pinky was so big that he had to hold the bowl for fear of falling in. Then she repeated her question.

'Prophet. You answer me, boy. Is your pinky that big? Are you top-heavy because of that big ol' pinky between your legs? I haven't noticed you stumbling around the schoolyard when you walk. And I ain't heard none of the boys talking about Prophet using his pinky as a baseball bat.'

By this time, I was on the verge of hysteria. My face had reddened like a blood clot trying to keep from laughing. For her part, Mrs. Brown remained as serious and stoical as a cigar-store Indian. This was no laughing matter to her.

'That urinal is state property, boy. If it gets broke, Mr. Conroy and I are required by state law to pay for it.'

By this time Prophet was crying, great tears rolling out of his eyes and down his face. Mrs. Brown continued, 'Mr. Conroy, I am going to leave this room. I want you to check Prophet's pinky to see if it is so big that he needs to lean on the pot to piddle.'

She left the room. Prophet unzipped his pants to give me a shot of his pinky. I grabbed him, told him to go no further, and waited a few salient moments. As I walked out of the latrine, I informed Mrs. Brown that according to my calculations the young lad, Prophet, did not possess a gargantuan pinky but a pinky of normal proportions. This is the most ludicrous scene I've ever been involved in, I was telling myself. After I delivered this factual information, Mrs. Brown grabbed Professor Medicine, her favorite strap, stormed into the bathroom, and beat the hell out of Prophet. I never did find out why Prophet hung from the urinal tank. Probably, like Everest, because it was there.

I believe Mrs. Brown sincerely believed that a child needed a beating every once in a while if he was to respect authority, do his lessons, and grow up to make a contribution to his community. She whipped children out of a sense of duty. We probably would never have crossed swords if she had let me work out my own system in the classroom and left my kids alone. For six months we worked together in an uneasy truce. Then total war raged through the two-room schoolhouse on the island.

Several events early in the school year told me that something was wrong between Mrs. Brown and the other black people on the island. One night I had left my set of school keys in Beaufort. I was still living in the schoolhouse and I needed the keys to get into the kitchen where I kept my food. It was already dark when I drove over to the 'white schoolhouse' where Mrs. Brown lived. The lights on the car swung into her yard. I parked under a tree and walked up the steps and knocked on her door.

A voice roared out defiantly, 'Who are you? I got a gun pointed at your head.'

A little bit startled, I shouted, 'It's me, Mrs. Brown, Pat. Goddam it, don't shoot me.'

She opened the door a crack, looked me over with one, great eye, then told me, 'Son, a man could get killed comin' up to somebody's house at night.'

'It will not happen again, I promise you. I just came up to get the keys to the kitchen. I need to eat, Mrs. Brown.'

'What happened to your keys?'

'I left them in Beaufort.'

'That's no place for your keys. That's state property.'

'I know, I am sorry. But I've got to eat.'

'Yes, sir. A man's got to eat.' She still had let me glimpse no more than her one eye peering out into the shadows at me.

'There are some people on this island, Mr. Conroy, who will shoot you deader than a door nail for coming up to their house.'

'White people?'

'No, colored people. There are some of the meanest, dirtiest people in the world on this island. That's why I carry fire in my pocketbook all the time. These people know that "Mr. Thirty-Eight" is always right near in case I need him. If you are smart, you'll get some fire too.'

'I would just like the keys, Mrs. Brown, if you please, ma'am.'

The door shut again, and Mrs. Brown disappeared from view. The door opened again and a large brown arm with keys dangling from two fingers was pushed under my nose.

'I would not advise sneaking up on someone in the middle of the night like that again, Mr.

Conroy.'

'Don't worry, Mrs. Brown.'

I never saw Mr. .38 but the idea of a loaded gun being pointed at my head by a woman who thought the Yamacraw people were out to get her made my stomach do handstands and somersaults. And I could not figure out why Mrs. Brown seemed to hate the people of the island, at least the black people. She thought Ted Stone was hot porridge, and that Ezra Bennington was conceived without original sin. There was something very wrong in the fact that a black woman in 1969 cast her lot with white men whose thoughts and actions dated back to 1869. Mrs. Brown, the principal, was showing signs that a blow-up between us was imminent. Small signal fires broke out for a long while, but the war would begin much later.

I left school early one day in November, for the supreme commanders in the educational hierarchy were clamoring for some form or document from Mrs. Brown. Mrs. Brown, unbelievably, was more inefficient than I was in compiling the drivel and trivia demanded by the higher administrators. Whenever they saw me in the county office building, they would curse Mrs. Brown with red faces and swear to the forces that ruled the underworld that she was personally responsible for sabotaging a hundred different sets of statistics in her tenure on Yamacraw island. And it was strange. For Mrs. Brown studied every document which she received from the top cats with religious zeal, as if she had just received the Ten Commandments from the burning bush. She would work all of a school day fiddling with figures and shuffling names, crying out that she was overworked and that the burden of teaching was too heavy a load. She was very cranky on these days and I kept my distance. Yet I could not help but wonder how she could botch them up when she spent so much time compiling them.

Anyway, she called me into her room one day, gave me an official-looking envelope, and commissioned me to take it across turbulent waters to the powers in Beaufort. Meek servant that I was, I consented to go. I left the gang an assignment on the board that I thought they would enjoy. We had talked about making a collage on the bulletin board. After going over with them what a collage was, and how you went about making one, and all the other rot, I brought out a stack of magazines. I told them to find pictures or portions of pictures that appealed to them or meant something to them. Art for art's sake. The joy of living. I wanted to return the next day to find a collage of such surpassing brilliance and shocking significance that it would knock my eyes out. O.K.? O.K., they murmured, each kid with a pair of those crummy elementary-school scissors that couldn't cut a fly wing. As I scooted out the door, each one of my scholars was thumbing seriously through the old editions of magazines I had brought to the island. The twin with the wart on his nose was meticulously excising a picture of a large, green Cadillac. He saw me watching him and said, 'I'm going to get me a big car.' Mary was snipping away at a model in a wedding gown.

The next day Mrs. Brown met me at the door. She was wearing one of those do-I-have-something-to-tell-you looks and her arms were folded beefily across her chest. Since Mrs. Brown took every action of my class as a sign of imminent conspiracy

197

or revolution, I strongly suspected, and was correct in believing, that the kids had somehow blown it, in Mrs. Brown's eyes, the day before. As I walked in the door, I looked to the bulletin board to see how the collage turned out. The bulletin board was blank. Mrs. Brown had retreated to the hall by then and was beckoning me with a seven-pound index finger. Like a well-trained spaniel, I trotted to the door.

'Mr. Conroy,' she intoned heavily, 'do you know what your babies did yesterday?'

'No, ma'am.'

'Well, I am about to tell you what they did.' Here she sighed loudly as if what she had to tell me was too painful to be divulged. 'They tacked up pictures of naked wimmin all over the room. Naked wimmin, Mr. Conroy, naked wimmin. They tacked up pictures of white wimmin naked as jaybirds.'

'I don't understand, Mrs. Brown. I didn't give them any girlie magazines in the stack,' I said, fearing for my life that a stray *Playboy* might have found its evil way into my stockpile.

'Don't know about any magazines. Just know that I walked in that room and my eyes nearly popped out of my head. There was a woman's bare va-gyna on that board. Bare va-gyna. I had to do some beatin' in there yesterday. I found out who done it and I set some fanny on fire.'

'Well, you shouldn't have done that, Mrs. Brown. I gave the kids the assignment and it was my fault if they screwed it up.'

'They knew it was sinful. They knew it was against the Lord's will.'

'They're just kids, Mrs. Brown,' I said.

'Man, you are lucky the preacher didn't walk in

198

this room. He would have thought it was Jezebel teaching in this school.'

'Hell, Mrs. Brown, he'd probably have gone out and bought the magazine.'

'Oh, I would be ashamed to talk about the preacher like that. The preacher is so good to come bring us the word of Jesus.'

'Yeah, he is a swell guy.'

'And what if some administrator had surprised us with a visit? I am the principal and in charge of this school.'

'None of those guys are going to come over here, I assure you, Mrs. Brown. It is getting cold on the river and I assure you we will see no one until the weather is pluperfect.'

'But wimmin butt-naked. Naked women. Naked women,' she repeated over and over. She paused, looked furtively around to see if any administrators were hiding in trees, then fished several pages from a hidden compartment in her pocketbook. She lifted the pages as if she were handling a tray of radioactive material. I looked at the pictures, then threw my head back and laughed like hell. Some esthetic student had discovered an article on Pablo Picasso in *Life* magazine. Indeed there were pictures of naked women.

'This is Picasso, Mrs. Brown.'

'It's naked women, Mr. Conroy.'

'If these were the originals, we'd be rich.'

'What would the preacher say. But the babies won't be playing with dirty pictures again. They got the belt yesterday.'

I left Mrs. Brown to her fulminations and returned to class. The kids were not amused. The singing belt of Mrs. Brown had found a sizable number of fannies the previous day. When I asked them about it, they would not talk. Somehow they felt I had set them up for the slaughter.

'How many of you guys like to look at naked women?' I asked.

No one raised his hand, nor did anyone speak a word.

'I bet I have a few guys in here that just love to look at naked women.'

'No,' a few of the boys answered.

'Well, you guys know what? I'd rather look at naked women than do anything. I love looking at naked women.'

'Conrack likes to look at naked wimmin,' Richard said.

'You know why I like to look at them?'

'No.'

''Cause they're naked.'

'Yeah,' the boys said.

'No,' the girls said.

Then the boys told me it was the girls who had hung the pictures on the board.

*   *   *

My own disciplinary philosophy, a frail and skeletal animal to begin with, never acquired the health or bulk I wanted during the year. The year became a search for what was right for the Yamacraw children: a magic formula to rescue minds stunted through disuse, a formula that would raise reading levels to Appalachian heights. The search was a failure because I did not and could not know how irrevocably my ideas about education, those sacred and pontifical utterances, would be battered, bullied, disproven, and changed. Like my bleeding-heart theory of discipline. Although I still maintain my right to claim bleeding heartship for myself, I had to modify my theory that a teacher does not have the right to lay a single digit on the body of a child. That notion worked fine at Beaufort High School, where my students had more or less reached the age of reason and could be dealt with and reached by words. Not so at Yamacraw. These children had known the leather strap too long to be controlled by the threatening modulation of the vocal chords. So when Lincoln would lean over his desk and slap the hell out of Fred, and Fred would turn around, blame Saul for the unseen blow, and hit Saul across the side of the head, and Saul, wailing pitifully, would pick up his ruler and flog Fred with it while Jasper was throwing a pencil at Cindy Lou, I would feel compelled to take some type of action.

'All right, gang. Now enough of this,' the bleeding heart would begin. 'Now, Fred, it's not right for you to pick on Saul. He's smaller than you.' This would cause Saul to cry more vehemently since he was more sensitive about his height than about Fred slapping his head. 'Come on, Saul. Relax. Take it easy. Head for the bathroom, wash your face, forget your troubles.'

Now at this point, Fred has discovered that it was Lincoln who socked him instead of Saul. Fred jumps out of his desk and plants five of his toes into Lincoln's ass, who is busy defending himself from the enraged and formidable Cindy Lou. Lincoln wheels and chases the fleeing Fred, who bumps into four desks on the way back to his seat, causing every occupant of a bumped seat to slap or poke at

Fred as he passes by. Then each one slaps and pokes Lincoln as he pursues Fred. Then Cindy Lou races after Lincoln and pinches him on the back. Oscar tries vainly to trip Fred, Lincoln, and Cindy Lou in succession. The noise level in the room has risen 5000 decibels, everyone is shouting and cheering on the gladiators as they battle their way around the arena, and the bleeding heart pirouettes about the room after them, armed with his theories about humanity.

Soon Mrs. Brown, whose ears are as sensitive to horseplay as American radar to a MIG, appears at the door, leather strap wrapped around one iron fist, death etched in her cold, brown eyes, and silences the room with a single, arctic glance. She then majestically turns her eyes to me after the waters have been stilled and says, 'You can't control these children without a strap. I know 'em. I know the only thing they listen to is Doctor Medicine.' After she leaves the room, I confront my class with the fury of one who has just been humiliated.

'Now, my friends, I am going to find out why you do not listen to me when I ask you to sit down and shut up, but you do listen to Mrs. Brown when she bops in the room with her strap.'

Pregnant, inscrutable silence reigns over all. Bleeding heart continues his soliloquy. 'I have never liked hitting kids or belting kids or slapping the hell out of kids in class. I don't believe in it. I am not going to do it. You are not going to make me do it. Does anyone want me to buy a belt and use it to keep you quiet?'

'No,' came the unanimous reply.

'Now, Lincoln, I would like to know why you hit Fred.'

202

'I didn't hit that boy, C'roy.'

'I saw you hit him, Lincoln.'

'No, C'roy. That boy hit me first.'

'What you say, boy?' Fred says angrily. 'You watch your mout', boy.'

'Who you tell to watch his mout'?'

'I tell you, boy.' Then Fred socks Lincoln and the whole festival of violence begins anew.

These small classroom brush fires occurred almost every day during the first three months of school. For a while I simply arm wrestled any body who caused a major disturbance in the room. The idea was if he could beat me in arm wrestling, he could continue fighting, talking, and disrupting. This took a great deal of guts and virility on my part since I outweighed every boy in the class by at least seventy pounds. All the boys took the arm wrestling very seriously, however, and all of them grunted and strained to slap my arm down on the desk. Oscar and Top Cat, the two largest guys in the room, would grimace painfully and breathe convulsively trying to bring the only white arm in the room to a state of humility. The only person I let beat me was Saul. Saul would take my hand, place his elbow firmly on his desk top, bend his wrist slightly, and drive my hand fiercely to the left. As my hand bit wood, Saul would turn to the much larger boys with a look of faint disgust in his eyes and say, 'I beat 'im.' The boys would shout foul and I would swear that Saul had the most powerful arms on Yamacraw Island. Of course, Oscar would then arm wrestle Saul and nearly break his hand driving it down upon the desk.

The arm-wrestling method was a great energy release, but it was not a foolproof method for putting down the skirmishes that raged through the class once or twice a day. The girls could be adequately controlled by simply appealing to their conception of womanhood, usually, that is. An enraged Mary or Cindy Lou could not be stopped, only contained or controlled by gentle proddings or removal to the kitchen. With all of the kids, though, I knew that I could never hit them with a belt, stick, or anything else. This was against my nature, philosophy notwithstanding. Yet with Mrs. Brown constantly lecturing me about the efficacy of leather on flesh and interfering when the fights did break out, I needed some way to control the kids instantly and silently. It was sometime in December that I remembered how to milk a rat.

Milking the rat was an art among my childhood friends. The best rat-milker of the group had the same status as the best marble-shooter, the best hitter, or the fastest runner. The boy who could milk a rat well could bring a bully whimpering to his knees in a matter of seconds. He could render Samson hairless or Goliath helpless. Nations have been conquered by notable rat-milkers. To milk a rat, you simply press the fingernail of an opponent's finger with your thumb. Your index finger squeezes the back of the bottom joint of the finger. Your thumb mashes the fingernail against the second joint of your opponent's finger. All three joints of your opponent's finger are brought into action against him. Milking the rat is an almost impossible maneuver to describe in words. It is extremely painful, but the level of pain can be controlled by modulating the pressure exerted by your thumb.

When I remembered this childhood protection from neighborhood toughs, I shouted aloud and announced to the class, 'My friends, I have got it. 1 can stop your stinking fights without bloodshed or raising my voice. C'mon. One of you guys make some noise or do something terrible.' I walked over to Oscar, who was sitting minding his own business pursuing his scholarly studies, when I suddenly grabbed his hand and milked his rat. He screamed, got out of his seat, fell on his knees, rolled his eyes, stood up, and then went to his knees again. I let Oscar go. Then I showed everybody in class how to milk a rat and explained as well as I could what an incredibly effective method of control it could be. All the boys practiced on each other after I demonstrated the basics. 'Press up with the thumb, Frank. Hold the back of his finger with your forefinger. That's it, right where the finger goes into the hand. Learn how to milk a rat and the world is yours.' Then I went around to every boy in the class, milked his rat, explained the physics of the maneuver, and how I was going to use it to break up fights, rebellions, or mutinies in the class. They loved it. Anything connected with violence, fighting, or the improvement of their skills as potential street fighters was always acclaimed by the boys. The rest of the day was spent with me milking the rats of boys causing a disturbance by milking other rats.

CHAPTER EIGHT

I gave up my house on the island at the end of October for three reasons. I wanted to live with my family, it seemed folly to pay rent for two houses, and my fear of rats. The last reason deserves some explanation. The Buckner house at night was quiet and dark as a mausoleum. Whenever I turned the lights out to go to sleep, the degree of darkness always startled me somewhat. It was the darkness of the womb, the prenatal darkness of embryos in that house, which was a little disconcerting but made for deep and luxuriant sleeping.

In the middle of October the man designated as official grasscutter on the island rode down on the island's lone tractor and plowed up the field outside the house, which had become choked with weeds and high grass. This pleased me since I still maintained a healthy respect for the diamondback rattlers that flourished on the island. What I did not realize was that the grass afforded cover for a multitude—nay, a plague—of mice who had settled permanently in this field. When the plow had ripped furrows into the land and destroyed scores of mouse homes, these mice, with infinite practicality, moved into my spacious quarters. Now mice, however small or harmless, are rats to me—snarling, needle-fanged wharf inhabitants whose fleas carry the black death and whose bite is rabid. Rats are dealers in death and ol' Conrack is scared to death of them.

After they had moved their belongings and their children in with me, I knew that my days in the house were numbered unless by some miracle of Hamelin I could lead them out of my residence and coax them, lemminglike, into the sea. Ted Stone recommended poisons virulent enough to kill a herd of mastodons and it seemed to clear out most of the rat population. But several hardy ones still crept around at night leaving their droppings as

206

reminders that they had no intention of moving on such short notice. The little round turds were challenges, like glove slaps across my face.

I might have won this battle had it not been for an extraordinary and strategic move on the part of one of my tormentors. Whether or not he sensed my phobia about his breed I will never know, but he acted in a drama convincing enough to draw me to the brink of coronary failure.

I was sleeping soundly on a fairly chilly night. The room was black as pitch, silent, with the vestigial odor of mildew left from the days of noninhabitation. I felt something on my foot, something palpable and heavy, something alive, something present, something breathing, but most seriously of all, something on my foot. Without moving, I tried to think of some rational course of action. I could not see my five fingers if I placed my hand against my nose, so very slowly I reached up and pulled the chain on my lamp—and saw a flash of movement and watched as the rat moved like bald-tailed lightning across the room and out the door. 'The rat was in bed with me,' I called aloud. 'The goddam rat was on my foot in my own bed!' Then I reasoned further that the rat could have just as easily been on my head—then a flashback to a scene from Orwell's *1984*, where there is a description of a starved rat chewing through the eyeball of the protagonist. A rat had bedded down with me. I had shared my pillow with the animal I feared most.

That was my last night in the house. Ted Stone was disturbed, probably because he would no longer receive his percentage of the rent. I did not tell him about the rat incident, since he was the kind of rugged frontiersman who would not cringe even if he found himself sleeping with a boa constrictor. My fear of mice would reflect on my manhood.

He came to check the house over a few days after I informed him of my decision to withdraw. I had moved all of my essential belongings back into the school; the avoirdupois crossed the river to Beaufort. There were still a few pictures on the wall and a couple of posters scattered in odd places about the house. As Ted inspected the house with an opprobrious tilt to his nose and something vaguely militaristic in his inspection tour of the damp bedrooms, he stopped suddenly in front of a poster and stared at it. The poster elicited nothing in me, not a single, controversial thought. It simply pictured Steve McQueen astride a German motorcycle he had stolen from the Germans in the movie *The Great Escape*.

'What are you doin' with a picture of this Nazi?' Stone hissed.

'What Nazi?' I asked.

'This Nazi here. I ought to know a Nazi when I see one. I killed enough of 'em.'

'Mr. Stone, that happens to be Steve McQueen.'

'I don't care who he is, he's ridin' a Nazi motorcycle.'

'It's a movie, Mr. Stone. In the movie, Steve McQueen steals a Nazi motorcycle and tries to get away from the Germans.'

'He looks like a Nazi to me. He got blond hair like a Nazi.'

'He is as American as hominy grits. That is Steve McQueen, Mr. Stone. He is a movie star. He is an American movie star in an American movie who steals a German motorcycle.'

'I fought Nazis from D-Day all the way into Germany. Killed a lot of Nazis. I don't like Nazis or Nazi motorcycles.'

'Mr. Stone, I'm glad it isn't a poster of the creature of the Black Lagoon. You'd probably go crazy.'

'I just don't like Nazis.'

'I got your point. I honestly did.'

Two weeks later, I became a commuter.

*　　*　　*

The boat ride to Yamacraw became a celebration of sorts. It was a time when I became aware of tides ebbing and flooding in accordance with the transcendental clockwork of the universe; a time of the pale, wafer-thin moon in the early morning sky and of the last star to vanish with the coming of the sun over the green waters. It was a time when I measured days by the flocks of birds winging south or by the number of porpoises that performed fluid and solitary ballets beside the boat. I would watch the egrets and herons, frozen in slender, graceful statues on the shores, and regret my intrusion when they flushed at the sound of the boat and passed over me in quiet, majestic flight in search of more private feeding grounds.

It was a good time, for I had never followed the hunters into the woods or the fishermen up the river. Nor had I ever been part of the enormous, grass-prevailing silences of the ever-shifting marsh. In winter mine was the only boat on the river, the sole craft desecrating the steel gray waters. In January and February the whine of my boat was heresy to the silence of the grasses. In winter, the marsh was anchoritic, reflective, and brooding; the presence of man was strange and unwanted. Yet I liked the feeling of being the only person in a vast stretch of water, the only index of civilization in the tenuous, light-flecked darkness of seven o'clock in the morning.

Each day Zeke would launch me, his every breath a short, swift cloud; his hands blue and copiously veined, his face as gaunt and weary as a tundra, his voice the only voice in a village unawakened. On days when the tide was sufficiently high, I would turn the boat toward Cannon Creek, a sinuous, narrow shortcut that wound through the heart of the marsh. Once in the creek among the brown, floating islands of dead reeds, I would watch the gradual coming of the sun, the swift resurrection in obedience to an eternal cycle, and the flooding of the land with the rich, incredible colors of early morning.

In this world of boat and river, I huddled low to escape the cold air that cut above the windshield like a blade. But I prized the aloneness of the trip, the beautiful isolation, and the knowledge that I was afforded a glimpse of the marsh at ease, a glimpse of the land at rest from the penetration and mindless barbarisms of man. But even then on clear days I could see the smoke towering above the Savannah skies. Tall columns of white smoke, graceful and almost feminine, rose like false gods on the horizons and from my boat they were salacious and impure reminders of the absolute insistence of man that he defile all that he touches. Man excreting, straight up, through the phallic smokestacks of Savannah. Still, the factories could not dull the sharpness of the air or despoil the natural sanctuary along the creek.

Often the river would be rough and the boat would fight through heavy swells and bitter winds on the way to Yamacraw. Other times, the water would be glass, hard, green and opalescent in the early light. I was always alone during the cold months. The winter ordained a cessation of motors, shrimp nets, and fishing lines. More than any other time, it emphasized the inaccessibility of the island and the isolation of the residents.

Because I was commuting and because I wished to prove conclusively that it was possible to commute, I never took a day off or failed to make the crossing on account of the prevailing weather conditions. Barbara went on an extravagant shopping spree in early November and returned home with enough winter clothes to melt a glacier. She bought insulated socks, jackets, gloves, and boots. She also bought a multicolored wool mask, which covered my entire head except for green-rimmed holes for my eyes, nose, and mouth. This wardrobe seemed adequate for even the worst conditions a South Carolina winter could offer. In the full majesty of my winter plumage, I felt that I could follow penguins to their homes. All through December I remained comfortable in the mild morning chill, but in the first week of January the most severe cold spell since 1952, according to Ted Stone, gripped the South Carolina coast. In this single week, my respect for the river turned into awe, and maybe a bit of fear. For in that week I met the father of cold, the grand cold, the inquisitor of cold, and the pope of cold, all huddled in my boat to supervise my trip to Yamacraw.

It began, as it always did, at Zeke's. The smell of coffee filled the yard outside his house. Zeke was sitting in his easy chair smoking a cigarette and listening to a nasal, twangy sound on the country-music station out of Savannah. Ida, cold-natured and crotchety when the thermometer dipped below fifty degrees, had her heater turned up high enough to simulate high noon on the Sahara Desert. In the bedroom I could hear the heavy, regular breathing of the two boys. The hounds whined and scratched at the front door.

'Cold as a witch's titty,' Zeke said, as I entered the room. 'Weatherman says it's goin' down to thirteen degrees this morning.' I peeled off several layers of clothes to insure my survival in Ida's makeshift steam bath. Momentarily, Ida shuffled into the kitchen, reached blindly for her mug, poured her coffee, then sat shivering on the sofa, claiming she was freezing to death.

'I'm sweatin' my balls off, Ida,' Zeke would say, winking at me.

'You would sweat, you son of a bitch. You'd live in a goddam icebox if I'd let you,' Ida would snap back.

Then Zeke looked at me and said, 'You're gonna be able to tell if you're a man this week. I wouldn't get on that river.'

'Be careful, Pat,' Ida would add, 'I get real worried about you on that river. You don't know your ass about boats.'

We drove to the landing. Zeke pushed the boat off the trailer. The wind whipped malignantly from the river and the waves crashed over the trailer to wash and numb his feet. It was this week more than any other that I ceased to like Zeke Skimberry and

212

came to love him. He put me into the water at sunrise and met me at the lowering sun at four in the afternoon. The last thing I saw as I lowered the mask over my face was Zeke smiling in the back of the blue pickup. 'See you at four,' he would shout. 'Don't get sunburned.'

I would start the motor and press my face against the windshield to protect myself from the terrible flow of air that swept over the boat. The water was choppy and a sharp, stinging spray covered me before I reached the first protected creek. The salt water soon froze on the windshield, making visibility very difficult. My breath came in frosty, labored clouds. Every drop of water was a fang, a single tooth of cold. My ears ached, my hands throbbed, and my feet deadened in the boots. As the boat passed the familiar landmarks of the journey, the sandbars and leafless islands, I noticed the absence of birds in the shallows and of life on the shore. The world was dead, soundless, and frozen. Nothing moved except the boat.

I also grew fond of the Stones that week. Each time I came to their dock, I tied the boat on the run despite fingers as supple as fence posts. I then sprinted for their house as quickly as my booted, frozen feet would carry me. I would have struck a stranger watching this ludicrous, quasi-athletic event dumb. At full tilt, arms pumping like crooked pistons, my breath steaming like an old engine, my face masked in orange and brown, I would charge up the ramp and race over the broken, rotted boards of the Stones' dock. Ted would see me coming and throw extra logs into the stove. Lou would have a cup of hot coffee steaming and ready for me as I broke through the door. It is

213

moments such as these that my belief in man's basic worth and goodness comes forth. I have cursed Ted Stone a thousand times before and since, but I will never forget how kind and concerned he was during those five January days. I would nearly embrace the stove in gratitude for its warmth, while Ted would discourse rather wistfully about the last time in his memory the edge of the river froze solid.

On one of these five days I cut my engine as I knifed toward the dock, grabbed the stern line, and jumped from the boat to the dock. I did not see the ice that glazed the dock in a thin, transparent sheet until I was in midair. I hit the dock and immediately went sliding across it toward the water on the other side. I grabbed for a piling, but could not prevent my legs from dipping into the water. Ted Stone clothed me in his son's leftovers when he saw what had happened.

I grew closer to my students that week. They huddled around the windows waiting for my car to pull into view. When they saw me, Fred would go to the woodpile and stuff small logs into the stove until he could stuff no more. I would come into the room and head immediately to the stove to warm up. I would pull my boots off and hang the wet socks near the stove to dry.

Then Richard would ask, 'You cold, Conroy?'

'No, man. Went swimmin' on the trip over. Just like taking a hot bath.'

'No.'

'You get wet up?' Mary would ask.

'You always get wet up when you go swimmin'.'

'You no swim, Conroy.'

Then I would spot Samuel and Sidney slapping their knees and giggling uncontrollably. 'White man got the blue feet,' Sam would cry.

The class would laugh and I would move my feet nearer the fire and admire their magnificent blueness. Blue feet were an occupational hazard of Caucasians. Blue feet remained with me until Friday afternoon. But when Friday came, Conrack also knew that he could take the river. And that seemed very important.

The river remained temperamental and full of surprises. When I was certain that the cold was my most formidable enemy, I was challenged one morning by a prowling, spectral nemesis that crept along the lowcountry as silent as an egret's flight—the fog. Fog caused no pain; it simply induced blindness and required one to navigate by faith instead of sight. It transformed the land into a terrible sameness; north became south and east became south and west became north. I had no compass and hoped that the routine of the daily commute would be enough to deliver me to the island. But the deeper I went into the soul of the fog, the more hopelessly lost I became, the more confused, and the more panicked.

I went from bank to bank, blind as a shorn Samson, searching for landmarks that would set my course aright. I felt the presence of Yamacraw for a moment, then lost it. I looked at my watch and saw that I had been circling and searching for the island for over an hour and a half. My eyelashes were sodden and flooded with moisture condensed from this earthbound cloud, this ghost born of warm air and cold water. Then I was paralyzed by the booming voice of an ocean freighter somewhere in the fog, though I could not tell if the foghorn had sounded miles or feet away. I thought for a moment that I had ventured into the shipping lanes of the Savannah River or, even worse, into the Atlantic. But I saw land again and I drove the boat almost onto the shore, lit a fire, and waited till the fog lifted and Yamacraw revealed itself. When the fog did lift, I found myself five miles away from the island and very near the Savannah River. In the contest of the elements, fog was more frightening than the cold. Later, in the spring of course, I was introduced to the winds and thunderstorms and the fog seemed almost maternal in comparison.

*   *   *

In early spring Bennington finally chose a contractor to come to Yamacraw to install the air conditioners for which the board of education had appropriated money the previous summer. Piedmont evidently wanted the air conditioners installed quickly, for the coming of warm weather brought with it an influx of the concerned and the committed who journeyed to Yamacraw to see firsthand the victims of southern society. Piedmont shrewdly moved at the end of February to insure the credibility of his boast that Yamacraw Island was 'one of the two climate-controlled schools in the county.' Since I no longer trusted any of these people, and no longer believed in them as educators or as human beings, it delighted me to see the intensity involved in their efforts to glamorize the two-room schoolhouse on the island. They were dressing up their most obvious wart. After the air-conditioning unit was in place, Piedmont and Bennington could say with utter conviction that they had done their best and had offered the island

216

buckets of sweat and an ulcer's worth of concern to make sure those little nigras had air conditioning.

Zeke was ordered to go out to the island with the contractor and do whatever he could to help them. My boat was loaded with tools, wire, and insulation. Zeke rode with me across the river. The sun had risen completely and its white light coming off the perfectly smooth water blinded both of us as I rounded the first sandbar and headed directly into the sun. I was talking distractedly to Zeke about something, when both of us felt the motor bouncing off solid land.

'It's the goddam sandbar,' Zeke cried. Zeke was absolutely correct. The sandbar I had passed safely and without error one hundred times in a moment of carelessness claimed me for its own. We were not on the edge of the sandbar, we were squarely in the middle of it. There was no way Zeke and I could rock the boat into deeper water. She was weighed down with equipment and too firmly entrenched in the sand to offer any hope, except for the coming of the high tide.

I was furious with myself and embarrassed as hell. The electricians, following us in another boat, sniggered convulsively as they circled around the bar. They tried to pull us off with a rope but to no avail. I finally put Zeke on my back, carried him across the sandbar à la St. Christopher, and deposited him with the electricians. He offered to stay with the boat, but unsullied guilt forbade me to do anything but suffer in the early morning cold with my wet, frozen feet, and wait for the water's coming. The giggling electricians soon disappeared down the creek.

My feet felt like the definition of frostbite. The

bitter cold of winter was over for the most part, but the water still had not accepted the coming of spring. I removed my tennis shoes and the heavy wool socks Barbara had bought me at the beginning of winter. My feet were blue, and somehow pathetic and vulnerable, as I tried, first, to wrap them in old newspaper. That did not work, so I took off my insulated green jacket and wrapped it tightly around my feet. This was the best I could do under the existing circumstances. The tide inched outward, slowly, imperceptibly, outward toward the sea, the eternal rendezvous, inexorably flowing with the tilt of the earth. For about thirty seconds it was nice reflecting on the ebb and flow of the tide over centuries, and how its progress had been marked and studied by Nelson at Trafalgar, Drake, and Leif Ericson. Soon the sandbar exposed its presence completely, and as Zeke and I both suspected, I had driven to the very middle of it before I cut the motor. The bar extended for a quarter of a mile down the right flank of the river. The salt marsh was still winter-brown, although if you looked carefully, you could spot a promise of green flavoring the dead, crisp grasses along the shore.

The spring tides had not come in full force, the great flood tides that would inundate the marshes completely, washing away tons of the Spartina grasses that had finished the life cycle, bringing the dead grasses in clumps from the inner marsh, and carrying it out to sea. Already clumps of grass had become a minor irritant while driving to the island, and often I had to weave between these tiny, floating islands like a downhill racer weaves between slalom poles. Once I hit one of these piles,

218

and the propeller was instantly clogged and overwhelmed. I had to lift the propeller and clear it.

So I had time to study the swamp in transition. I even wavered on the edge of thinking deeper thoughts, of time and timelessness, of now and eternity, of my own impermanence as compared to the marshes, the river, and the tides. In fifty years I would be seventy-four, an old curmudgeon with a hairless, toothless head; the geriatric remnant of the forties, whose blood had dried, whose youth had withered, whose dreams had died like the grasses and washed out on a spring tide.

But the deeper thoughts became vestigial as my feet once more started to ache from the cold. I looked to the Bluffton shore and saw a man with a blue coat standing beside his car looking at me in the boat. I looked for something to read—the backs of oil cans, the instructions for starting the motor manually, the ingredients used in the composition of the stale potato chips I had bought a few days before. Heavy stuff. After I had exhausted all reading matter and had tended to the defrosting of my feet once again, I decided that the most prudent and intelligent thing to do at this particular moment of time would simply be to drop off in a deep sleep; no, a coma, a state of suspension that would eliminate the tedium of waiting for the earth to tilt the other way and the waters to reverse their flow and race inland toward the fresher waters and the brighter rivers upstate. So I rewrapped my mummified feet, hung my socks on the windshield to dry, lay down among the oil cans, and used one of the boat cushions as a pillow. At first I thought I would never sleep because of the cold, but as soon as I started thinking that and consciously worrying about it, I slept.

I awoke some time later, alarmed at an engine roar above me. I had slept soundly and perhaps for a fairly long time, for I could hear a slight rhythm of water against the bottom of the boat. The roar grew louder, until I saw a helicopter hovering just above me, then circling in a long arc over the boat. The pilot's head craned over the edge of the cockpit, and he tilted his craft as he swerved by the boat again. He looked worried.

It must have been boredom, or some unforgivable streak of black humor that took over from there. I knew that this pilot was probably a young warrant officer being trained in nearby Savannah, was on maneuvers, and had spotted my prone, seemingly lifeless body in the boat below. I had often waved to these guys as I went to work and on occasion they had come low enough for me to see them waving back. Anyway, I did not move from the bottom of the boat but lay there squinting maliciously through slitted eyes, contorting my body into a grotesque posture of death. The helicopter came lower and lower: the concern of the pilot grew, the closer he drew to my beleaguered craft. I chortled to myself that this was a mighty fine joke, but that I had better rise from the dead and wave to the pilot that I was alive and well, though stranded and helpless. As this thought was being bandied about in my head, the pilot headed his helicopter to the west. I heard the great propeller turning, but it was now a distant sound, and the pilot no longer was sweeping low for a firsthand look at my body. Yet he had not left the scene. I could hear him. My curiosity finally bested whatever impulses I had to remain horizontal, and very slowly, snaking my way across the bottom of the boat, I lifted my head just over the side of the boat. I could hear the helicopter. My eyes glanced first to the right, then my eyes met the eyes of the helicopter pilot who had landed on the far shore and was looking straight at me.

It shocked both of us. I immediately rose and stretched like I had been asleep in a back-yard hammock. I beat on my chest a couple of times and exulted in the crisp, cool air of late morning. I waved to the pilot. He had not shut down his engine, and the prop whirred above him. He was pissed. He shouted something at me that was lost in the tumult of the rotating blades. He then shot me the universal American symbol of derision and contempt—his middle finger stood isolated and defiantly raised on his right hand. He shouted something again, then clambered back aboard his craft and took off angrily, sort of like a teen-age dragster laying rubber in front of his girl friend's house after a spat. I quickly checked the water level and decided that, with luck, I could extricate myself from this throne of sand. I took my paddle, drove it into the sand, and pushed according to Newton's law. The boat moved. In a couple of minutes I had paddled into deep water, pulled the rope, started the engine, and headed barefoot for Yamacraw. The helicopter followed me for a while, buzzing over my head like an angry mosquito, then roared off toward Savannah. I waved cheerfully.

★   ★   ★

It is hard to pinpoint accurately the precise moment when I lost favor with the administrative juggernaut of Beaufort County. This disintegration was a gradual, progressive awareness on both sides that gained momentum every time we dealt with each other on a professional or personal basis. I have mentioned the letter of fire I sent to Piedmont after a couple of days on the island. I learned later that Piedmont liked his subordinates to grovel a bit before they presented a proposal, shuffle a bit before they offered a suggestion, and lie prone on their faces before they dared proffer a bit of advice. Therefore, my first letter, written with the sap and arrogance of youth offended, put Piedmont on the defensive. Piedmont had told me that his first job as a boss man in an upstate mill had imparted to him a virulent distaste for labor problems. With my first letter I was instantaneously transformed from a number on a teacher-ratio chart to a labor problem. It was many months later before I learned how Piedmont had probably handled vexing problems with the semiliterate though obstinate workers who greased looms on the midnight shift and rocked the vessel of obedience in defiance of the invisible capitalists who ruled the mills from far away. These same capitalists hired the gravelly voiced, production-conscious Piedmont to keep the occasional sparks of resentment extinguished. I learned this much later, this was still the period of innocence.

And my innocence continued *ad nauseam* during the year. Piedmont had told me in that first meeting that he worshipped truth and 'dealt in facts.' I took his word for this and each time I saw him during the year, hunched behind his desk, peering at me over the thin horizon of his half-glasses, I told him firmly, forcefully, and with conviction that I considered the Yamacraw School a tragedy, a mockery of education, a condemnation of our county, and a situation that called for desperate, radical ideas and methods. Almost always he nodded his head affirmatively, delivered an oily, ingratiating, and hollow sermon about the good job I was doing and how much he appreciated the letters I was writing him and how I reminded him of the young Henry Piedmont—idealistic, capable of sacrifice, and sweating for the improvement of mankind. Yet his office was filled with ghosts and unnamed spirits of resentment. His name struck fear in the soul of all his employees and his hand ruled the passages of his carpeted bailiwick with the subtlety of a sword. Bennington quivered when Piedmont's name was mentioned. I was warned again and again that he did not tolerate criticism under any guise; woe to him who entered Piedmont's tabernacle with the bitter tongue. Yet each time I spoke with him during the year, the good Dr. Piedmont told me, 'I have the most democratic school system in the country.'

Our initial dispute was fought over the boat's gasoline bill for the month of October. By this time, I had relinquished the principalship to Mrs. Brown and the figure-shufflers at the county office had discovered that Mrs. Brown was incapable of shuffling figures to their satisfaction. So Piedmont had appointed an administrative head to supervise the questionable reports submitted by Mrs. Brown and to act as a buffer between Piedmont and me. By November Piedmont had evidently tired of my carping and unrelenting bitching about conditions at the school. The man appointed administrative head of the Yamacraw School, like Piedmont, had never set eyes on the Yamacraw School. His name was Howard Sedgwick and he was the principal of Bluffton High School. He had recently moved to Bluffton to assume dominion over the high school. I had once heard him talk about blacks to a group of white teachers; ideologically he was somewhere between a backwoods Baptist and a Klansman. Every time I saw him, he was yelling about something or at somebody. Piedmont had appointed him as the titular head of a school he had never seen. I now had to deal with a principal who acted as though she wanted to be white and an administrative head who was sorry there were blacks.

The gas bill for October was the first shot fired in a long embittering war. Piedmont addressed his letter to Sedgwick, following the prescribed rungs of the ladder of command, and asked him to look into an 'exorbitant' gas bill and to make recommendations and regulations binding the use of the boat. Sedgwick dutifully composed a letter that ruled that I could use the boat on Mondays and Fridays only and that I must incur the expense of any additional trips. In his letter his sycophantic inclinations bubbled to the surface a couple of times, as did his complete ignorance about the island. Mrs. Brown by this time was concerned about the dilution of her authority by an unseen white man and told me so. I agreed that the positioning of Sedgwick over her had 'strange symbolic value' and I promised to lodge a complaint. I began my second letter to Piedmont in prototypical Conrack style—self-righteous, angry, undiplomatic, unapologetic, and flaming. Colonel Conroy, the chieftain of my clan, issued a hard-shell rule in my youth that the most unforgivable of sins was for a Conroy to beat around the bush, put garlands of roses around his thoughts or ideas, or—horror of horrors—for a Conroy to drop to his knees, pucker his potato-famined lips, and kiss somebody's rosy red behind. Dad did not admire the ass-kissers of the world and he passed this prejudice on to his offspring. So I will quote the first paragraphs of my second letter to Piedmont. Notice the youth, naiveté, and indignation of the young Conrack enraged. Dressed in green, insulated boots, and a torn, red sweater, eyes afire with self-righteous piety and wrath, I wrote Piedmont a letter with his epigram 'I deal in truth' lighting my path.

DEAR MR. PIEDMONT,

 I did not like your letter. Since it is rather inconsequential whether a public school teacher agrees with a dictum passed down from his superintendent or not, my only recourse is to answer you without regard to our positions. First of all, if I was expected to come to Yamacraw Island to preside over the intellectual decimation of forty kids, you selected the wrong boy. If I was expected to remain silent when intolerable conditions presented themselves, then once again, I should not have been sent to the island. Even though these kids were unfortunate enough to be born on Yamacraw Island, it will take you and a team of varsity scholars to convince me they don't deserve the same quality of education received by children in Beaufort itself. If you disagree with this, then I feel it is you who must question your suitability for the job of superintendent for the entire county.

My letter went on to justify the extracurricular voyages of the boat.

The boat has transported supplies, films, guest speakers, exchange students, groceries, and injured students to and from the island. The boat has brought the Sullivan Reading Program, an overhead projector, a tape recorder, a record player, and a film strip projector, thereby bringing Yamacraw into the audio-visual age. The boat took me to Beaufort five days in a row one week to arrange a Halloween trip for children who had never heard of trick or treat. The boat, Dr. Piedmont ... has opened vistas, horizons, and possibilities that never existed before.

I ended the letter with a pronouncement that I am sure Piedmont interpreted as a threat, a gesture of incredible and unforgivable defiance.

Neither Mrs. Brown nor I was pleased with the latest memorandum. We will be present at the next meeting of the Beaufort County Board of Education. I will give an introduction to the problems and tribulations of Yamacraw Island. I will also pay for the gas I use that night.

Sincerely,
PAT CONROY

The letter was full of the usual bombast and fustian I reserved for my periods of anger, but I wanted to appear before the board of education very much. I felt it could not know the conditions on the island if it were dependent on Piedmont and Bennington for the information. The board was the one group that could initiate measures strong enough to reverse the hopelessness of the Yamacraw School. In it lay the Christ-powers to revive the prone Lazarus of education. And I wanted to ask it if the whole county stunk with ignorance and brain-rot; if Yamacraw was an isolated example of decay, or if this were an acceptable standard in schools with all black populations. Something was dawning on me then, an idea that seemed monstrous and unspeakable. I was beginning to think that the schools in Beaufort were glutted with black kids who did not know where to search for their behinds, who were so appallingly ignorant that their minds rotted in their skulls, and that the schools merely served as daytime detention camps for thousands of children who would never extract anything from a book, except a page to blow their noses or wipe their butts.

I wanted the members of the board to tell me this. I wanted the board to know that I had graduated from one of their all white schools with an education I was proud of, with an education that prepared me well for any goddam thing life wanted to shove in my way. I required an explanation from them. What was it I had stumbled on, why was it, and what were they going to do about it? It was incomprehensible to me that a group could serve the public in such a capacity and not be frothing at the mouth when confronted with pure, crystalline evidence that a generation of Beaufort's children lay slaughtered in the mortared recesses of her classrooms. I was very young then. I really thought people would care.

I penned the letter on a Wednesday and planned to appear before the board at its monthly meeting the following Tuesday. Mrs. Brown dropped by Friday to tell me that she did not want to make any waves. I told her I understood. I jotted down notes and tried to write a speech with lean and muscular prose, prose without diplomatic accouterments, prose that was strong, masculine, and direct. Each day at lunch I planned what I would say to the board. I wanted to cause an explosion that would reverberate through the attics and cellars of its ivory tower. Every time I glanced at Sidney or Samuel, Fred or Prophet, Richard or Lincoln, I grew angrier. I had something to say. I planned to say it on a Tuesday night in the middle of November. But I was young.

At ten o'clock on the Tuesday of my appearance before the board, I saw a car drive in front of the school. From the car emerged Ezra Bennington, Morgan Randel, the deputy superintendent of administration, and a bulky, bald-headed man I had never seen before.

Mrs. Brown nearly blanched when she saw this august group emerge from the car. She fixed her hair, froze her students to silence by threatening death or worse if they misbehaved, then went out her door to act as welcoming committee. The bald man came into my room with Bennington and introduced himself.

'I'm Charlie Miller,' he said. 'I'm on the school board.'

'I'm Pat Conroy. I'm going to talk to you guys tonight.'

Miller flashed a quick glance to Bennington, whose eyes were roaming like water bugs over the

228

classroom. The room was in its usual disarray: papers, books, magazines, and games littered the desks and tables and spilled over onto the floor. Miller motioned for me to follow him to the hallway, which I did. Bennington followed close behind me. They closed the door. Miller looked at me with what I interpreted at first as malevolence. Then his face sweetened into what might be mistaken in some circles for a smile. He leered, cleared his throat, and tried to arrange his bulldog features into something approaching amicability.

'I talked with some of the board members about your visit, Conroy.'

'Yes, sir?' I asked, a trifle intimidated at the show of power.

'We decided not to let you appear. We got a lot of serious business to tend to on that there board. We can't be listening to every teacher who thinks he's got a gripe.'

'Then you are refusing to let me appear.'

'That's right, son.'

Bennington hovered on the edge of this conversation, a hint of a smile etched into his face. I wanted to knock hell out of both of them, but the intimidation factor was too large. And besides, Mr. Randel had come with them.

Morgan Randel was the deputy superintendent in charge of administration and personnel. He had once been in control of the Beaufort district until Piedmont had eclipsed his star along with Bennington's during the consolidation of the county systems. Whoever sent him along merited a decoration for strategy, for Bennington and Miller could have no greater assurance that I would not erupt and tell them to kiss my fanny than Randel's

229

presence. He was my single ally in the administration.

Our friendship had been sealed since March 14, 1962. On that day I played a baseball game against Wade Hampton High School from the next county. Mr. Randel's son, Randy, was scheduled to pitch that day. Randy had become one of my best friends over the year. We had sat together in Gene Norris' English class, had both played football and basketball, and had planned to go to his grandmother's house in Newberry to play golf the weekend following the Wade Hampton game. We were incurable jocks.

Randy was a brash, witty kid, fifteen years old and six feet four inches tall. He joked incessantly, mimicked his teachers and classmates, and took infinite pleasure in teasing Gene Norris during class. Randy was also an extremely gifted athlete. He could throw a football fifty yards, sink a ten-foot hook shot with monotonous regularity, and throw one of the finest curve balls I had ever seen. The general consensus was that baseball was Randy's finest sport. It was widely assumed that the tall, gangly Randy would one day pitch in the major leagues. He was that good.

The day we played Hampton was cloudy and threatening. It was a day between seasons, bizarre and somehow portentous, strange with gray clouds and eerie patches of light. But Randy pitched well. His fast ball looked untouchable from my vantage point and no one came near the curve. He struck out five of the first seven batters who faced him. Not one Hampton player had succeeded in reaching first base. On this day, Randy looked serious as he rocked forward in his long, patient wind-up, then flung the ball with impressive speed toward the catcher's mitt. An opening-day crowd cheered him on and grew more excited each time another Hampton player struck out. His father shouted encouragement to him from the stands.

In the fourth inning Randy threw a hard, fast ball and the umpire called it a strike. Then, suddenly, Randy lurched forward on the mound and fell to the earth. In that moment—though none of us knew it, and though all of us would try to deny it, and though none of us would ever understand it—Randy was dead. There was a confused rush of coaches toward the mound. The coach of Wade Hampton became hysterical and, in a voice that was ancient, haunting, and terrified, began screaming, 'The boy's dying.'

At this moment, I saw Mr. Randel coming over the fence, striding toward his fallen son. He was a strong, handsome man with a stern, capable face. I cannot remember if Mr. Randel ran to his son, because, somewhere in the panic, everything slowed down for me and the world softened into a nameless, agonizing dance that dulled the screams of women and the pain of men who could not bring the boy back to life. I watched Mr. Randel as he looked into his son's face and felt his son's heart and held his son's hand. And in that instant was born the terrible awareness that life eventually broke every man, but in different ways and at different times. I saw Mr. Randel's strong face loosen up at the seams and melt from strength to horror. I saw his face at the moment he surrendered his son to the earth, when his loss was driven like a nail into his soul, when he understood that his oldest son was dead and that nothing would ever be

231

the same again. The sinew of Mr. Randel's face relaxed, his jaw grew slack, and grief spread along his face like a rash. It was like watching a second death.

An ambulance came and a doctor emerged, took one look and drove a needle full of adrenaline directly into Randy's heart, but there was no heart, no soul, no movement, no laugh, no smile. Mr. Randel turned his head away from his son as though tomorrow was too painful to face or want to face. The ambulance left the infield in slow motion. Randy's feet dangled from the back window. As I watched his feet through my fog, I prayed on my knees that Randy would somehow be spared. But the dangling feet of my friend—that was the looseness, the complete looseness of death.

So I could not argue with Bennington and Miller when Mr. Randel was with them. I had gone to Randy's funeral and seen his mother and father paralyzed with grief among the flowers encircling the casket. I went to see them soon after the funeral to give them a poem I had written about Randy. My first poem. A poem that offered Randy to God when I secretly could not envision the necessity for any god to strike such sorrow in the midst of a family.

Years passed and I became a part of the Randel family and subliminally tried to become a substitute for the lost Randy. Julia, his lovely, soft mother, for years after Randy's death would cry whenever I came over, and I would cry with her. When I went to The Citadel, the Randels paid for most of the first year with a scholarship established in Randy's memory. We wrote frequently during those years at college and I saw them often on vacations. They came to see me on Parents' Day at The Citadel.

So when Mr. Randel acompanied Bennington and Miller to Yamacraw that day, there was no way I could tell the group what I was thinking. Mr. Randel and I had an unwritten, unspoken law that we would never cross swords professionally, that our friendship was too intense and personal to be tarnished in some abortive, temporal crusade concerning our jobs. He did not want me to be on the damn island. It embarrassed him to be a part of this mission. He winked at me when he passed and we later talked basketball in front of the school.

When they left, I realized that Piedmont's empire was not going to be assaulted easily. I also knew that I was too young to handle the blitzkrieg that had just rolled over me. I had accepted Miller's ultimatum without a fight. I, along with the school, was just being shoved under another part of the rug.

*　　*　　*

Piedmont was a firm believer in that ancient, time-destroying remnant of the Paleolithic era, the chain of command. The greatest of all sins in his administrative lexicon was for someone far beneath him in rank to catapult over a series of links in the sacred chain to confront him or even worse, unspeakably, to present a complaint to the school board. This is why I was honored with the show of power, the flexing of the administrative biceps, the flashing of the talons when I wrote Piedmont that I was going to appear before the board. According to the stone tablet of administrative procedure, I should first have presented a complaint to Mrs. Brown, who would refer it to Mr. Sedgwick, who

233

would mull over it for several weeks, then submit it for perusal by the antique Bennington, who would eventually and very timorously lay it on the tabernacle of Piedmont's desk. Piedmont thought the chain of command was the next best thing to organized religion. I thought it was the most inefficient thing since the stone wheel. It simply did not work. In November I asked Mrs. Brown if I could take my class on a field trip in the spring. She said no. I asked that she pass my request to Mr. Sedgwick for approval. She said no again. End of chain of command. But Piedmont had studied several books on administrative procedure from the groves of Columbia University. All of these books concurred that the successful superintendent demanded strict adherence to the chain. In my chain Brown was terrified of Sedgwick, who trembled at the wrath of the unforgiving Bennington, who trembled at the thought of annoying Piedmont. Piedmont did not realize that his staff reserved the same affection for him that Russian peasants held for Ivan the Terrible. Nor did Piedmont ever quite understand or forgive my writing him letters instead of writing to the three other frail and rusty links in the chain. Piedmont, regardless of his ruthlessness or the fact that he could be a genuine son of a bitch, got things done. He could deal in facts, figures, numerals, air conditioners, pencil sharpeners, chalk, water pumps, and groceries. He could relate to people.

Piedmont wrote me in the middle of December and asked me to meet with him and Mr. Sedgwick. In this meeting we would discuss the 'exorbitant' gas bill. I looked forward to this meeting, especially since I felt I had chickened out of a confrontation with the board of education. Face to face, I thought I could challenge Piedmont to come to the school, visit with the parents, and decide for himself what the school needed. Sedgwick had fulfilled his obligations as administrative head with a mercurial visit to the island at the end of November. He flitted through the school building in a five-minute sprint, congratulated me on using the Sullivan and SRA reading programs, and left as quickly as he could. An officious man, Sedgwick now could look Piedmont in the eye and declare he had analyzed the Yamacraw situation firsthand by braving the river brine for an eyewitness visit. He never returned to the school as long as I was there. He also infuriated Mrs. Brown by completely ignoring her presence. Nor did I wish to be the one to explain to her that ol' Sedgwick had this thing about niggers.

So Piedmont, Sedgwick, and I would form a strangely diverse triad when we assembled to discuss the future of the Yamacraw School. Sedgwick selected a Friday in January for the conclave to meet in his Bluffton office. The Friday happened to coincide with the last day of my endurance test in the river, the terrible week of cold along the coast. I was in no mood to pander to the tender sensibilities of administrators who needed to flex their biceps for my benefit. Nor did I feel like waging war about my commuting. In my mind, I was not wedded to the island, nor would I be guilty of bigamy if I went home to Barbara each night. I had never heard of a school board in America with the authority to force a teacher to live in a certain place. I planned to fight Piedmont tooth and claw for the right to commute.

235

Only Piedmont did not show. He sent Bennington in his place. Bennington and Sedgwick were to conduct the meeting and report its results to Piedmont—all praise to the chain of command. I walked into Sedgwick's office garbed in my winter splendor, boots dripping, gloves sticking out of my jacket, and hat arranged haphazardly over tousled hair. Zeke had informed me that Bennington would preside at the meeting instead of Piedmont. Zeke also told me that he had heard they were going to make me pay for the upkeep of the boat.

'Wanna bet, Zeke, me fine man,' I said.

'Just telling you what I heard. I'd quit that job so fast it'd make their eyes open, if I were you.'

Bennington greeted me effusively when I came in, grinning his cunning, endearing grin and asking me how I had withstood the cold that week. This, evidently, was a big moment in Sedgwick's life, a chance to impress his superiors with his ability to handle the niggling problems that arose on his end of the plantation. He was nervous and plucked absently at his chin while he stared intently at a piece of paper on his desk. He shook his head negatively, painfully, as if the piece of paper were a moist dung sample deposited before him for reluctant analysis. But Bennington, the lead mule in the odd pack, began the discussion by apologizing for Dr. Piedmont's absence. He blamed the absence on the ubiquitous whipping boy of southern education—the Department of Health, Education and Welfare.

'Doctor Piedmont has asked me to take his place and to let his feelings in this matter be known.'

'Now, Mr. Conroy,' Sedgwick started, clearing his throat impressively, 'this gas bill is out of the
236

question. It is entirely too much money. Thirty-four dollars, I believe. We cannot be expected to pay for the gas you use to get yourself to work each morning.'

'Yes, you can,' I answered, pleasantly, I hoped.

'We don't pay any other teacher to get to work,' said Sedgwick.

'How many teachers go to work in a boat?' I asked.

'That's beside the point. The county has no travel allowances for teachers to get to school. You are no different from anyone else,' said Bennington.

'That's crap,' I answered. It was about this time during the exchange that I felt the great, ancient Conroy temper rising like an air bubble to the surface. Whenever I am going to lose control, whenever I am about to assume the emotional and psychological responses of the Peking man, my upper lip quivers reflexively and I find it very difficult to enunciate even the simplest of words.

When Bennington said, 'We have come here to tell you that we will pay for your gas to the island on Monday and from the island on Friday. No more, no less. Nor will we pay for the upkeep on the boat if you continue to commute.' My upper lip fluttered like a butterfly wing.

'O.K., guys,' I said. 'Thanks a lot for the meeting. I'll see you around. I'm going to have to talk to Piedmont if I'm going to get anything solved.'

'You can't just walk out,' gasped Bennington, as if I had urinated in the holy grail.

'Like I am leaving, man. This week has been too damn cold and this year has been too damn long to give it up because of this lousy gas. Eventually

237

Piedmont and I are going to have to fight it out anyway. You guys are just doing what he told you to do. You really don't have any power to compromise at all.' And I headed for the door. Sedgwick sputtered incoherently and Bennington made an abortive attempt to block the door.

'You can't leave. You can't just leave.' Ol' Bennington really was concerned about me leaving. 'You are the most unreasonable young man I have ever dealt with in my life.'

'I'm not unreasonable,' I fired back, lip aquivering. 'I just ain't going along with what you guys say, so I'm taking off.'

'You can't just walk out of this office while we have things to discuss,' said Sedgwick.

'Sure I can.'

'Sit down, young man,' Bennington said. 'Please sit down. I've never had a meeting end like this. It's not proper.'

'We can work something out,' said Sedgwick.

'Good, that's all I wanted to hear.' So I returned to my seat and sat down. 'Gentlemen, all I am asking is you to continue to pay for my gas and upkeep of the boat this year. I will continue to act as a stevedore, guide, ferryboat captain, and anything else the county might want to use me for in relation to the boat. I would like you to think of the boat as a lifeline to the island. Five days a week in the morning and afternoon, I will be coming to and from the island. Mr. Skimberry has also suggested that I start carrying fresh milk for the children of the island so they won't have to drink that crappy powdered milk.'

'Sounds like a good idea to me,' said Sedgwick.

'I know where we can get cheaper gas,' said

Bennington.

So the discussion progressed and got more detailed. It was decided that I could indeed commute, that it was an excellent way to serve the needs of the island, and that a fresh-milk program should be initiated immediately. As I left the office, I shook hands with Bennington and Sedgwick, apologized for losing my temper, and told them that the cold weather had frayed my nerves somewhat. Sedgwick intimated that he liked to see teachers fired up about their jobs. Bennington agreed, but there was something in his eyes that told me I had earned the enmity of a man who would never forget my impertinence, a man who would not rest until the wolves cut my flanks from behind. He smiled at me and it was the first time I ever knew that a smile could communicate hatred. I also realized that neither of them would have had the guts to report to Piedmont that I had simply walked out on them.

CHAPTER NINE

The older boys played basketball almost every day at recess. The basket was only eight feet high and the playing area was pure sand. But the games themselves served as emotion-cleansing rituals where the strong and tall waged war against the fiercely determined small and weak. Oscar was the acknowledged prima donna of the group, the golden boy of island athletics, who used his height and weight effectively under the boards to shove out any lilliputian who challenged his right to that domain. I have mentioned the competitiveness of these children before. These basketball games at recess were serious business that sometimes degenerated into violence, one player sitting on top of another player pounding his head. Yamacraw basketball had several variations and modifications.

Since Oscar was the tallest and the game naturally centered around him, he was the number-one target for the hatchet men who swarmed all over him like angry bees. It was not unusual to see Oscar under the basket preparing to shoot with Frank punching away at his stomach and Fred, directly behind him, punching away at his kidneys. Oscar would generally manage to get the shot away, then he would lean down and punch both Frank and Fred.

Saul was the out-man. Since he was the smallest and frailest of the players, he hung far outside the brawl under the basket. If a ball accidentally was flung in his direction, he would scurry over to intercept it, then feed it to one of his teammates before the thundering herd engulfed him. If he held the ball a fraction of a second too long, he would be pounced upon, relieved of the basketball, then cast aside like a troublesome fly on a cow's tail.

Since the court was sand, the game was a mixture of football and basketball. The flying tackle was a main stratagem of defense, as was the cross-body block and the flying wedge. To dribble was to suffer the loss of the ball, so the skilled player developed fakes, feints, and a stiff arm that carried him near enough the basket to shoot. Of course, if he could not get close enough to the basket, he shot anyway. The kinds of shots staggered the imagination. Fred had developed the most interesting and versatile repertoire. To arch the ball over arms outstretched to block his shot, Fred would fall to the ground while at the same time hooking the ball high into the air. If this failed to score—and it almost always did—on the next occasion he would turn his back to the basket and simply hurl the ball over his head toward the goal. Fred almost never scored, but he was hell to watch.

When I first attempted to put a little form and rules into this madness, the kids listened respectfully, but continued to play the way they always had. Whenever I tried to inject a little order into their chaotic interpretation of the game, they looked at me as though I had lost my mind. They loved their game too passionately to allow me to ruin it with a flurry of rules.

In March I read in the paper that the Globetrotters were coming to Charleston and I thought it would be fun to take my noontime stars to see them. I asked the boys if they had seen the Trotters on television. Man, they loved the Globetrotters; they worshiped the Globetrotters. Since it would not be a school-sponsored trip and since I would not have to go through the crap of asking Mrs. Brown's permission or collecting written slips from the parents, I told the boys to fight with their parents and talk them into allowing the Globetrotter trip. I told them I would not enter this battle with the parents but save my energies for the great campaigns that lay ahead. (The parents trusted me for the most part; some kids were even allowed to spend weekends at our house.)

Top Cat was going, along with Oscar the Large, Fred the Hooker, Saul the Small, and Lincoln the Dirty. Frank told me of his gallant attempt to talk Edna into giving him permission, but her fear of the water prevailed. On the appointed day, eight of us piled into the boat—five boys plus Chuck and Al, the two new California boys, and I—and started the long, tortuous journey to Bluffton. My poor boat poked along the waterway with the blinding speed of a manatee. It took an hour and a half to get to Bluffton, twice the usual length of time.

We drove to Beaufort. Chuck and Al took one group in one car; Bernie, Barbara, and I took the rest. We stopped off once we got to Charleston for a quick hamburger at McDonald's. It tickled the hell out of me to see the guys fumbling with their change and trying to act like big-time operators accustomed to dining out in the big city. They bought enough food to feed half the city of Charleston.

The Globetrotters were playing in County Hall in Charleston, a large, sterile arena that looked like a throwback to the declining years of the Roman Empire. Most of the crowd were seated when we arrived. The crowd itself was a wide mixture of people. More white people than blacks sat in the arena, but at four dollars a ticket that formed no real enigma. Fat cops ambled up and down the aisles chewing gum and looking bored. Women with the faint aura of high society sat rigidly erect, trying to look chic in an atmosphere of stale popcorn and jock smells.

We had a hell of a time finding seats and finally stood near the Globetrotter dressing room, where we had a fair view of the court. Bernie and Saul had managed to inch up to a spot that afforded them a good view of the game. The rest of us were standing on our tiptoes and seeing as best we could.

A roar from the crowd told us that the

Globetrotters were emerging from the locker room. They ran right past us on the way to the court and one of them, the greatest Globetrotter of all, Meadowlark Lemon, won a place of honor in my heart for all time. When he ran past Bernie and Saul, he reached out and patted Saul on the behind. With that simple gesture, Meadowlark immortalized Saul's fanny—at least for a week.

Eventually we clambered up on a bandstand and had an excellent view of the entire game. The boys loved every stinking minute of play. They watched in amazement as Curly Neal performed his classic dribbling exhibition and gasped as these huge, black athletes went high into the air to jam the basketball into the hoop. They laughed at every joke and whooped it up at every gimmick. Sometimes they would just look at each other and grin in disbelief. They learned many tricks which they would utilize in their blood games on the island. From this night forward the behind-the-back pass and the between-the-leg pass became staples of the island brand of ball. This was basketball, man, and it was good.

As we left that night, walking to the car through the milling crowd, all of us talking about the Trotters and relating firsthand our favorite parts, Saul paused on the side of the road, people walking all around him, and took a piss. Bernie watched in shock, and I tried to figure out a proper response. None came. When Saul had finished, he zipped up his pants and continued to walk toward the car. It struck me then that the boys probably just let fly on the island when the occasion demanded it and Saul saw no reason not to follow his urges on a Charleston street just as naturally. I said nothing.

On the way home I learned that this great journey to Charleston was the farthest any of the guys had ever been from Yamacraw Island.

*   *   *

Once I started teaching on the island, a great many of my friends clamored for a trip to Yamacraw. At first, I entertained no thoughts about running a ferry service between the island and the mainland, but I swiftly changed my mind after the first few cataclysmic days that I spent exploring the void that gripped my eighteen students. I soon decided that any human that had not been entombed on Yamacraw since birth had a vast repository of experience to share in my classroom. I reasoned further that if my friends were coming to the island to learn something about the culture of the Sea Island Negro, then they, in return, could impart some measure of their own existence to the children of the island.

When I first started dating Barbara seriously during September, I met two friends of hers at dinner one night, Dick and Marie Caristi. Dick was a dentist in the navy, stationed in Beaufort. He was also an avid amateur photographer, and my descriptions of the island instantly caused some Nikon gland deep within him to salivate. A week later he became my first official visitor in what was to become the favorite part of my program. Dick was successful in breaking down the incorporeal barriers that separated the children from strangers in the early days. He provided an excellent opportunity to introduce another part of the country to them. Dick was from Boston and his accent was as thick as Bunker Hill. I gave him the tape recorder, let him talk about himself, his work as a dentist, healthy teeth, and the city of Boston. We replayed his voice and analyzed his speech, the silent *rs*, the articulation, and finally, the speed of his presentation. Then I played a speech Cindy Lou had given the previous day with her island dialect racing with jackrabbit speed from the first word to the last.

'Lawd, that girl talk so fast,' laughed Ethel.

'You shut yo' mout', girl,' cautioned Cindy Lou.

Then we went to the map to find Boston. Dick started to cite its preeminence in the Revolutionary War, but this quickly led to a staggering amount of new material. Since the kids knew nothing about Boston, or Massachusetts, or the Revolutionary War, or New England, or England, out of necessity we had to restrict the scope of conversation. Compared to the Yamacraw children, everyone I brought to the island was a compendium of ideas and experience, and the one transcendent problem of all who came to the classroom was the intelligent condensation and control of the material they wished to present. This was my own greatest problem. How much did the kids know and what should I teach them that they didn't know?

Dick was the first in a long procession of visitors. His success that first day convinced me that associations with a multitude of people would be beneficial and instructive to my students. Before the year ended, forty people made the voyage to Yamacraw. Some of them were only mildly successful in leaving part of themselves in the classroom and some simply could not relate to children and made little imprint on them. One man, not a friend, patronized the kids badly and spoke to them as though he were addressing an assembly of cretins. But of the forty or so who came to the island, there were several who implanted their names and personalities forever in the memory of eighteen very impressionable children.

My sister was one. Carol Ann was a senior in college then and decided to come down for a week to get to know Barbara and the children better. She also wanted to see the island. When Zeke put us in the river it was a cold, wind-driven Friday in December. Before we hit deep water I watched as Carol delivered a vigorous incantation against the shark gods who ruled salt water unchallenged. Carol was always a kind of high priestess in our family circle, a wry and demonstrative oracle who read eastern philosophy with sophomoric intensity and who tried to implement the lessons she derived from her readings in our household. Carol had difficulty enlisting Dad's interest while she lectured about the teachings of Vishnu, as he watched the White Sox games on television.

I relished the thought of introducing Carol to my students. Nor did she disappoint me. Along with my father, she is one of the world's great undiscovered actors. Whatever she does or says is burnished with an almost vaudevillian touch. She longs to write and act in a play where the heroine combines the pragmatism of Scarlett O'Hara, the wit of Falstaff, and the destiny of Ophelia. Until she does, only her family and friends will benefit from her dramatic gifts.

She entered the classroom when we got to the island, moved about the room talking to the kids and making herself comfortable. Then she told me

246

she was ready to perform. Her performance that day was superb. She recited poems from our childhood, poems of adventure, and scenes from plays. She did this with typical Carolian flourish. Her eyes gleamed, her voice ranted, then whispered, then rasped, then quivered. The kids sat transfixed. They neither smiled, nor cheered, or moved. They had never seen anything like it.

Pleased by her reception, she delivered her rendition of the witches' scene from *Macbeth* with such macabre passion and blood-chilling authenticity that the children without exception grew restless, wide-eyed, and frightened. Carol sat in the middle of the floor, her eyes blazing at an imaginary cauldron, her lips quivering as she summoned double the toil and stinking trouble, and her hands worked diabolically as she bent over her fire on the schoolroom floor. It was a good act; she had performed it frequently for an appreciative family when we gathered for the holidays. But the students did not fathom the relatively important fact that it was a performance and not the utterances of a madwoman I had imported for the occasion. To further complicate matters, Carol had performed a few magic tricks just to loosen things up a bit.

She was delighted to discover what she had wrought. It pleased her to think that her performance had been so dazzling, credible, and convincing. I pointed out that she had not played before the most sophisticated audience in the western hemisphere, but the actress in her was undaunted and her ego soared.

The kids bombarded me with questions the following Monday.

'Your sister really a witch, Conroy?' Lincoln asked.

'Of course not. She was just acting,' I answered.

'No,' other voices interjected.

'She bad,' said Samuel.

'She tell me she turn me into a hoppy-toad,' said Sidney.

'She was just kidding. She was pretending to be a witch.'

'How you know?'

'Because she's my sister.'

'Witch gotta be someone's sister,' Ethel reasoned.

'Witch bad.'

'She tell me shark get 'um if I fall in river,' Lincoln said.

'For Chrissake, she's been talking about sharks since she was a little girl.'

'That girl was a witch,' Jasper said with finality.

So my sister literally and figuratively left the classroom with her witchdom intact, nor could I ever mention my family again without conjuring up visions of boiling pots and Carol's bent shoulders crouching over toad-filled concoctions. The aura of Carol's performance lingered long after she left the island. She had fired the imagination of my students and brought the magic of theater into the classroom. She had mesmerized the kids by simply tossing around a few lines by Shakespeare. She opened up a wonder in the art of pretense, the fantasy world of drama, where witches and teachers' sisters can be the same people.

One of the more memorable visitors came by accident. Mrs. Brown dismissed school early one chilly day in March when the water pump inexplicably quit working. She commissioned me to

248

go to Bluffton for the sole purpose of eliciting help from the long-suffering Zeke Skimberry. Whenever the pump froze, it suited me fine, since there was something rather melodramatic in the endless procession of small boys heading for the pissing tree in the woods. Whenever the pump broke, Mrs. Brown would come in the room, heave her shoulders dramatically and say, 'Tell your babies to put on the brakes, Mr. Conroy. The commode will not flush, so just tell everybody to put on the brakes.' At noon, I pointed the boat toward Cannon Creek and the public dock in Bluffton.

As I pulled in view of the dock and was making the final elaborate preparations for landing, I spotted George Westerfield, a teacher at the high school and a solid regular in the Skimberry bull sessions. He was sitting with his feet dangling over the dock, chewing tobacco and periodically spitting into the river. On his left sat a startling, exotic man, slender and well over six feet tall, who was staring intently at my boat. The man did not have a single hair on his head.

They helped me tie the boat up and George introduced me to his college friend, Peter Walter. I learned in the ensuing conversation that Peter and George had anchored a strong soccer team at the University of the South during their undergraduate days. Peter was on a break from a private school where he taught in New England and had brought several of his students with him on a leisurely tour of the South. He spoke rapidly, a machine-gun patter of words and phrases that flew out of his mouth like small, harmless cartridges. I liked him immediately. He professed a genuine interest in the island and the children I was teaching and asked me what methods I was using to improve the kids' reading ability. When I had carefully explained the cabalistic ritual of my teaching secrets, he affably informed me that those methods were all wrong.

'Pat, I teach with this fabulous man who has developed a foolproof method for teaching kids to read. He takes kids who can't read a word and has them reading on a third- or fourth-grade level by the end of one year,' Peter said.

'Come to the island tomorrow and show me your stuff,' I said.

'You'll take me to the island? That's great. That's simply fantastic. Can I take the kids I brought with me? They would love it.'

The next morning the boat was filled with Peter and his three students. Zeke Skimberry, who had also fallen under Peter's spell, went along with us to fix the inscrutable water pump. Peter talked incessantly during the entire trip. He had joined the Peace Corps but dropped out during the training sessions because he could not tolerate authority figures controlling his life. He switched to the Teachers Corps, but opted out once again during the training sessions for the same reason. To make the cycle complete he planned to join the Job Corps and the Marines, wash out during both preliminary trainings, retire to the wilderness, and write a definitive confession on life in the American Corps. His enthusiasm infected everything he touched, magnified life about him; his students worshiped him openly and laughed convulsively whenever he cracked a joke, no matter how corny.

When we entered the classroom, Peter's hairless head and tall form striding gracefully to the center of the room froze my critical bunch for several moments. I waited for Prophet to utter some endearing salutation like, 'Man ain't got no hair on his haid,' but the gang contented themselves with staring and whispering when Peter first made his entrance. One of Peter's students was from Hong Kong, so I had him go to the map, pick out his country, then let Peter tell about the country. (The boy from Hong Kong spoke English about as well as I spoke Cantonese.)

It did not take Peter long to capture the attention of my entire class. He had a way of talking, gesturing and bouncing along—hypnotism by words and movement—that fascinated my group even though, at first, they nudged each other with their elbows and flashed each other amused glances. Peter remained oblivious. He gathered everyone in the room around him, including me, and initiated math games, word games, and geography games.

'Take the number five. Add seven. Subtract two, and multiply times three. What do you get? Think now. We have to learn to think fast on our feet. We have to be quick and bright. We've got to enjoy learning. Enjoy doing. I'll do it again. Slower this time, but not too slow. Take the number five. Add seven. Subtract two and multipy times three. What do you get?'

'Don't get nothin',' whispered Richard.

'Get thirty,' said Frank.

'Great. That's right. That is great. Who are you?'

'Frank.'

'You are really smart, Frank. Any other smart kids around? Sure, everybody's smart. Everybody's smart. They just need a chance to prove it. They need to find something they like.'

Peter worked these games for half an hour. The

251

kids never took their eyes off him during his entire, spirited performance. His hands moved beautifully as he spoke and his hands were very important to his teaching. They were like twin batons controlling the mood and tempo of an orchestra. When he tired of this, he called for a volleyball. Oscar retrieved one from the closet, a spongy, deflated ball, which Peter claimed would be good enough. He then launched into the history of soccer, told us how it was the world's most popular game, how its popularity was limited in the United States, and how the game could be played with ease in the Yamacraw schoolyard.

'Soccer is a game played with the feet,' he said, controlling the ball expertly on the floor. 'All of us are so conditioned to use our hands when we play sports that it is very difficult for us to use our feet only. It takes lots of practice. Now get these desks out of the center of the room and I'll show you some real footwork.'

We shoved the desks to the corners of the room, leaving the center entirely bare except for the wood stove.

'Now, some of you boys and girls try to steal the ball from me using only your feet.'

Naturally all eighteen of my students surged forward, kicking and booting their feet at the ball. Peter took about thirteen direct hits on his shins as he maneuvered the ball through the gauntlet of shod feet. After his legs could take no more punishment, Peter led the thundering herd to the playground.

Mrs. Brown went crazy when she saw my babies swarming over the playground before the time designated in the sacred rule book. I convinced her that Peter was a scholar of some renown, a gifted wanderer who traveled the country demonstrating the joys of soccer to rural children. He would even teach her class if she so desired—but she insisted indignantly that her class studied more important things than games. 'You don't learn a thing by having fun. You gotta work. You gotta work.'

By this time Peter had miraculously divided the class into two opposing squads, put Lincoln as goalie at one end of the field, Ethel at the other, and was leading a hopelessly chaotic pack of soccer neophytes up and down the field. Saul kicked at the ball, missed by two feet, fell to the earth, and was immediately trampled by Sidney and Richard. Cindy Lou tried to boot the ball and kicked Anna instead. Samuel and Sidney chased after the ball, kicking conscientiously, until finally they stood on the perimeter of the field, kicking the hell out of each other.

'Cut it out, man,' I yelled.

'Boy kicked me,' whined Sidney.

'Who you call boy, boy?' answered Samuel.

They resumed kicking each other. Meanwhile, Peter broke loose from the crowd and was heading expertly toward Lincoln's goal. Lincoln, a passionate defender of his imaginary net, saw Peter approaching formidably and decided that it was better to retreat than to face Peter's kick with resolution and courage. Lincoln fled from his position and Peter rolled one home. The game lasted a half-hour. Peter then rallied the entire troupe, marched them into the classroom, and demonstrated his control of the ball. Without using his hands, he bounced the ball off his shining head fifty straight times, then repeated the performance with each of his feet.

His soccer was excellent, but what impressed me more was his communication with the kids, so natural and spontaneous. They followed him around the entire day, pawing at him, talking to him, laughing at his jokes, and trying to hold his hand. He listened to their stories, laughed at their jokes, and answered every question they directed to him, carefully and with enthusiasm. This guy Peter was a natural teacher, I thought later, one of those rare human beings who loved and responded to children more than to adults and who could draw children to him as effortlessly as a magnet gathering iron filings. It rained on the trip back, a slashing, driving rain that limited visibility to a few feet, and it was interesting to note that Peter entertained the entire miserable boatful of us the whole way back. Soaking wet and shivering, we pulled the boat up and Peter said, 'Wasn't that a magnificent ride?'

By far the most successful visitor, according to my students, was Richie Matta. Richie was a stocky, powerful, and irrepressible Italian who had entered my life with a flourish the last year I taught at Beaufort High School. He crashed a party at my house during the middle of winter, made friends with everyone three the first hour, then took over the whole party during the second. When one nostalgic group commenced to sing old rock-and-roll favorites from the fifties, Richie startled the entire burping, beer-sodden chorus by stepping back from the record player and singing like a deep-voiced seraph. He was a songbird amidst insects and frogs. We eventually gravitated next door, where Tim Belk, another friend, banged away at a piano while Richie traced the history of rock and roll in the previous decade. His repertoire seemed unlimited, his energy seemed boundless, and he sang for three hours.

Richie's life history was revealed to me after we became friends that night. He came over frequently to talk. He was raised in New Orleans in a fragmented, rather chaotic childhood. He had sung professionally on Bourbon Street. He had gotten a good break in music, cut a few records in Memphis, and became a minor rock sensation in the Delta region. Then the Marine Corps intervened, drafted him, and sent him to Vietnam. His musical career had died the moment his draft notice arrived. He had come to Beaufort with the Marine Corps and planned to get a college degree when he was discharged. He envied Bernie, Tim Belk, and me because we had been to college, received degrees, and spoke with phony authority about the contents of a sophomore literature book. Richie, a lesser man, could tune a car, tear a motor boat apart, plaster a ceiling, build a house, and sing an aria from *Carmen*. But Richie wanted to be a teacher. He was a boat mechanic for his last year as a Marine and he had tired of a life whose trademark was grease under the fingernails. He longed for a life of scholarship and contemplation of Greek urns and things. Bernie and I used to gag when we considered the possibility of the hairy, swarthy Richie, sipping sherry from a fragile glass, dressed in rumpled tweeds, reciting poetry from a frail leather volume. The vision was so out of character—like Attila the Hun wearing ballerina shoes. We preferred our own mythology of Richie Matta.

I brought Richie and his new bride, Aldie, to

Yamacraw in early spring during the season of the fog. Richie held to the common theory that I could not zip my pants, much less navigate a boat, and I wanted to demonstrate the skills of boatsmanship acquired over the year. I wore my official winter wardrobe with the flashy scarf and impressive boots, and the wool hat tilted rakishly on my seasoned head. I coveted Richie's respect and played the Admiral Nelson role during the preparation for landing. I even dismissed the fog, which was starting to rise thickly and ominously, as a minor irritant and one that would not deter a master seaman. We left Zeke and entered into that strange world of swamp and fog, Nelson at the wheel, Aldie sitting prettily on the passenger seat, and Richie asking me if I was sure I knew where I was going or what I was doing.

'Of course, Richie. Just shut your big mouth and let Admiral Conroy do the driving. I know this run like the palm of my hand.'

Midway we were hopelessly lost. We crossed the widest stretch of water on the trip, turned when we reached a familiar oyster bank, and hit a sandbar that was not supposed to be there. Richie pulled us off the bar, I retraced my path, figured out what I had done wrong, embarked on a new direction, and hit the same sandbar again.

'Hey, Admiral Conroy,' Richie said mockingly.

'O.K., Rich. Do not say a word. Promise? Don't ever bring this up to Bernie and wipe it out of your own mind, son. It's all a mistake.'

We finally found the right shore line and followed it unerringly to Ted Stone's dock. Driving to the school, I asked Richie what songs he would sing.

'Any song they want to hear, son. I know them

all.'

His performance that day was indeed notable. Top Cat whispered, 'Oh Gawd,' when Richie warmed up with Otis Redding's 'Dock of the Bay' and ended with 'Proud Mary.' He sang for a solid hour, singing soul and folk, traditional and rock. He told the kids about New Orleans, about singing in the clubs, about the underworld and crooks. He briefly described his experiences in Vietnam. But mostly he sang. When he discovered their love of church and gospel music, he lit into 'Down by the Riverside.' Ethel responded by singing 'Blue Burying Ground' accompanied by Anna and Cindy Lou. Soon the whole class erupted in sounds of feet clapping and feet stamping and voices singing. Mrs. Brown poked her head in the window, her face a portrait of disapproval, and grimaced in displeasure. Richie did not see her and at the precise moment she appeared, he roared out his highest glass-shattering note of the day, which caused Mrs. Brown to jump, the kids to go into convulsions, and me to scurry into the hall with apologies to the highly offended principal. Later on in the day, Richie distributed records he had made in Memphis to every kid in the class. I put one of them on the record player and we listened to a much younger Richie crooning the top song of his aborted career, 'Time Out for Love.' Each day at recess, after Richie's appearance, the girls gathered by the record player and danced to the voice of Richie Matta. One of the California boys, on first arriving at the school, asked one of the girls if she had heard of James Brown.

She replied, 'Yeh. You hear of Richie Matta?'

'No.'

'He sing "Time Out for Love,"' she explained.

I also taped Richie's performance that day and periodically when boredom settled in, I would flick on one of Richie's brighter moments.

'Lawd, that man sing good.'

'Not as good as me, Saul,' I said.

'Shoot, mahn,' said Oscar. 'You sing like a frog.'

'Oh, that boy say Conrack sing like frog,' cooed Ethel.

'I sing good,' I insisted.

'You sing so bad, Conrack! I laugh so hard when you sing.'

'Man hurt my ears,' someone said.

'"Time out, time out for love,"' I crooned.

'Gawd, stop.'

'Gawd, that sound so bad. Man dyin',' said Cindy Lou.

'I taught Richie to sing.'

'That not so,' said Frank seriously.

Then we would settle down to listen seriously to Richie's legacy to the classroom for one of the world's most appreciative audiences. Richie Matta, whose career sparked brightly then faded like memory when he left the Delta, made his comeback and made it big with eighteen kids on Yamacraw Island.

★   ★   ★

Lincoln forced me back onto the kindness-to-mute-animals platform when he told me he hog-tied his dog every summer to pick ticks off him. I once more railed against cruel bastards owning animals, and if he could not treat a dog right, why in the hell did he have one anyway? Lincoln giggled and said

258

he was going to tie the dog up again next summer and do the same thing. There were many times when my sermons fell on ears of stone. The kids could not understand my concern for animals. They loved their dogs and cats, but treated them with far more cruelty than I thought was necessary. Ethel gave me the clue that this attitude toward animals was a pervasive part of the island culture when she told me about her uncle. Her uncle's name was Charlie and was rather well known around the island for his prodigious drinking. Ethel told this story about Charlie and her aunt.

'They had this ole cat, Mr. Conroy. Lawd, that cat could ate anything. Anything you put out that cat snatch 'em up before you could look around. One night Uncle Charlie say, "Man, this liver I buy sure look good. So red and fine. Honey, fick this here liver up tonight so I can eat it tomorrow at lunch." So my aunt fick up the liver with salt and leave it on the table. In the morning she wake up and look fo the liver and found it nowhere in the room. She look all around and never could see that liver. So she say, "Charlie, did you eat that liver? I don't find it nowhere," and Charlie say, "I don't know. That goddam cat musta eat it during the night." So he say, "Here, kitty. Here, little kitty, you want some good food." The kitty hear Charlie callin' and comes runnin' out from under the bed. Then the kitty follow Charlie out the door and Charlie grab a hoe and chop kitty's head clean off.'

With this magnificent punchline, the class laughed hysterically. I stood there hoping that an appropriate sermon would form on my lips.

Then Ethel said, 'But Gawd, that cat sho' could eat.'

And Oscar said, 'Cat don't eat when it ain't got no head.'

Spurred by the success of her story about kitty's decapitation, Ethel continued in the same vein. 'One time Charlie didn't like this little chicken-eatin' dog. Dog pop chain many times and gobble up one, two, maybe three biddies before we catch 'im and chain 'im up again. Once he got himself four biddies before we see 'im. Charlie go get 'im but dog see 'im comin' and run under the house. He peek his head out a few minutes later and Charlie grabs him around the neck. He gets the chicken-eatin' dog by the tail, and swings him 'round and 'round and then breaks dog's head against tree. Eye pop out and brains bust. Dog dead when Charlie let 'im go.'

'What a nice story, Ethel,' I intoned.

'Dog bad,' Prophet said. 'He eat biddie.'

'Would you kill a dog that ate biddies, Prophet?' I asked.

'I shoot 'im daid,' he replied.

'I shoot 'im in the haid,' Oscar added.

'Dog that suck egg is bad, too. I shoot 'em daid,' Jasper said.

'Oh Gawd, egg-suckin' dog suck all egg up. Gotta kill 'im or you don't get no eggs,' Lincoln said.

'Egg be suck dry,' said Cindy.

It took me a long time but I soon became aware of an underlying, pervasive fixation for violence among the people of the island. Violence was part of the culture and it erupted periodically during the year and affected the children in my class. I had only superficial knowledge about their homes and families and it took me a very long time to realize that classroom depression or exhaustion usually

260

indicated that fathers were drinking too much or mothers were down at the club too late, or worse.

To begin with, the island was a small arsenal. Every home, black and white, contained enough firearms and weaponry to hold off a platoon of Marines for a fortnight. The people supplemented their food supply with squirrel, possum, and an occasional deer, and the boys in my room continually bragged about their marksmanship. Guns were as necessary and vital to the island as fishing poles or crab traps.

The most impressive collection of rifles on the island belonged to Ted Stone. In one of his rambling dissertations on what's good and what's bad for Yamacraw, he intimated that his formidable array of hardware was added insurance that the natives would never venture into his compound uninvited. His gun rack was antlered with high-powered carbines and short, heavy shotguns. 'I can handle any trouble on this island. My only worry is outside agitators. Communists trained in Havana. Nigger-lovers comin' to make trouble.' I thought at the time he was referring to the California boys, but I later realized he could have been saying this as a warning to me.

Alcohol always precipitated the violence. Drinking was a way of life on the island. Both the men and women consumed great quantities of liquor and beer, drinking themselves into a stumbling, muttering limbo from time to time. Of course, I understood very well why people drank on the island. It was the single form of entertainment, the social medium that bound the island together, the only sport, the only recreation, the focal point of island activity. And alcohol brought the same

261

relief to poor farmers and crabbers that it brought to emperors: its particular, elusive magic could dull the cumulative effects of being poor, jobless, isolated, and frustrated. That it could cripple, ruin, and summon cruel demons from the darker side of a man's soul was secondary. On Yamacraw its most important function was to bring joy, relief, and euphoria; it desensitized a person into not caring whether he had a job, clothes for his children, or money for food.

One of the younger kids whispered to me one morning that Anna's grandmother had been shot the night before. When I asked how it happened, all I got for an answer was a grin and a silent tongue. Whenever some crisis welled up on the island, I had learned that the children would never come to me directly and narrate the story as it happened. They would drop hints, let me overhear conversations, give me fragments of the story, until I more or less knew what had happened.

It was through this piecemeal gathering of bits and pieces that I learned an unnamed man had gotten drunk, come to Anna's house, swaggered and stumbled about the house brandishing a pistol and 'talkin' big.' The end result was a bullet entering her grandmother's side. Whether the shooting was accidental or attempted murder I never learned or was meant to learn. A woman had been shot, the kids wanted me to know, but they did not want me to know the circumstances surrounding the shooting or the name of the dark stranger who wielded the gun. I asked Anna if she needed any help or if there was anything I could do to help her or her grandmother. I did not mention the shooting. Anna simply shook her head

262

negatively and smiled her beautiful, inscrutable, profoundly silent smile.

Several months later I entered the classroom one morning to find the kids uncharacteristically silent. I was very unaccustomed to introspective, confessional silences any time during the day, but I was especially suspicious of morning quiet. It generally meant that Mrs. Brown had set a fanny afire. But this morning was different. I saw three of the guys with their heads on their desks crying—Oscar, Fred, and Prophet. I walked over to them and asked, 'Did she hit you?' Everyone else shook their heads. 'Then what in the hell happened?' Still no answer, and by this time I had realized that there would be no answer for right now. I knew that the story wpuld be revealed in scraps and tiny portions over the day. I also knew that the story would not come from Oscar, Fred, or Prophet, but from the others. And it did.

At recess I heard one of the kids whisper too loudly about 'their momma gittin' shoot up.' Then someone mentioned that she was shot in the foot. Lincoln walked up behind me and said she would be all right. One of the girls said that Oscar's father had done the shooting. Carolina said he had been drinking. Through this random method of communication, the full story evolved and took form. The father had gotten very drunk and abusive; the mother had gotten very drunk and acrimonious. A pitched, screaming battle ensued with the boys cowering in the back bedroom until they heard a shot, ran to the kitchen, and found their mother bleeding. The scene must have been terrifying. I know it was traumatic. It took several weeks for the shock of the event to wear off the boys. They cried easily and pitifully for many days after the shooting took place. Fred seemed to be particularly affected. His attention span, normally short, became almost nonexistent. During a phonics rally, Fred suddenly started crying when Jasper teased him about his speech impediment. He ran to the bathroom, where I followed him. He put his head on the sink and wept as if something was breaking up deep inside him. I rested my arm on his shoulder and told him to cry all he wanted, that sometimes a man just felt like crying and it made him feel better in the end. He cried for an hour.

The shooting incident made me take a closer look at Prophet. The kids had told me that no one messed with Prophet, even the boys in the class much larger than him. It was said that Prophet went crazy when he got angry and would kill anyone who crossed him during his smoldering rages. A fifth grader who killed, I thought? The smiling, mischievous Prophet I knew in class did not seem capable of the violence attributed to him by his peers. He was a tough kid, very scrappy, but not a killer. Oscar, his brother, however, traced the history of Prophet's eruptions one day after school. On one occasion, Oscar had beaten Prophet up, the birthright of every older brother. Later in the day Oscar was running down the hall, when Prophet stepped out from a room and flattened Oscar with a brick slapped against his forehead. A man, it seemed, should exercise discretion when bullying Prophet. At another time Prophet reduced a much older brother to weeping and begging for his life. Prophet led him all over the house with a loaded pistol at his head, threatening to blow his head off at any second. Frank told me, 'That boy go wild when he gits hold of a gun.' I do not think I even looked harshly at Prophet for the remainder of the year.

The final paroxysm of violence involved me and the class directly. It was in the spring when the fringe of forest around the school celebrated the renewal of leaf and bud and the wildflowers began to color the edges of the dirt roads. It was late in the morning. A knock sounded on the schoolhouse door. It was Ethel's mother, Lois.

'May I please see Ethel, Pat?' she asked.

'Sure, Lois,' I answered, sensing that something was wrong. 'What's wrong? You look like you're hurting.'

'Oh Gawd, that damn husband of mine. Oh Gawd, he hurt me bad.'

'What's wrong, Lois? Where did he hurt you?'

'On my back. He hit me on my back,' she answered, leaning against the door. 'He nearly kill me.'

'What did he hit you with?'

'A chair, Pat. He break a chair over my back. He try to kill me. Chair break up when he hit me. I think my back break when he hit.'

'You wouldn't be walking around with a broken back.'

'Oh, somethin' break. I know somethin' break,' she wailed. By this time Ethel was standing beside her mother with an expression of complete stoicism on her face. Not a flicker of emotion crossed her eyes or moved her lips. Whatever storm she felt thundered in a place neither I nor the world could see.

'You O.K., Mama,' she said quietly.

'Oh, Ethel, I hurt so bad. He hit me with a chair.

265

He break the chair on me.'

'We git 'im back, Mama,' Ethel said impassively.

'Pat, will you drive me to my house? I got some money hid that I don't want him to git hold of.'

'I don't know, Lois. If John is still down there, he's liable to break a chair over my damn head.'

'Oh, he go 'way. Go down to the club to get drunk up. He ain't in the house no mo'.'

'Are you sure, Lois? Are you damn sure?'

'I pretty sure.'

It was lunch time, so Ethel, Lois, and I got in the car and drove over to Edna Graves' house. Edna was Frank's grandmother and the first lady I approached about the Halloween trip. She was also, I found out, Lois's mother. Lois wanted me to drive her to Edna's house so she could narrate her latest domestic misadventure to a sympathetic ear. Edna's ear was far more murderous than sympathetic. When she heard how John had demolished a chair over her daughter's back, she went insane.

'You tell that dirty son of a bitch that if he ever comes here again that ol' Edna gonna shoot him daid. Daid, I say. Did everybody hear me? I mean I am gonna git Betsy out of the house, load her up, point Betsy at his head, and put him in the ground. He ain't gonna mess with me and Betsy. And I ain't gonna talk to that son of a bitch no mo'. I done through talkin'. Betsy's gonna do all my talkin' now on. And when Betsy done do the talkin', that son of a bitch ain't gonna be doin' no mo' list'nin',' ranted Edna, her body bent and trembling in anger, her index finger slashing the air for emphasis. 'He hit my daughter. Beat my daughter. Make my daughter cry. Make her bleed. Now I'm gonna

266

make him bleed. Edna and Betsy are gonna git his ass. You hear me? Git his ass and git it good.'

'Oh, Mama,' Lois said.

'Don't you "oh, Mama" me, girl. Go git your stuff and your chillun and git up to this house and leave that son of a bitch. Leave him. You hear me. Leave him 'fore he kills you or Betsy kills him.'

To a do-gooding, bleeding-hearted Pollyanna, the whole scene seemed incredible, exotic, savage, and ritualistic. From Ethel's reaction I could tell that this was not the first time her grandmother had delivered this same speech, nor was it the first time her mother and father had waged war against each other. I had heard from the island grapevine that John and Lois were alcoholics and that their battles under the influence were epic in their turbulence and fury. The family had an impressive history of broken heads and cauliflower ears. John, in fact, had been blinded in one eye during a fight. As he was beating his wife with a club, she threw a potful of potash into his eye, and darkness instantly ruled his left side. It was a very physical family.

After Edna's long soliloquy ended, we continued down the road to Lois's house. All the way down, the thought that John might still be in the house, inebriated and feeling his Schlitz, caused me a great deal of anxiety. He was lame in one foot, but I knew that my swiftness would be as the wind if John made a threatening move toward me. I also knew that bullets had been known to travel a bit faster than feet. So with these cheerful thoughts I steered the car toward the house. Ethel sat beside me in the front seat. Her mother occupied the back seat, chattering about leaving her husband for good, and how much her back pained her. I looked over

267

to say something reassuring to Ethel and saw her fiddling with a shining object in her hand. It was a razor blade.

'What in the hell are you doing with that thing, Ethel?' I demanded to know.

'Jes' for a little protection.'

'You don't need it. Put it away.'

'No.'

'Ethel, I am your teacher. Other kids at other schools listen to their teachers and do what they say.'

This seemed to tickle her and she smiled. Then she said, 'I'll put it away, but I'll take it out if he's there.'

'You don't have to worry, man. I'm here,' I said heroically.

'He may git you too,' she said, confirming my worst fears.

'Well, what are you gonna do with that thing if he's there?' I asked.

'I'm gonna cut 'im,' she answered without smiling.

'Oh, that's nice,' I replied, wanting to fling myself under the wheel of the car.

The house finally came into view. I rolled the car easily into the front yard, got out, and with a voice that tried to be virile, but came out with a squawk of axle and a squawk of poultry, I said, 'John. John. It's me, your good friend Pat.' When I discovered that he wasn't home, Lois went into the house, extracted her money from a secret place, and returned to the car.

I took Lois to Bluffton to see Dr. Wohlert. He x-rayed her back, discovered that it was just badly bruised, and gave her some medicine. She spent that night with Barbara and me, returned to the island and her mother for a few days, then went back to her husband. The strange thing was that John and Lois really liked each other.

*   *   *

Barbara invited my whole class to our house for a Valentine's Day party. Her class at Beaufort Elementary was coming over and she thought it would be a nice gesture to bring the two groups together. Barbara crafted an ornate, lacy valentine for me to pin on my bulletin board inviting the class for the holiday weekend. Only the girls decided to come. The boys glanced suspiciously at the lace and the enormous red heart, then decided there was something intrinsically feminine about this gathering at the Conracks'. They said they would rather hunt and kill in the deep woods. The girls bounded in joy when they discovered they would be going on the trip without those nasty boys. So on Friday of Valentine's week, four of the girls and I laboriously fluttered and putted in choppy waters toward the landing in Bluffton.

This was the first time the girls had stayed at our new house. We had recently bought a two-story, seventy-year-old home on The Point. We put them in the downstairs bedroom to sleep. They demanded they be allowed to sleep together. I later learned why. Mary had felt the presence of ghosts in the house from the moment she saw it. She spread this notion to the other girls, and by nightfall the four of them had clustered in the living room, clucking about imagined noises, footsteps on the dark stairs, and faces pressed against windowpanes. I had not realized how real and palpable the spirit world was to them, and even when I heard them voicing their fears, I was more delighted than alarmed.

'You got a ghost in this big ol' house, Mr. Conroy,' Mary muttered.

'We hear 'im in the stairs,' said Jimmy Sue.

'I ain't stayin' in this ol' scarey house,' said Cindy Lou.

'Oh, Gawd, I so scare. I don't want no ghost to git me,' said Carolina.

So then I did a very foolish thing. 'Girls, I didn't want to tell you this. But you're right. We've got a ghost in this house. Barbara and I just didn't want to scare you.'

'Oh Gawd, I knew it. I feel it. I feel it all the time,' wailed Mary.

'It's not a big ghost. It's a dwarf ghost, a little fellow. He murdered his wife with an ax and was hung by the neck until he was dead. He walks around this house at night now, looking for his murdered wife. I saw him once. He had long fingernails, more like the claws you would find on an eagle. His teeth were long and white and sharp. Some people claim he drinks blood, but only a certain type of blood. The blood of young girls who live on Yamacraw Island.'

'Oh Jesus!'

'Oh, Gawd, I leave this house now.'

'I'm just joking, gang,' I said. 'It's just a big joke. There's no such thing as a ghost.'

'You crazy. I see ghost on Yamacraw.'

'You ain't never seen a ghost befo'?' asked Cindy Lou.

'No,' I answered. 'That's because there's no such

270

thing as ghosts. They do not exist. There is no such thing. Never was and never will be.'

'If you ain't never seen no ghost, how do you know there ain't no ghosts around?' Cindy Lou asked.

'Do you believe a dwarf ghost lives in this house?' I asked.

'Yeh,' they agreed.

'Do you know where he lives?' I asked macabrely. They shook their heads negatively. 'In your bedroom,' I uttered with the voice of a gravedigger.

They screamed, ran about like beheaded poultry, then huddled on the couch.

I was still not taking their phobia seriously and was trying to think of a way to eliminate this nonsense once and for all. I did not realize that I was not dealing with nonsense but with a culture, a history, and something very kin to religion. I was determined to laugh them out of their belief in the other-worldly. To do this I chose to perform a very improper, very insensitive, but very typical Conroy drama.

'I am going into your room right now to see if I can find the dwarf ghost. I am going to prove that he does not exist and that no ghosts exist in this house. I will not turn on any lights but will go in alone in the dark,' I said, going into the hallway that led to the haunted bedroom. I closed the bedroom door and remained absolutely quiet. The girls grew fidgety as the minutes passed by. Finally they started calling my name and pleading with me to come out. I remained silent. They became more agitated and the entire group gathered in the darkness of the hall, huddling together, half-smiling, half-whimpering. When they got near the door, I crashed through it and fell to the rug like a dead man. I lay on the floor moaning that the dwarf ghost had done me wrong by sucking on my jugular vein. Of course, by then I was talking to myself, for the group had shot through the doors, screaming and yelling for Barbara.

Mary was half-delirious with terror. The others were hiding their heads under pillows by the couch or cowering behind living room chairs. It took several hours to restore equilibrium to the scene. I had not only traumatized the four girls, but Jessica, my three-year-old daughter, had also been in the hall when my limp body had plummeted to the floor. She was hysterical and would not let me within three feet of her. As Barbara, who had rushed into the living room as soon as she heard the Armageddon erupt, shot me disapproving glances, I tried to explain how I was simply attempting to dispel this superstitious belief in ghosts. Nowhere in the frantic, fear-ravaged room could I find a sympathetic eye.

This was the first time that I realized how seriously the kids took the supernatural. During the planning sessions for the Halloween trip, we talked about ghosts, witches, and warlocks, but had done so in a lighthearted vein. We had also talked about these things in daylight. The Valentine's Day experience told me that the mythology of my childhood was the frightening reality for Yamacraw children and that they were actually spirit-haunted and aware of silent demons lurking on deserted trails and behind fallen trees. We would talk about these beliefs in class. A bit wiser after the dwarf-ghost fiasco, I listened to the children recite

272

story after story of ghosts who walked the island by night. Nor did I try to ridicule the stories or make the children renounce their fears as superstitions. It would be like trying to convince a religious child that he worshiped a myth instead of god.

Everyone had seen a ghost or knew someone who had.

The ghosts were often the spirits of people who had recently died on the island. A spirit would roam the island for three to six months after its body was buried. Then the spirit would tire of wandering and return to the grave. Mary told of her cousin who had seen a ghost.

'He walk down road in dark. He alone when he walk by fence at Cooper River end. He look in front of him and see a man walk through the fence to him. The ghost have his head in his hands and it walk straight through the fence. My cousin be so scare. He scream but the ghost keep comin' at him. The head make awful noise like dead man in the ghost's hand. Cousin run all the way to his house. He scream so much. Then he git sick. Stay sick for days and almost die.'

Then Saul told of a ghost his mother had seen on the road to the club. 'She be walkin' to the club. She look over at some tree. She see sumpin' move a bit. Then she see a ghost. Jes' the ghost's legs though. Nuttin' else but two legs. Legs start walkin' to my mama. She scream and run. Legs come to get her, but she run too fast.'

'Did she ever find out whose legs they were, Saul?' I asked.

'Legs of a dead man,' he answered with authority.

'Then I'd have run like hell too.'

273

Top Cat lowered his voice to relate his story of the underworld. 'I be out one night walkin'. I so scare. It dark and I able to see nuttin'. I hurry fast to git home 'cause I know there be ghosts around. Then I see it. Ghost come fast ridin' on a horse. It Adam. Man what been drowned a couple days befo'. He ride fast and I be scare. I fall down and wait for him to be past. He go by and not stop for nuttin'. He ride until he be gone. I run home so fast.'

Everyone in the room had felt the presence of the supernatural and every child believed implicitly in the presence of ghosts. No one doubted a single story and all listened with an intensity and fascination difficult to describe. Ghosts without heads, without bodies, without hands, without feet; ghosts dressed in white, black, or naked; ghosts of all sizes and descriptions; ghosts who floated, who walked, who ran, who rode cows or horses. Frank had once felt a ghost sitting beside him on a wagon. His horse had stopped suddenly and refused to go farther. He looked to his left and the ghost was seated beside him—a strange, eerie figure who remained rigid and silent even when Frank yelled. The horse was frozen with fear and stood motionless in his tracks. Frank very prudently fled.

When the kids finished telling about the ghosts who dwelt on the island, I tried to tell about the dwarf ghost who lived in my house but was hooted down.

*   *   *

In March there was a death on the island. Like most deaths on Yamacraw, it came with unforeshadowed swiftness; there was no lingering or gradual wasting away or bedside farewells. A heart attack felled Blossom Smith on a Saturday, an islander raced to Ted Stone's house, Stone immediately radioed for a rescue helicopter from Savannah. Blossom was carried to an open field near the nightclub, where half the island gathered around her wailing and praying. The helicopter appeared, landed rapidly and efficiently, received the motionless Blossom into the dark angel with the rotating wings, lifted into the sky in a maelstrom of debris and air, then disappeared over the top of the trees. It was all very quick, very impressive, and very futile. Blossom died that night in Savannah surrounded by strangers and the ammonia smells of a death ward.

Death meant the cessation of all activity on the island and, though school was in session, no children appeared at the door on the day of the funeral. Though it was a time of intense emotional sorrow, a funeral was also an important social event. Relatives in Savannah and Hilton Head hired an excursion boat to transport mourners to the island. The immediate family was fed and consoled. The old women of the island sat around and reminisced about their girlhood. They also wondered out loud who was going to be called to the Lord's bosom next.

Early Tuesday morning a contingent of island men went to the 'colored cemetery' to dig a grave. Two dapper undertakers accompanied the body from Savannah on the excursion boat. The whole proceeding exuded the air of a ritual performed so many times that everyone knew exactly what was expected and everyone had a part to play. As I

275

drove to the cemetery, I was taken aback by the number of mourners who had come to the island. The road leading to the cemetery was thick with well-dressed black people slowly walking toward the open hole that would serve as Blossom's final resting place.

Many of my students were already at the gravesite when I arrived. They looked faintly bewildered by the fuss and rising sadness. The procession of people continued unbroken through the woods. Most of them talked animatedly, laughed with mild restraint, and seemed to be enjoying the festival beneath the trees. Several relatives threw their arms around each other in greeting. But all grew rather silent as they neared the deep, rooted scar gouged out of the earth near a large, straight pine tree in the cemetery. Three saplings, freshly cut, lay perpendicular across the open grave. Beside the grave, her face powdered and rough in death, her body neatly dressed, her hands folded across her small bosom, her casket decorated with ludicrous frills, lay Blossom Smith.

Behind the big pine trees, a vast and greening marsh stretched for a mile before it paused for the river. Magnolia trees towered and presided over the ceremony. The cemetery was hauntingly beautiful. Yamacraw's lone deacon, a bespectacled man named William Brown, bowed his head reverently to begin the ceremony. 'Jesus took you from us. He took you to be with him.' His voice was plaintive, immensely evocative, and profoundly sad. His sermon was almost a cry, a lament from one who did not understand death, but who accepted it as a calling of man by his creator, a manifestation of a larger, unfathomable, mysterious, yet loving presence in the universe.

Then everyone present walked beside the open coffin and viewed Blossom for the last time. A chorus of older women sang a spiritual with voices of ancient, incomparable sorrow. The column moved slowly, laboriously, as each mourner paused to look deeply into the image of death. Some reached out and lightly touched Blossom's face. Others looked at her, then covered their eyes and wept. Some spoke to her aloud and bade farewell as though she would be gone for only a short time. Some became slightly hysterical and had to be comforted by a team of women who seemed to be present for that purpose. Some spoke the name of Jesus aloud. Some stared at Blossom, then joined the grieving chorus that rallied new voices with every breath.

Flowers abounded beside the casket, carefully tended by the two undertakers, who seemed to encourage the atmosphere of sorrow and hysteria by their dramatic presentation of each new part of the ceremony. Most of the flowers were plastic, a vivid example of a twentieth-century incursion of Yamacraw. Aunt Ruth's husband had been the island undertaker before his death. He had fashioned pine coffins in a shed near his house. He would have none of the tacky death chambers wrought by factories and peddled by the oily undertakers of Savannah. Death on the island was cleaner and less packaged when he was alive. The plastic flowers, with their senseless bid for immortality, added an ugliness to the ceremony hard to define.

As I mused upon the plastic flowers, an attractive black man darted from the viewing line, grabbed a

277

handful of plastic flowers from Blossom's stockpile, and walked swiftly to a grave fifty yards away. This caused an audible rumble from the crowd and for a few dramatic moments it looked as though a band of men were going to pursue the brash thief through the graveyard. Then the man with the flowers stopped abruptly and placed the flowers gingerly on the grave. 'That's his mama,' someone whispered. 'He still loves his mama and miss her so much.' Everyone was visibly moved by this show of filial devotion, except one man who uttered, 'Why don't that boy buy his own flowers?'

After every single person filed by the open casket and responded appropriately to the sight of Blossom's lifeless body, an old lady stepped out of the crowd holding a small girl not more than three years old. To my utter disbelief, the woman very slowly passed the girl over the casket into the arms of a waiting man. The little girl looked down and saw Blossom's dead face and became hysterical. Three times the girl was passed over Blossom's body, and her screaming grew louder each time. I was horrified but did not feel that it would be enthusiastically applauded if I rushed in and rescued the girl. I seemed to be the only one upset by this ritual. I learned later that the little girl was Blossom's granddaughter, who had lived with Blossom before she died. To protect the girl from Blossom's spirit returning from the grave to haunt her, the girl had to be passed over Blossom's body three times. Thus freed, the girl disappeared into the crowd still screaming.

A little while later, the singing having subsided and the weeping having become softer, the two undertakers gave a signal to the six men who acted as pallbearers. The six men lifted the casket and placed it on the saplings that lay across the grave. They then looped ropes around the casket and lifted it slightly into the air. Several other men slid the saplings out of the way. The casket was then lowered into the hole. Four men started shoveling dirt. At this time there was a stirring among the crowd. A palmetto tree near the marsh was rattling and shaking as though a powerful wind was blowing through it. Only there was no wind blowing and no other trees around it were affected. A few women screamed and the entire crowd shrank back to size up the significance of the event. I tried to scientifically explain what I was witnessing and found no ready or easy explanation. The palmetto then grew still again, and I heard someone behind me say, as in a prayer, 'That's Blossom tellin' us she still around.'

★   ★   ★

When Conrad, Gordon, and Bean blasted off from Cape Kennedy, amidst the swirl of thoughts that passed swiftly through their minds, the hundreds of fragmental recollections that flashed before them at the instant of takeoff, the one that never occurred to them was that eighteen children and one teacher on Yamacraw Island shouted the last ten digits of the countdown and cheered as the rocket lifted off the launch pad on the first step of the journey to the moon. After we cheered, Mrs. Brown popped her large head in the doorway and informed me that the state government was paying me good money to teach the children from the textbook.

'We are required by law to finish the textbook,

Mr. Conroy. Required by law. If we don't do it, no tellin' if we get paid or not at the end of the year.'

'Yes, ma'am, I am just getting ready to rip through the textbook. All you punks haul out your textbooks,' I shouted.

The kids dutifully reached into their desks, knocked the layers of dust off these neglected tomes, and spread them officially on their desks. This seemed to satisfy Mrs. Brown, and she retreated back to her side of the cave.

'Now take those dusty books, those worthless pieces of garbage, and put them back in your desks.' I had yet to find a single textbook that I felt could be utilized in the class. All of them were too difficult or too irrelevant to force on students already killed by a system that demanded certain progress through textbooks. To keep Mrs. Brown off my back, though, I would go to extensive trouble.

'Now my dear Yamacrawans, we have three brave men going to the moon to walk around looking for big rocks. Conrad, Gordon, and Bean are their names.'

'They not gone to moon,' Frank told me.

'Of course they are. We just heard them blast off.'

'They ain't goin',' Oscar agreed with Frank.

'Didn't you guys watch Armstrong and Collins on the moon this summer?'

'Yeah.' They all nodded their heads.

'Didn't you see the pictures of the moon on television?'

'Yeah,' they agreed again.

'Well, then you know people have been to the moon.'

'No,' Lincoln said. 'They ain't goin' to the moon. They burn up if they go to the moon.'

'That's the sun you're talking about. The moon isn't hot,' I said.

'They still ain't goin' to the moon,' Ethel said.

'Why do you think that?' I asked.

'They just ain't,' Ethel said.

'They flyin' off somewhere, messin' around, then comin' back and tell people they have done been to the moon,' explained Big C.

'Gang, as your teacher, as the person responsible for stuffing knowledge into your porous little brains, I am ordering you to believe that those men are going to the moon.'

'No, Conrack,' said Sidney.

'Men just foolin',' added his twin, Samuel.

'Moon too far, Mr. Conroy.'

'Moon too hot.'

'Moon too cold, girl. Not hot.'

'Shut yo' mout'. I say moon hot.'

'Moon got man,' Prophet said.

'The man in the moon, Prophet?' I asked.

'See 'um at night,' Prophet went on.

'There are really going to be some men on the moon tomorrow night.'

'Oh, Conrack,' Cindy Lou said, 'you believe anythin' on radio. They ain't goin' nowheres.'

'Why, Cindy?'

'Just ain't. Don't ask me no questions no mo'.'

CHAPTER TEN

Somehow my days on the island seemed numbered and I grew restless and impatient with the sluggish pace of learning in the classroom. I wanted the twins to become brilliant readers and writers and my stomach knotted each time I heard them stuttering and wrestling with the incomprehensible mysteries of one-syllable words. I wanted Richard to leap and bound ahead of his peers in other schools in other places, wanted him to devour books, write witty letters to congressmen, speak to rotary clubs, and shine like a fallen star on his abandoned, lovely island. I wanted to remove the tongues from Prophet and Fred, replace them with silver and brass, and assure them that they never would have to cower before strangers again, that their speech would never humiliate or embarrass them again. I wanted to give Saul the gift of height and Lincoln the gift of slimness. I wanted Mary to be aware and proud of her aloof, unspoken beauty and Anna to somehow fathom the wonder of her smile.

I have read a number of books by teachers who had brilliant success by using certain methods. I would stumble upon an idea in the morning that seemed surpassingly clever and relevant, then find it foolish and absurd by afternoon. Or what appeared ordained by the gods in the autumn seemed commonplace and senseless by spring. What fired the imagination of my students one week bored and stultified them the next. So there was constant shifting in emphasis, approach, and material. The one great knave that I hunted was boredom, and if I caught him lurking anywhere in the room, in corners, by blackboards, behind the covers of books, or in glazed, anesthetized eyes, we went to something else quickly, shifted in midstream, danced, sang, fought, or milked rats. But always we spoke of the world beyond the river. The cities with their stables of cars, their flow of people, their massive stores, their baseball teams, and their hidden dangers. The kids would ask questions ('Tell us 'bout New York?') and I would tell of my first trip to the City of Stone and they would tell me of letters from cousins, of the hard living, big drinking, music-loving city where the lucky relatives had migrated. Always we turned outward to where they would drift when they left Yamacraw, to the world of lights and easy people, to the dark cities that would devour their innocence and harden their dreams.

The one goal I developed the first week that never changed was to prepare the kids for the day when they would leave the island for the other side. Their experience in driving oxen, cleaning fish, and catching crabs could not be classified as excellent preparation for the streets of large cities. Anything that I could construe as relevant to the day when they would leave the island had a place in the classroom. Thus Jimmy Sue could look through the Sears Roebuck catalogue without encountering too much lip from her teacher. And Saul could practice tapping his desk with two pencils because he dreamed of playing drums in a jazz band. Yet I worried that I did things more by instinct than by logic and would be hard-pressed to explain why I let the twins mold clay when their literacy was

283

questionable, except that they seemed to enjoy it.

During the winter these thoughts flowed about the classroom like uninvited birds. We were prisoners during the cold months, for the parents would not entrust their children to any man to cross the waters in the bad season. So we created a world in the classroom, chained to seats and the same walls, looking out the window at the same trees, waiting for the time to move and travel again. In discussions I found that the kids liked the idea of leaving the island for other places among other people. I promised them that we would hit the road again when the weather warmed. It was during the introspective, wood-burning days of winter, when a kind of malcontented lethargy gripped us, that I found the letter that would provide the means to the grandest, most improbable voyage of all.

The letter was from a lady in Falls Church, Virginia, named Judy Hanst. It was a year old and was addressed to Mrs. Brown. The letter lay fallow on the bottom of a Himalayan stack of catalogues and debris that Mrs. Brown had thrust upon me during my interregnum as principal. Mrs. Hanst had heard about the island during Senate subcommittee meetings on hunger in America. She was moved to write a letter to Mrs. Brown and offer to help her in any way she could, with books or supplies, money or food. The letter reflected a sincere author. She said she had friends who would help financially and spiritually. The letter was a passport, a ticket, a commitment of the soul. Something about the phrasing of the letter convinced me that the unseen, unsung, and unanswered Judy Hanst would not have forgotten the island and still would want to help. Looking up from my desk, I said, 'Gang, listen up. A hot-dog announcement: we are going to Washington, D.C.'

I immediately wrote a long letter to Mrs. Hanst explaining how her letter had been unearthed from the elephant burial ground in my desk and how excited I was that someone near Washington had offered help. Then I splashed a few adjectives about the page describing the isolation and deprivation of the children, how they needed to have their horizons expanded, and how we would just love to hike our young arses to Washington. I designed my letter carefully, assuring myself that it was plaintive and rueful enough to pluck the heartstrings of every human residing on both sides of the Potomac. This was not necessary, for this magnificent discovery, Judy Hanst, sanctified herself in my eyes even further by replying a week later that she and her friends would be delighted to sponsor a trip.

Mrs. Brown, whose primary job on the island seemed to be resident crapehanger, forbade all plans to leave the island for any reason. 'Those children have had their fun. Now it's time to work. Fun time is over. They need drill in readin', writin', and 'rithmetic. They don't need no Washington, D.C. The state department says we gotta get through the books. You aren't even usin' the books, Mr. Conroy. Not even usin' the books.'

'Yes, ma'am,' I answered, 'but I want you to know, Mrs. Brown, that I want to take the kids on this trip and will go higher if you insist on saying no.'

'No,' she quickly insisted.

The month of March was spent working out the innumerable details of the trip. Transportation was the most serious. Flying was out since I would have to flog the kids with a cattail and a bullwhip to get them into an airplane. A bus seemed like the most pragmatic form of transportation, but when I inquired about prices I was continually staggered by exorbitant figures. I eventually decided that automobile was the cheapest, most versatile, and most readily available form of transportation. The two new California boys, Frank Smith and John Richford, volunteered immediately to drive and chaperone. Father John Becker, a northern priest who had migrated south to labor in more temperate vineyards, offered me full use of a large station wagon. He also contributed $150 for the trip for gas, food, and incidental expenses. Barbara and I planned to pay for the trip insurance, which ran somewhere around $40. Barbara also informed me that she, Jessica, and Melissa were going to Washington if at all possible. It was about this time that Barbara told me that she was pregnant with an unknown creature, who would ultimately emerge as our third daughter, Megan. So her bargaining position was immeasurably strengthened.

In April I drove around the island visiting the parents, describing the wonders of Washington in vivid, glowing, purple prose, and asked them to sign their names or marks on a form I placed before them. Expecting a cakewalk after the unqualified success of the Halloween trip, I was a bit surprised when every parent I approached refused to sign anything. When I asked the kids why in the hell their parents were playing the same game they played before the Halloween trip, as if on cue all eyes lowered balefully and Lincoln said, 'We ain't gonna go to no Washing-ton.'

'The hell we ain't, my friends,' I answered.

So each day I would depart at noon to browbeat or beg the reluctant parents to allow their children to cross the water again. Carolina's father, Alvin Pinckney, wanted to talk more than argue. 'Well, Mr. Con-roy, I let my girl go 'cause she's a good girl. Kinda like her momma was. Good with them books. Eat them books up. Myself, I do some travelin'. I born in All-Benny Joe-gia. Ever hear of it? Spen' mos' part of my life away from Yamacraw. Come back when money git poor. When fish come summer I make good money. A couple fish now. Not many. No fish come. They come, I catch 'em. Go to Savannah to git stamps. You know, food stamps. All that tape. Red tape. Shit. Me payin' for the stamps and still got to run through shit. No mo'. Me and mine gonna tough it out. No mo' shit. About that trip. Sho' she can go. Ain't got no money to give 'er. But she can go wit' you.'

Soon after this I had the signature and consent of every parent except Cindy Lou's mother and the obstinate earth mother, Edna Graves. Edna was critical since her approval or disapproval controlled the destiny of Frank, Big C, and the twins. All of them dwelt under her roof and her word was law the moment it spilled from her lips. Cindy Lou's mother was eight months pregnant and had taken up residence in Savannah to await the coming of her child. Since Aunt Ruth, the midwife, was forced to retire, the black women had to emigrate to the city to deliver their infants. Cindy Lou mournfully told me that she was 'sittin'' for her brothers and sisters until her mother returned. When I asked if her grandmother could take over for a week, Cindy just said she didn't know.

Cindy's grandmother was a squat, whimsical old

287

woman who offered me a beer soon after I sat down in her kitchen. I accepted. As I sipped it she asked, 'How's Calyfornya?'

'Pardon me, ma'am?'

'How's Calyfornya doin'?'

'I am not a California boy. I teach Cindy.'

'Oh Gawd. You the white teacher. Oh Gawd, give me that beer.'

'Why? I want to drink it.'

'You the white teacher. I thought you one of the boys.' Then she paused. 'You gonna drink it?'

'Yep.'

'Teachers drink?'

'Yep.'

'That's good. Oh Gawd, that's so good. I got some gin in that there paper bag when you finish.'

Mrs. Barnwell and I became instant friends. She agreed to babysit for Cindy Lou's brothers and sisters, and to intercede with Cindy's mother for me. She said I might have to take a trip to Savannah to reassure Cindy's mother (which I did), but she was sure that everything could be worked out. 'That chile needs to be in that Washington,' she added.

Edna Graves was much more formidable and contrary. Her wolf pack treed me for the second time when I entered her domain and, as she swept the dogs out of the way with vicious blows from a scraggly broom, she shouted, 'You might as well head on down that same road you come up 'cause I ain't lettin' none of my children go. Ain't none of 'em goin' to no Washington. You hear me, mahn. You hear Edna talkin'. Once is once too many time and they done be off this island for Halloween and they ain't goin' no hunnert mile to no Washington.

288

Those are my grands and ain't nobody takin' them cross no river to go a hunnert mile up the road.'

Nimbly keeping away from the multifanged pack, I egg-shelled my way into Edna's kitchen. Her finger wagged at me like an old and oft-remembered friend. She towered over me and her voice grew louder and more volcanic the longer she spoke. 'Gawd, these chillun pester me all day sayin', "Cain't we go to Washing-ton, cain't we go with Mr. Con-roy on a trip up the road?" And I say, "Hell no, ain't nobody goin' nowhere wit' nobody." You hear Edna talkin'. You hear what I say.' By this time she was veritably screaming.

'I can't hear you, Edna,' I whispered.

'Ha-ha-ha,' she thundered. 'Ha-ha-ha.' Then she paused and said, according to her standard formula, 'Gawd, you is a good-lookin' teacher. A good-lookin' white teacher.'

'Jesus, Edna. Not this stuff again. You told me you wouldn't start that anymore.'

'Yes, you is a fine-lookin' man. A fine-lookin' teacher.' She grinned, her eyes twinkling devilishly.

'When I was in college, Edna, someone once told me that I had a nose like a pig's.'

'No,' she cried, 'you got a boo-tiful nose. Gawd, a pig nose look so bad.'

'He said my nose looked exactly like a pig's nose.'

'That man crazy. If I see that man I tell him he crazy.'

'Can the kids go to Washington, Edna?' I asked abruptly.

'Ha-ha-ha. Hell, no. I tell you straight. I ain't gonna let 'em go cause I don't wanna lose my grands. Gawd, if anything happen to Frank. Oh Gawd, I don't know what I do. He's my boy, you

289

know. I have him since he was a tiny baby. He's my boy. Anything happen to Frank, you know I might have to use Betsy on you. Gawd, I don't want to use no Betsy on a nice-lookin' teacher like you.'

'I got a nose like a pig.'

'No, Gawd. Now let me talk. Edna feels like talkin' and I want you to hear what Edna say. The trip on Halloween was nice. So nice and my chillun talk about it so much. They need to see things. You take 'em off the island to places I ain't never seen. So I might let them go.'

'That's great, Edna. I promise nothing will happen to the kids.'

'Nuttin' better happen to my grands. 'Cause I still got Betsy when you gets back.'

'You are a magnificent creature, Edna. A queen. A saint.'

'Oh Gawd.'

When Edna relented, the last major bulwark of opposition or doubt among the parents tumbled to the ground. Once the decision was reached the parents shared in the general excitement of the children's crusade to the nation's capital. Now, with the trivial details of finances and travel arranged, with the full and supporting consent of the parents, the most difficult and vital hurdle stretched across Henry Piedmont's door.

'Why, Pat, it's a pleasure to see you. I swear it's a pleasure,' said Dr. Piedmont, as I entered his office. 'To what do I owe this privilege of your visit? I've been meanin' to get out to the island to pay y'all a visit, but HEW keeps me so tied up I'm lucky to be able to go home at night. How's everything goin'?'

I then explained very quickly why I had come to

290

waste his priceless time, that Mrs. Brown refused to authorize the trip, that the trip was being paid for by private resources, that the children would benefit from this trip a hundredfold, and that God and man considered it peremptory that he grant his approval. He leaned back in his leather chair, placed one hand on his massive, brown desk, and said, 'Pat Conroy, you are the spittin' image of Henry Piedmont years ago. Young, brash, idealistic, always trying to help people out. I look at you and see myself and think of young Henry Piedmont wantin' to do good in the world with the help of Jesus.'

Oh God, I thought, here comes the second variation on the sacrosancy theme of Henry Piedmont. From my first meeting with him I knew there would be a comparison of him and me, followed by a biography of his days of suffering and self-denial in his mill town, and finally a rousing testimony of faith in Jesus. A few sentences or paragraphs later he said, 'After I served my country proudly in the United States Army, I went back to my hometown to help poor kids like myself who just didn't have a prayer. I taught just like you're doin' now, Pat. Only I taught mill kids where you're teachin' colored children. I was a mill kid myself. These colored people think they know prejudice. I knew prejudice, too. I was called lint head. And being called lint head is just as bad as being called nigger, believe me.'

After retracing his career as a company boss, teacher administrator, and finally, the holy of holies, a doctorate from Columbia University, he croaked the secret of his success to me for a second time. 'I don't know how you feel about religion.

291

But I can tell you that faith in the Lord has put me where I am. He has guided me along the way. He has brought me success and more money than I ever dreamed of making. His hand has led me down the path He chooses. I just fall to my knees each night and ask His guidance.'

Like some purifying ritual, he repeated his life story to me, the Protestant ethic, the unassailable formula of the American dream, Horatio Alger in the cotton mills, Henry Piedmont, child of poverty, man of paramount success, a golfing buddy of Jesus, had given me the green light to go to Washington. But something else came out of that meeting. For some reason, I realized that I really liked Henry Piedmont.

*　　*　　*

The odyssey began just after dawn on the first Monday in May. The kids were well primed for the journey. The previous two weeks had been a time of brochures, pictures, facts, history, art, and trivia about Washington, D.C. I had brought road maps to school and we traced our route north on Interstate 95, listed the towns we would pass, and charted the mileage. I told the kids about the first time I saw Washington during the magic, impressionable season of my tenth year, when I first reached the summit of a Virginia hill above the Pentagon and looked down to the Potomac River and the majestic city growing on her banks. 'When I was ten, gang, I didn't think anything could ever be so beautiful or fine,' I told them.

So it was early morning when we left Beaufort. During the trip I would see through the eyes of children who had seen little, and who had never ventured away from the smell of salt marshes and the sound of incoming tides. I do not need to describe in painstaking detail what we did in Washington. We made the endless treks to the proper monuments to pay homage to the proper Presidents. We gasped appropriately at the bones of dinosaurs, at the plaster-of-Paris blue whale, and at the unfortunate elephant set in perpetuity to welcome visitors to the Smithsonian Institution. The kids registered most of the proper responses, said the predictable things, and marveled at the incredible herds of bleating Fords and Chevies during the morning and afternoon cattle drive to and from the city. They liked the statue of Lincoln, because he 'freed the colored folk and did the Mancey Pation Decoration,' and they looked upon the Jefferson Memorial as a worthy thing because he, too, had issued some famous 'decoration.' At the art museum I marched them to a painting of a man being attacked by a great white shark. They dutifully followed me around trying to feign interest in exhibits that would strike my eye but bored them to extinction. They salivated heavily as we walked over the ramp at the U.S. Bureau of Engraving and Printing and gazed upon the acres of currency being churned out below us.

The museums and monuments were nice, but other things made the trip memorable and significant to the kids. My terrible instincts of wanting the kids to learn potfuls of knowledge, to absorb the entire culture of the city in a single week like dry sponges were ridiculous and generally ignored by the kids. Their pleasures were simple. Neither Barbara, nor Frank, nor John, nor I could keep the gang away from the souvenir vendors that flourished on every corner. 'Don't buy that crap, Saul,' I would shout, and the next moment Saul would appear bejeweled with peace medallions, Kennedy buttons, and rings with pictures of Lincoln and Martin Luther King, Jr. Cindy Lou soon sported enough junk jewelry to start a shop of her own. Before long, each child glistened with cheap baubles, three or four necklaces, plastic Washington Monuments, and Capitols of fake bronze. Beside the junk salesmen stood the peddlers of hot dogs and Popsicles hawking their wares and spotting easy prey in the wide-eyed Yamacraw contingent, who did not wish to insult anyone and therefore bought almost everything. After the first day of extravagant spending, the kids took inventory of their finances and discovered to their chagrin that the trinkets for which they had bartered so generously that day were priced like crown jewels.

The kids also really liked the neighborhood where Ken and Judy Hanst lived. It was a suburban neighborhood with manicured lawns and sloping hills, a neighborhood where ladies played bridge, frequented shopping centers, and had their hair done once a week. Judy was an attractive, shapely brunette who had convinced her neighbors to participate in housing the visitors from Yamacraw. The neighbors had responded enthusiastically. So the kids went in pairs to houses all along Judy's street. Throughout the week they played with the neighborhood children, spent the rest of their money buying candy and other trinkets at the large drugstore up the street, and rode bicycles for the first luxurious time in their lives down a paved hill.

'Oh, Gawd, I ride bike so fast down a hill. I sho' like ridin' on a hill,' they would say excitedly.

Meanwhile, all of us honored with the title of chaperones would answer the questions of Judy's neighbors, who seemingly were expecting a ragtag tribe of starving pickaninnies with loincloths and bones through their noses. 'These kids look well fed to me. I was led to believe these kids are poor,' one man said. 'Why are they so well dressed? I thought they were supposed to dress in rags,' a lady said. 'They won't carry on a conversation at dinnertime. They just look at us,' another lady said, very distressed. So we would try to explain to the distraught suburbanites that things were not always what they seemed, that the parents and relatives of these children spent a great deal of money so their children would not be 'shame' when they went to Washington, and that the children were often taciturn and remote with strangers. It was during this same week that I read about students in a Washington ghetto school who had never seen the Potomac River.

Yet the neighborhood responded with warmth and humanity to the kids. The ladies made lunches for our sightseeing expeditions and held cookouts in the evening. Most of the kids made a point of telling me that 'these sho' is fine people. They so nice, Mr. Conroy.'

On the final day, we took the kids to the zoo, where, as I expected, they went berserk. We had studied every picture of every animal we could find in encyclopedias, books, and magazines. We had watched every film on wildlife I could lay my hand upon, but nothing could equal the drama of seeing the great cats, the animated bears, the pool of seals, the elephants, and reptiles alive and moving before their eyes.

'That monkey look just like ol' Conrack,' Cindy Lou squealed, as I walked up to the chimpanzee cage.

'That snake made out of rubber. Too big to be real. He just lay still 'cause he not real. Rubber snake. I tell you that right, boy. Oh, Gawd, snake move. He 'live,' Richard said, as he lurched back from the glass enclosing the boa constrictor. The zoo won all plaudits when compared to bloodless visits to all the notable monuments put together. Animals were alive, breathing, being fed, bellowing, roaring, and among the animals, no matter how exotic, the Yamacraw children felt at ease.

After the zoo we went to Great Falls. I wanted the kids to get the feel of a hill, the sensation of height in nature, and wanted them to know the joy of clambering among rocks and hearing water rushing through narrow gorges and leaping over impediments on the way to the sea. For two hours we climbed up hills and looked down at the water below. We maneuvered along cliffs which bordered the rapids, played silly games, took pictures, made plans to live in Washington, then headed back to Virginia in the full spring tide of afternoon traffic.

It is difficult to calculate the value of an experience. I never created a test to evaluate the trip, nor did the thought ever occur to me. On the way to Washington, it struck me that the trip was a good thing in itself and needed no defense. Barbara and I were riding in the front seat of the station wagon, not far outside of Beaufort, when Jasper leaned up and asked me, 'What those ol' lines for?'

'What ol' lines?' I asked.

'Those ol' lines all over the road.'

I still didn't know what he was talking about. 'I don't see any lines on the road, Jasper.'

'Yeh, they all over on the road,' he answered.

Then Barbara said, 'You mean the lines that divide the highway, Jasper. They tell the driver which side of the road to stay on. The yellow lines tell the driver if he can pass another car or not.'

'Oh,' said Jasper.

I sat there trying to comprehend what had just happened. I had seen the lines so often that they had disappeared from sight and were no longer part of my consciousness. To Jasper, who was accustomed to unpaved roads, they represented something strange, unexplained, and beyond his framework of experience. For the rest of the trip Barbara and I decoded road signs, billboards, and numbers painted on bridges and overpasses. Things I had not noticed for ten years now assumed great significance. I regretted that I could not be making this trip with the freshness of insight and beautiful innocence of Jasper and the others. I regretted that I was old, that I could no longer appreciate the education afforded by an American highway, and that I could not grasp the mystery of a single line painted down a road going north.

CHAPTER ELEVEN

Graduation was on a lovely June morning before the sun removed the dew from the ground. The two male graduates, Frank and Top Cat, had bought flashy dark blue suits for the occasion. The girls, Mary and Jimmy Sue, were dressed in the traditional white. The parents trudged up the dirt road to the school. Everyone was dressed in their 'Sunday-go-to-meetin's,' as one of the mothers said.

The graduation was held under the oak trees in the schoolyard. A ceremonial white picket fence was pulled from the hall closet by Mrs. Brown and placed in front of the speaker's podium, where the graduates would deliver their farewell addresses. The guest speaker of the day was the ubiquitous Ezra Bennington, whom Mrs. Brown introduced as 'the best friend Yamacraw ever had.' Ezra delivered his speech in his slow, avuncular manner.

'I think Yamacraw is as fine as any school in the county, despite what some people say. We've got problems here, but we've got problems in all the schools.' He then related several stories that reflected his concern over the island and its children. 'When I was in charge of this district, there was one year, around Christmas time, when all the schools were going to have turkey for the last meal before the holidays. All except Yamacraw, of course. It seems the luncheon supervisor had decided it was too much trouble to send a turkey over to the island. So I went to the freezer and got two big turkeys out and sent them over to the children. Some people might call that stealing, but I felt that what was good enough for the mainland was good enough for Yamacraw.' Ezra was smooth as good bourbon, the consummate politician who could talk honey as well as he could act vinegar. He did not realize what the people who listened to his speech were thinking.

I had taken up a small collection among the kids

298

who wanted to contribute to buy Zeke Skimberry a gift. I walked up to the podium after Bennington's speech and said I wanted to present a gift to the man who had done more to help me than anyone else this year. Then I called Zeke up and presented him a copy of *The Family of Man* signed by all of my students. Zeke got choked up. His blue eyes glistened as he accepted the book. He then gave a small speech. 'I just want to say thanks for this wonderful gift and that I've worked on this island for a long time and have got to know the people and they have got to know me. I think the people of this island are some of the finest people in the world. This year I've gotten to know the children in Pat's class real well and I've learned to love them. I love all kids. I just want to say if any of you ever need me in Bluffton, for anything—for anything at all—just come to my house and I'll be glad to help you. This gift means a lot to me. An awful lot.' It was the speech of the day.

On Monday after graduation seven of the kids took the island boat to Bluffton. Barbara and I met them there and drove them to camp at St. Mary's. Father Becker, the northern priest who had contributed to the Washington trip, had given me full use of the camp and swimming pool for one week. In this week I hoped to accomplish another dream. I wanted to teach the kids how to swim. It had astounded me that the people who lived on the island, exposed constantly to the perils of storm and rough sea, did not know how to swim. None of the kids in my room knew how to swim and their fear of the water was so pronounced that I felt gratified when I was able to talk seven of them into accompanying me to the camp. I could not find a place on the island to serve as a place for swimming instruction, since the kids refused to enter the ocean because of the currents and the fresh water because of the water moccasins and alligators. I wanted them to learn how to swim and swim well. Throughout the year while talking with the adults, I had heard the islanders recite litanies of their friends and relatives who had fallen into the water and sunk like stone. The bodies would generally resurface later bloated and discolored, salt water pouring from the ears, nostrils, and mouth. One source of drowning was the 'snowbirds.'

Anyone familiar with the inland waterway that runs along the East Coast of the United States knows of the great white yachts, driven by the captains of industry and their wrinkled ladies, that point their bows southward toward Miami when the first breath of winter is manifested on Fifth Avenue. The shrimpers around Bluffton and Hilton Head call these boats the snowbirds, for like the migrating fowl from northern skies, those boats, too, seek refuge from the bitterness of the cold. The people of Yamacraw Island fear these boats with good reason. Several times in the history of the island, a snowbird has passed an islander crabbing or fishing in the river, failed to cut its engine to a lesser speed, and capsized the bateau with a huge and dangerous wake. The result is nearly always the same: an islander is dead. The captain of the snowbird does not see the bateau overturned, for he is looking to the next channel marker and does not witness the drowning of the sometime crabber behind him.

So the snowbirds, if nothing else, made it important that I try to teach my students to swim.

There was another reason. It also occurred to me that the people of Yamacraw spent an inordinate amount of time on docks fishing, socializing, and waiting for boats. Falling off a dock is not the most uncommon accident on riverfronts nor the most serious. But it is fatal to the nonswimmer. I learned from Edna Graves that she had lost a close relative the previous summer in this manner. He had gotten drunk in Savannah, fallen off a dock while trying to board a boat, and was fished out three hours later—which brought me back to the original premise that people who lived near the sea should not have to perish in the sea.

Of course Barbara and I soon discovered that simply because we had succeeded in getting seven kids to come to the camp was no guarantee that seven kids would enter the water. The three boys who came, Lincoln, Frank, and Top Cat, entered the water quickly, if not eagerly. They splashed about the shallow end of the pool an arm's length from the edge, nervously daring each other to go deeper. The four girls lingered beside the fence surrounding the pool, chattering like parakeets, shrieking wildly whenever I implored them to come near the pool.

'I ain't comin' near that ol' pool,' Mary screamed. 'Git away from me, Mr. C'roy. Git away now. I ain't playin'. I ain't gonna drown. Don't you play no games with me.'

The upshot of the whole scene was that the girls never overcame their fear of the water during the entire week, nor could I coax them into even the most basic discussion of swimming. They would have none of it. Barbara talked to them and other people who came to the camp to help talked,

301

cajoled, and pleaded with them to moisten a toe or two in the water. All to no avail. Toward the end of the week they would sit by the edge of the pool when no one was around, cool their feet, put their hair up in curlers, and listen to soul music. I would lecture to them about the critical necessity for at least mastering the art of dog paddling.

'Man, you girls are going to fall into that water around the island and sink like bricks. Mary, you will go straight down swallowing about eighty gallons of water before you hit bottom. You are gonna swell up like a toad, float back up all blue and purple, and they are going to stick you in the ground.' Even with this macabre vision I could not convince Mary that swimming was for her. She and the others had developed a phobia about water so strong that it would take several weeks just to get them to enter the pool. All of them had attended funerals of relatives killed by falling into the same medium that I wanted them to enter voluntarily. They would have none of it.

The three boys came to the camp wanting to learn to swim. They fished the island waters during the summer, lifted crab-pots into the tiny bateaux, and played around the docks or on the beach all day. They saw the need for swimming and understood that it could conceivably save their lives. They entered the water hesitantly, but it did not take long for them to put their heads under the water, dive off the side of the pool head first, and after the third day, to dog paddle formlessly and desperately across the breadth of the pool. By the end of the week I could take them into deep water and let them swim to the safety of the shallow end. On Friday they bragged to the girls about their miraculous, Christlike powers to stay above the water. Though they could hardly endure a twenty-yard test, they were convinced that they could swim and referred to themselves as 'the three man swimmers.'

During the week we played softball, hide and seek, freeze tag, and went crabbing. The kids loved their crabmeat savagely peppered and stoked with hot sauce. On Wednesday afternoon I took all of them into Beaufort to hear my good friend Tim Belk play the piano. Tim was a teacher at the university extension in town, a distant relative of the Belk department-store clan, and a very fine pianist. I had wanted him to come to the school during the year to give a concert for the whole island, but Tim suggested that it would be easier to raise the dead than to transport a piano to the island.

So after failing to bring Tim to the island, I was very pleased to bring some of the kids to Tim's house in Beaufort. Tim was a master of style and I was glad the kids could see him in his own domain, against the dark woodwork and faint whiff of southern decadence he loved to cultivate and discuss. He had peanuts in bowls and cheese and crackers set out for the kids to eat. I had given him a list of the 'great works' that we had played during the year. I asked the gang to see if they recognized any of the songs Tim played. As soon as I said this, Tim suddenly and with the timing of an experienced ham, let loose with Beethoven's Fifth Symphony. Naturally, Lincoln, Top Cat, and Frank nearly catapulted off the couch, over the peanuts and cheese and onto Tim's keys to shout, 'Bay Toven the Fifth!' Soon Tim's fingers moved

303

again; his audience shouted and screamed the names of the identified pieces.

After exhausting the list they knew, Tim gave a brief, impromptu concert. He would first introduce the composer with a brief biography, tell something about the music, then play something from his works. Tim had an incredible ability to tailor his performance to his audience. After a bit of classical music, he played songs from *Porgy and Bess*, rock and roll classics, and even a little soul. Then he rose majestically from the bench and sat each child down and taught him to pick out a song. Then, ever the cordial, impeccably mannered host, Tim winked at me, discoursed on Mozart, congratulated the kids on their knowledge of music, and passed the peanuts and cheese. It was a good afternoon. Mary told me later that she 'just loved ol' Timbelks!'

On Friday, just before we drove the kids to the boat, I received a phone call from Howard Sedgwick in Bluffton. 'Hello, Pat. This is the axman. Doctor Piedmont gave me the dirty job. He doesn't want you back on the island next year. He's not paying for your gas bills. He's also had a lot of complaints about you.'

'You mean I'm fired, Mr. Sedgwick?' I asked, a trifle stunned.

'Well, let's say you are expendable.'

'Thanks for the call,' I said. Then I told Barbara and the kids.

*　　　*　　　*

The next day I entered Piedmont's office on the run. We shook hands like two gunfighters about to draw back thirty paces at high noon. I wanted him to explain the phone call from the axman, what had prompted it, and why he had not called me himself. He stared at me with malevolent, falcon-yellow eyes burning behind his brown half-glasses. He made no effort to be civil, or his normal unctuous, ingratiating self. For some reason he had assumed the role of the terrible godhead of authority wronged or authority challenged. He crouched in his seat, bent and misshapen, staring at me with a contempt born over a long and trying year. His stare was calculated to wither me and Piedmont had risen to minuscule greatness by his uncanny ability to melt underlings or other prey with his rapacious glance. I sat in a chair across from him staring back. And in that single moment I realized something very important. Piedmont could not scare me. Nor could Bennington. Nor could the assembled board of education in all its measly glory. For in crossing the river twice daily I had come closer to more basic things. I had come to know the singular power of a river advancing toward the open sea and the power of tides regulating that advance. I had seen how fog could change the whole world into its own image. The river, the tides, and the fog were part of a great flow and a fitting together of harmonious parts.

Because I had seen this for the first time over the year, I could not be intimidated by guys who wore expensive shoes and flashy ties. Piedmont could fire me, bawl me out, abuse me, put it on my record that I was an incorrigible son of a bitch, make sure I never taught in South Carolina again, or cut off my teacher's pension. That was all he could do. His power was economic and emotional, not spiritual or supernatural. Compared to the river that flowed even as we stared sullenly at each other, Piedmont

305

was a nothing and so was I. Soon though, the great doctor commenced to handle an irritating labor problem.

'Pat, I've been informed that you have been late to class this year.'

'Who informed you, Doctor?'

'Let's just say I've been informed and leave it like that.'

'No, just tell me who informed you and we'll leave it like that.'

'Have you been late?'

'Yes sir. I was lost in the fog three times, late because of rain four times, and I walked to school from the dock for the last three weeks because Ted Stone took the use of the car away from me.'

'We simply can't have our teachers bein' late to school.'

'Why?' I asked.

'Because it's against the rules. In my school system I treat all teachers alike. All teachers keep the same rules. No exceptions. You've been tryin' to make an exception of yourself all year. You are no different than any other teacher in this school system,' he said, leaning forward across his desk to emphasize the point.

'You're wrong, Doc,' I answered, the blood rising like hot sap to my head. 'If you think teachin' on your little island is exactly the same as teachin' anywhere else in this county, you're crazy. That is so ridiculous that I can't even figure out a good answer for it. It just shows that you have been sitting in this office so long that you have forgotten what the world is like.'

'I know an awful lot about what goes on over at your schoolhouse. A lot more than you think I

306

know,' he said defensively.

'Sure. You get your information from Bennington, who gets his from letters from Mrs. Brown, his hired stool pigeon. Bennington whispers in your ear that I am an impudent punk who's going to make trouble. Bennington is the same guy who was in charge of that island for forty years, Doctor Piedmont. Forty stinking years he was the king of the dump. And he didn't do crap, but let those kids rot over there.'

'Mr Bennington worried himself sick over the Yamacraw School. He worried about those children as much as I have.'

'If you are so worried about the kids, Doctor Piedmont, why haven't you been over to the island?'

'I haven't had time. HEW has kept me so busy I have barely had time enough to go home at night.' (I badly wanted to ask him how he had had time to win the golf championship at his country club, but prudence held me back.) 'I've been meaning to get over to see the school and meet Mrs. Brown, but things keep coming up. Anyway, this is beside the point. You've been late to school. I've been receiving all kinds of complaints about your long hair and your appearance.'

'I do not have long hair.'

'Yes, you do.'

'You better be glad you live in South Carolina if you think this hair is long.'

'Young people don't realize how important personal appearance is. If you're neat and well groomed you can go anywhere and talk to anybody. People will listen to you and respect you.'

'Young people know that some real sons o'

307

bitches hide behind coats and ties.'

'This is all beside the point. You were late to school. You didn't work with the chain of command. You commuted against my orders. And you charged the gas to the county. We can't afford to pay for your personal transportation to and from school. That's not fair to the other teachers. What if they ask me about my payin' your gas bill to school? How could I look them in the eye?'

'I drive thirty miles to Bluffton, Doctor Piedmont. I pay for my gas until I hit water. Since I can't walk on water, and since I can't swim twenty miles, and since I teach on an island, I don't think it extraordinary that the county pay for my transportation. Especially since I had a meeting with Mr. Bennington and Mr. Sedgwick to discuss the gas bill and they authorized it.'

'They did?' he said a bit incredulously.

'Of course, they did. Remember the meeting in January you were supposed to attend—when you sent Bennington in your place? Well, I got extremely mad when they told me the county would not foot the bill and was ready to stomp out when they calmed me down and told me a place to buy cheaper gas—and to keep charging it to the county.'

'They told me they had settled the matter. They didn't say anything about approval of gas money.'

'That's the old chain of command for you. You don't think I'm stupid enough to go on using county funds after a principal and a deputy superintendent told me not to, do you? That was just a breakdown of communication between you guys. I should not be blamed for that.'

'It makes no difference. The county is not paying for your free ride to and from work every day. If you want to live on the island, that's fine, but we aren't footing your transportation bill any longer.'

'Then I'll go to the board.'

'Go to the board, then. I've got the most democratic school system in this country. If you are not satisfied with a decision of mine, then I invite you to appear before the board.'

We talked and argued for an hour that day and I have only recorded the essence of the conversation. We talked again of his youth in the mill town, his journey toward the doctorate, his belief in education, and his allegiance to Jesus and country. The meeting was full of strange cross-currents: the nostalgic Piedmont, the religious Piedmont, the authoritarian Piedmont, the paternal Piedmont, and the one I would come to know most intimately—the vengeful Piedmont. He once again asserted that I reminded him of the young Henry Piedmont, but he also made apparent his desire for me to leave Yamacraw Island for good. Bennington had talked to him, that much I could tell, and I strongly suspected that they wished to dine on my teaching career.

And so it came to pass that there was a board meeting to decide whether I would return to Yamacraw Island the following year. The meeting would be extremely important for both Piedmont and me. I wanted to return to the island desperately, but I also felt a substantial obligation to bring the board out of shadow into the clear light of day. I felt it should know and understand the real problems of the island without the benefit of Piedmont or Bennington's interpretation. Piedmont, on the other hand, smelled a rat in his system and wanted me exterminated as cleanly as

309

possible.

Bernie and I went over to Yamacraw to tell the people what had happened. I traveled from door to door and explained to each parent what the situation was and what I was trying to do about it. Their response was to initiate a petition to get me back to the island. Every black on the island signed the petition, although many of them had to enlist the help of friends to write their names. The petition was a rambling, disjointed diatribe, almost more of a condemnation of Mrs. Brown than a vehicle to retain me as teacher. In part it said,

Our children do want Mr. Pat Conroy to come back and teach the childrens. But Mrs. Brown don't do nothing for our childrens she believe in beating them and hollow at our childrens. But Mr. Conroy love both childrens white and color it doesn't make any different with him. If we lose Mr. Conroy the island will go down ... Mr. Conroy come to school in the rough whether sometime he fall overboard and come to school all wet up. But he still teach our childrens.

It was a very strange document filled with references to esoteric events that had occurred over the year. I could not guess the authorship until I came to the most telling line in the petition, which said, 'Mrs. Brown told my childrens that they are so skinny and when March wind come they better put rock in their clothes so the wind wouldn't pick them up.' Mary, still very sensitive about her height and weight, had never forgiven Mrs. Brown for making this unfeeling remark. Her anger burned and seethed across every page of this long, strangely

310

eloquent communication with the other world. Three of the mothers also made plans to attend the board meeting and present the petition to the board.

It was a hot, sticky night when the board convened to hear my arguments about the price of gas and education in America, but the board room was new and air-conditioned, with yellow carpets surging along the floors and bright colors flaming along the newly erected walls. On a borowed Ping-Pong table I placed thirty photographs of this island directly across from where the board members would sit. I wanted to suggest to them that the discussion tonight would concern a place without yellow carpets and pasteled walls. I wanted them to stare at a few rags, a few shacks, and a few skinny kids while they pondered the weighty decisions of the evening.

The board members came in singly and in pairs. They were mostly a lot of calories under gray suits, a lot of talk behind bright ties, and a lot of coarse laughter. Yet Beaufort had an eclectic and educated board. On it were a judge, a lawyer, a doctor, and a dentist. Two black women had been recently elected, but their votes meant little or nothing, since they were overwhelmingly outnumbered. A pretty lady from Hilton Head whose husband was an architect had been appointed to the board due to a vacancy in the last month. Overall, the board made a nice impression to the outsider: a lot of smiling, educated people serving their community in an enormously expensive building they had allocated money to build.

My friends flooded the board meeting that night. I had gathered them together for one grand assault in the board rooms. Board members, like all politicians, base their opinions on community response and support as much as any other factor. Neighbors control men and the way men act more than convictions do. Some of my friends were pillars of the community and others were barbs in the community's behind. My friends were a strange conglomerate of long-hairs, Marines, and the attractive wives of powerful husbands. My mother, who had just moved to Beaufort while Dad went to Vietnam, sat by Bernie and Barbara. My brothers and sisters took up half a row of chairs. My friends had come to pressure the board and the superintendent. For this is the way of small towns.

Piedmont controlled the board as effectively as an organ grinder controls a chimp. Minor differences of opinion might arise, but generally Piedmont's education dogma was law before he had even opened his mouth. As Piedmont drifted among his board members before the start of the meeting, I was mildly impressed by his unctuous, lubricating manner. His etiquette of power had been honed over the years and he floated atop the waters of his dominion like a grease bubble.

For an hour the board shuffled figures dexterously. Piedmont, peering through his half-glasses, quoted prices for new schools, additions to schools, and wall-to-wall carpeting. I rested in a chair toward the back of the room, listening with a mild nausea rising, a combination of fear and anger repressed too long. As Piedmont's voice droned over the crowd, I thought about the change in me since the beginning of the year. And the change had to do with the children of Yamacraw.

312

According to tradition I was supposed to speak in a quiet voice fresh with honey, shuffling, and humility. Piedmont had convinced me that an appearance before the board was a rare and unspeakably sacred privilege. In the hierarchy of schools, teachers are the most expendable of creatures, the fauna of classrooms who can be replaced as easily as light bulbs.

But I wanted to tell them about Yamacraw Island, the way it was and not as others saw it. I had spent a year hearing administrators telling people how cute the island was, how unusual and exotic it was, and ignoring the fact that it was a disgraceful depository of ignorance and a hundred years of neglect. The building was not bad, the materials were not bad, the food in the cafeteria was not bad, it was the single fact that the kids did not have a chance and no one seemed to care. I wanted to boot the board members in their asses and welcome them to the unhappy reality of the twentieth century. I wanted to stick their noses into the island sand and let them feel the hurt and sorrow of history. So despite my impulses for survival and despite my absolute knowledge that people do not like to be faced with the cold, ugly deathbed of truth, I abandoned myself to those passions that rumbled below the surface. On June 30, 1970, before mother, wife, and friends, Conrack let the bastards have it.

I started my speech by telling the board I had gotten a haircut for their edification and to insure that they would listen to what I had to say. In a voice rather creaky and unimpressive, I traced my background on the island very briefly. Then I told them:

313

'I am not here tonight for the love of the school board. I have been on the island and have seen the conditions there. You have been presiding over an educational desert. Children who grow up on that island don't have a prayer of receiving an adequate education. They grow up without hope. They leave the island without hope. They drift into the big cities of the East Coast and rot in some tenement slum—without hope. They are not taught to read, to write, to speak, or to be proud of themselves or their race. Their parents are not influential, literate, or vocal, so this educational system is perpetuated. If these parents were white and important, their school would be as fine as any school in the county. If their parents were white, the question of a gas bill and maintenance bill would never come up—even if I were driving a battleship to work. But the school is black. The people on the island are black. And, my God, the hopelessness of teaching in a black school, cut off from society by water, is an agony few people have experienced. Yamacraw requires sweeping reform of your thinking. It demands for a brief moment that you forget about money and budgets and balanced books. Forget about your building plans, ordering new volleyballs for the high school, and how many tractors to purchase next year. Think instead about children. People. Human beings. Feel for once that education is about people—not figures.'

I then recited the litany of ignorance I found the first week.

'Six children who could not recite the alphabet. Eighteen children who did not know the President. Eighteen children who did not know what country they lived in ...' I slammed twenty-three of these

314

strange facts down their throats, hoping they would gag and choke on the knowledge. My voice grew tremulous and enraged, and it suddenly felt as if I were shouting from within a box with madmen surrounding me, ignoring me, and taunting me with their silence. My lips trembled convulsively as my speech turned into a harangue and the great secret I had nursed in my soul thundered into the open room.

'If you are not disturbed by all this,' I said, 'then you should not be on the school board. Or perhaps you will be like one county administrator who told me, "Don't worry about the kids not being able to read. Lots of schools have that problem." Well, I worried about it and tried to do something about it.'

I then listed activities and trips the class had done. Once again I tried to crush them with a mountain of facts. I wanted to bury them under the weight of a single year. I ended the speech with a blustery declaration.

'And so we are here. I want to go back to Yamacraw next year. I cannot go if I have to assume transportation costs for the boat. The superintendent told me I was exactly like any other teacher in the county. That is nonsense. When I taught at Beaufort Hill School, I did not have to chop wood for the stove, haul seven hundred pounds of groceries, walk two miles to school, wash dishes during lunch time, spoon food into plates to help the cook, drive cows and pigs out of the schoolyard at recess time, send my students to the woods if the toilet broke, or fix soup when the cook was sick. Because of difficulties with the boat, I sometimes did not make it to school. But in the framework of an entire year, look around the county, talk to all of your teachers. Show me a better investment of county money—an investment that produced more significant human results—and I will quit.'

Piedmont had a look on his face as if the floor had caved in under him. The board members sat like old buddhas with their hands resting on ponderous pot bellies; their mouths agape with disbelief or incredulity. My friends peeked back at me to see if I was frothing at the mouth. It was a very funny scene.

Piedmont counterattacked. I had been recalcitrant, had not gone through the chain of command, had cheated the county out of gas money, had obtained the gas fraudulently, had lied, broken promises, and failed to live up to obligations and commitments. If he had been armed I am sure he would have leaped across the table and we would have grappled on the floor until either he or I had succumbed. His face was red and veins stuck out of his neck and head. Bennington was sitting near Piedmont and shot me a few vituperative glances that could have turned back the angel of death. And Piedmont continued to cast accusations my way, which I caught on the first hop, if I could, and fired back at him. Both our jaws were rigidly set and we argued out of a sense of survival more than anything else.

The three Yamacraw mothers stood up during the middle of this backbiting war and delivered very eloquent pleas for my return to the island. They also handed out copies of the petition to all the board members. Piedmont considered their talks mere intrusions in the meeting, having no bearing on the matter at hand. He grew impatient

316

as Mary's mother tried to explain about the island and how much she wanted for her children. He tried to ignore Edna's raised hand, but I could have told him that Edna's elongated, work-sculpted hand would be in the air all night if need be. When Edna wanted to talk, it took more than a board of education to silence her.

Then the audience jumped in. There were catcalls and hisses, groans and gasps of disbelief. The whole scene was unruly and angry. My mother yelled at Piedmont several times, much to my keen embarrassment. (Mothers have no sense of restraint when it comes to the honor of their children.) People shouted, 'How much is the gas bill?' and none of the administrators knew. 'It's too much,' Piedmont shouted in desperation. 'How much?' the voices shouted back.

Finally Piedmont called for an executive session. The crowd moved outside, where loudly and profanely they attacked the stolid immovability of a system run amuck. I shook hands with happy, sweating people who had blown off enough steam to energize three revivals. It was a street circus loosened upon that alley behind the education building. Everyone hugged the Yamacraw ladies, who declared they had never met such wonderful people in their lives. Later that night I called one of the black members of the school board. She told me that the board had voted to give me the gas money. I had won.

*   *   *

But the victory, if one could call it that, was ephemeral and elusive, a brief and strident shout

317

atop a mountain that was more noise than substance, more smoke than flames. Piedmont and I had locked horns in a furious encounter, separated by an insurmountable gap of thirty years. The victory strengthened my belief that a man could speak the truth to his elders, to the new scribes and pharisees, and not be crucified or vilified because of it. My faith in the democratic system was renewed by the puzzled, scowling cluster of men and women who composed the board of education.

But that was when I was young. I underestimated the dark part of mankind that is rarely seen in the light of day. I failed to reckon with the secret beasts that reside in the lightless forests of men's souls. The beasts were watching me at the first board meeting, and in the flush of victory I failed to hear the baying of those hounds in the unlighted thickets ahead. The great unpardonable sin I had committed was this: I had embarrassed the superintendent of schools. It was Homer who had written again and again about the dangerous folly of mortals challenging the gods. I fought with words and youthful ardor. But Piedmont fought with thunderbolts. And time was his greatest ally.

September came and the new school year began almost too quickly, before the sediment of bitterness over the summer board meeting had time to settle. I saw Piedmont once, very briefly, and he conveyed the warmth and glowing good humor of a tundra during our fifteen-minute conversation. Whenever Bennington spied me, his face contorted into a wrinkled mask, as though staring at me was equivalent to chewing on cow chips. It looked as though my punishment was going to be a cavernous silence from those who ruled the kingdom. This I interpreted not as a punishment but as a blessing. And I had much to do during the year and did not wish to waste it wrangling with two crotchety administrators nursing their wounds.

I had written Piedmont a letter saying that I only wanted to spend one more year teaching on the island. I did not elaborate the reasons for this in my letter to him. I felt the reasons were personal but sound. When Bernie and I went to the island over the summer, I heard many of the people express an idea that was very disturbing to me. They constantly derided Mrs. Brown and said that she was a bad teacher simply because she was a 'colored teacher.' When I tried to erase this thinking, the people would shake their heads and say, 'It true. All dese colored teachers no good for the chillun.' I had unwittingly created a new stereotype among the island people and it seemed insidiously pervasive among the parents. The great danger of this thought lay in the fact that I might be tempted to establish myself as an educational Ted Stone on the island. I would try to be well meaning and dedicated, but would reinforce the myth of white supremacy in all things. Therefore I wrote to Piedmont, offered my resignation for the following June, and offered to help find a replacement. I wanted to find a sharp, young black couple who would live on the island as part of the community and provide a sound image with which the kids and parents could identify.

But this lay in the distant future, and my brain teemed with ideas for the present. I wanted the final year to be a great carnival to the children filled with the magic and beauty of their own island. The year before I had concentrated too much on opening a

319

window to the outside world and had failed to illuminate and sanctify the island around them.

So in the first weeks of school we began a zoo in the classroom, scoured the forest for various types of flora and fauna, planted a garden that would eventually be a cooperative, and took a deliriously happy walk through the woods to the beach, where we gathered sea animals washed ashore and swam fully clothed in the afternoon surf. We made plans to raise pigs and chickens in an ambitious extension of our fledgling cooperative. We would draw, paint, laugh, and read like hell. The first few weeks of school passed joyously, as in a dream.

Mrs. Brown seemed more subdued. She was quieter, more brooding and reflective than she had been the year before. She seemed to have conditioned herself to a laissez-faire policy concerning me and my ill-disciplined class. And in the second week she disappeared without a trace or a single word of farewell. She was in class on a Friday morning, then, without a word, she got in her car and left school. She did not return to the island for ten days. She did not offer an explanation for this absence, nor did I demand one. Her absence had provoked the most stimulating week of teaching I had ever enjoyed.

And the kids were responding well to the presence of Jim and Vivian Strand. Jim and Vivian were VISTA volunteers who had been assigned to Yamacraw Island. They were both from Detroit, Michigan, and both of them got along with kids exceptionally well. Jim was a skilled guitarist who had once earned plaudits singing in the smoke-filled environs of coffee houses at the University of Michigan. I envisioned him being an afternoon troubadour in the school, telling the history of America and the black experience through songs, ballads, and spirituals. I could also see him putting the multiplication tables to music and giving guitar lessons to interested students.

Vivian was a sprightly, attractive Italian girl who had majored in special education at Michigan. This made her about ten times more qualified to teach the Yamacraw students than I was. She bubbled with ideas to help the twins read and Jasper add. In fact, their coming to the island instilled a hope that many of the children's problems could be solved by saturation of fresh ideas and faces.

I had also made plans for three long trips. The first would begin in the middle of October. Dale Hryharrow, a childhood friend, was attending Emory University in Atlanta. She had solicited room and board for the kids for a week from Emory professors. She had planned to enlist a noted instructor in survival swimming to teach the kids this pragmatic art in the early part of the morning. We had talked about the trip all summer and Dale had already made the preliminary arrangements by the middle of September.

In the spring Bernie and I had planned to take the kids to Boston. Bernie had left Beaufort and the principality in Port Royal in order to obtain an advanced and blue-blooded degree from the holy of holies, Harvard University. He phoned several times during his first week in Cambridge to tell me he thought we could get a federal grant for a trip to Boston. He even thought we could combine it with a visit to New York, if I could convince the authorities to go along with the plans.

The last trip was by far the most ambitious.

When school was out I wanted to load a couple of Volkswagen buses full of Yamacraw kids and head for California. The California boys promised to meet the caravan when we arrived on the West Coast and take charge of showing the kids their state: camping trips in the Sierras, visits to Disneyland, classes at Santa Cruz, wine vineyards, Hollywood, and Death Valley. I did not know how I would finance this expedition, but I did know that I could and would finance it. If I could carry the kids 600 miles, then I could carry them 3000. It was all a matter of geography, good automobiles, and greenback dollars. Nothing more. And Cowell College people had promised to help with the money.

My first major problem of the year was to find money to finance the trip to Atlanta. The school board would not pay for it, nor would Dr. Piedmont be inclined to siphon funds from another project for the trip. Indeed, it started to look as though the Conroy bank account would be a bit pale and wan when November rolled around. Then Bill Dufford called.

Bill was my high-school principal, a handsome, athletic man who was an extremely capable administrator and one of the finest men I had ever met. I probably chose teaching as a career because of him. To him education was as holy a profession as the priesthood. It was one of his greatest gifts that he could convey his sense of mission about education to the kids who came under his jurisdiction. A whole tribe of us went into teaching because of his influence. Some, like Bernie Schein, even became principals.

Yet Bill was required to undergo the same

transitions we faced during the 1960s. He had once made the statement that he would never be principal at a school that had a nigger in it. When he was a segregationist, he was a rabid defender of white supremacy and all it stood for. He had been my principal during the years of total segregation, those mindlessly happy years of my dead youth when Beaufort High School was a beleaguered Camelot, still white but troubled by rumblings from the Supreme Court. Those were joyous years, though. Bill walked the halls laughing, speaking to every kid he saw, and creating a sense of community and belonging that I had never known before. Two years later, Roland Washington, a slender black, walked into Beaufort High School in an act of singular bravery. He probably did not hear the walls of Jericho crumble behind him.

Bill left the year after Roland integrated the high school. He went to the University of Florida to pursue his doctorate. I wrote him frequently while he was there and visited him several times during the summer months. Though forty years old, Bill Dufford was undergoing a miraculous change. The change was similar to what was happening to tens of thousands of other people around the South, but with Bill the change was not enough. It became a religion and the religion had ultimately to lead to action. He eventually became the principal of a high school in Sumter, South Carolina. In a single year he transformed a plodding school rife with racial tension to the finest school in the state. His sideburns were a little long, though, and he was known to be openly sympathetic to the problems of the black students. The board of education pressured him constantly and decided it would be

323

best if he pursued his career elsewhere. Bill accepted this setback as a wound in a holy war.

He then took a job with the Desegregation Center of South Carolina. This rather controversial group was composed of South Carolinians dedicated to easing the strain of total integration in the state. They would go to a school district, talk to the teachers reluctant to accept change, talk to students, and initiate programs to aid the district in the transition to the unitary school system. It was in his capacity as assistant director of the Desegregation Center that he called and offered me a job at Ridgeland, South Carolina, as a consultant. The job paid sixty-five dollars a day, lasted five days, and would provide enough money to get my kids to Atlanta. I jumped at the chance.

I could not tell Dr. Piedmont about the job, since he associated the Desegregation Center with the bubonic plague. He had made his feelings known during the preschool teacher conferences, when he blasted the center as a bunch of 'outside agitators.' I planned to teach until noon, made an excuse to Mrs. Brown, turn my class over to Vivian, and get to Ridgeland by three o'clock. Mrs. Brown would become apoplectic if she discovered what I was doing, but I was determined to follow this schedule. If I could not follow it, I planned to take five days of personal leave to earn the money. In Beaufort County teachers are entitled to ten days of leave a year.

But before I could initiate this plan of action, Vivian went to see Dr. Piedmont and Mr. Bennington to talk about her own plans for the school on the island. When she got back to my house, she told me that Piedmont and Bennington did not hide the fact that they despised me and were out to get me. She was afraid that I would be fired if I left school at noon to go to Ridgeland. She was worried that the administrators would find out.

This was a serious blow to my plans. I did not wish to fight Piedmont again. Nor did I wish to give him an excuse to drive his foot up my behind. So I decided to take the second plan of action. I drove Vivian and Jim to the dock where I had put the boat in Bluffton. I gave Vivian lesson plans for the week, told Jim how to run the boat, and told Vivian to tell Mrs. Brown that I was taking personal leave. I would be back the following Monday. 'Tell the kids we are going to Atlanta,' I shouted to them, as they pulled away from the dock.

The week proved fascinating. The Desegregation Center was the first I had ever seen of a coalition of blacks and whites operating together for the same purpose. The group was southern, well educated, and articulate. The town of Ridgeland had considerable trouble acclimating itself to total integration. A few boycotts of white students soon led to a boycott of black students. Parents of both races were screaming that the school system could not survive unless desperate measures were initiated. Thus, the invitation to the Desegregation Center.

The week was full of meetings, sensitivity groups, films, and conversation. Many of the white teachers parted with the old ways reluctantly, but there was a certain magnificence in seeing white-haired old ladies sincerely attempt to understand the coming of the new age. Black teachers told the whites of the old days, when a glance at a white girl meant the flow of blood. The

325

week was a poignant ceremony of opposing forces trying to find common ground for the good of the community's youth. In all it was an emotional week, not a miraculous one but one in which I was glad to have been a part. And including expenses and travel, I had earned over $400 for the trip to Atlanta.

That Sunday night I recounted several scenes of the week in Ridgeland to Barbara. I had just finished taking a bath with Jessica and Melissa, when the phone rang.

A familiar voice on the other end of the phone said, 'Hello, Pat, this is Doctor Piedmont. Where have you been this week?'

'Working for the Desegregation Center of South Carolina,' I answered.

'Well, I don't want you goin' back to the island. You hear me? I don't want you to go back there.'

Then the receiver clicked on the other end of the phone. My first reaction was to reflect momentarily on Piedmont's tone of voice. I had never heard such raw, physical hatred emanate from a human voice before. His tone was malignant. It shocked me that I could inspire such hatred from another human being. Only a little later did I realize that I had been fired.

Then it was war. My days of walking the streets as the golden-haired jock returned to the community to teach were officially over with that phone call. Piedmont was not just making idle threats on a Sunday night; he meant to destroy my teaching career and drive me out of town. The day after the phone call I received a letter from Piedmont. In the letter he specified the reasons I had been fired: disobeying instructions,

326

insubordination, conduct unbecoming a professional educator, and gross neglect of duty. Along with the letter was a severance check, which would be my final remuneration from Beaufort County. The cold precision and organization of the death blow were extremely impressive. On the following night, the board met and enthusiastically concurred with Piedmont's decision. In a span of forty-eight hours, I had been exorcised from Yamacraw Island.

I do not react well to crisis. My first thought was to race over to Piedmont's house, knock at his door, and put a fist against his jaw. I never function with dignity when a crisis confronts me, but rather with a terrible emotionalism that is childish and soon regretted. But after my initial volcanic sputtering and railing against the demons who plotted my downfall, I took stock of the weapons I had at my command.

I had been in Beaufort longer than Piedmont, seven years longer, and I considered that a great psychological advantage. Friends that I had gone to school with now ran gas stations, fixed air conditioners, sold dresses, and cut hair around the county. I could turn to them, ask them for their help, and be assured that their bitching would be loud enough to reach the sensitive ears of the board members. I could turn to old students and ask for their help. I could go to local politicians. And finally, I could go to the newspapers. Before I could be officially fired, I had a chance to appeal before the board. It took no towering intelligence to conclude that this appeal would be crucial to my career as a teacher. I wanted public opinion to be stirred up, whether for me or against me.

There was an excellent chance that it would be against. In this eleventh hour, there was but one fact that stacked the deck against me, and I knew it well. In the previous spring Barbara had received a letter from Mary's mother. The letter was barely literate, but its message was clearly elaborated and needed no translation. She asked if Mary could live with Barbara and me the next year when she had to leave the island for high school. Mrs. Toomer said that Mary loved our home, felt comfortable there, and wanted to live with us. Evidently Mrs. Toomer had managed to live in twentieth-century America and retain a startling innocence about the relationship between blacks and whites. Or perhaps she thought that since Barbara had frequently invited the children over for weekends, that it was only a natural extension of these visits for Mary to stay the entire year. Whatever her thoughts, she put the dilemma into Barbara's hands.

We discussed the request in depth. Both of us feared the reaction of the neighbors. We were sure The Point would not exactly embrace the idea of an integrated household. Yet we both felt that Mary had a fighting chance to make it in the world if she received the proper encouragement. The pregnancy rate was quite high among girls leaving the island and the supervision of their parents. So Barbara wrote back to Mrs. Toomer and said we would be delighted to welcome Mary into our home and family the following year.

Of course we immediately received letters from mothers of Frank and Top Cat asking if their sons could live with us the next year too. When the smoke had finally cleared away and the school term began, we had three black ninth graders living in our spacious white home on the historic Point. I had a theory that if you did something quietly and without fanfare, you could get away with it, but the presence of three black kids irritated some people with far more power and influence than I wielded. Some ugly talk circulated behind our backs and some felt this ugly talk encouraged Piedmont to place my head on the chopping block. Indeed I had trouble choosing my most heinous crime. I had embarrassed Piedmont in front of his board, and I had brought niggers into my home. It looked as though the Old South was still alive and well, a little more subtle, without the sheets and night riders, but a force that still tolerated little deviation from the norm.

On Tuesday I went to see one of the local politicians to enlist his help. I recited the entire story to him from the beginning, let him know I had voted for him in the last election, and finally, received a valuable lesson in survival from him. I learned that politicians are not supposed to help people. They simply listen to people, nod their heads painfully, commiserate at proper intervals, promise to do all they can, and then do nothing. It was very instructive. I could probably have enlisted more action from a bleached jellyfish washed ashore in a seasonal storm.

The great powers of Beaufort would not help me. So, in desperation, I turned over my only trump card. I went to the people of Yamacraw. I called a meeting at the community house on Wednesday afternoon. I sent word that I wanted to talk to all of the people about my dismissal. Richie Matta, my singing friend, offered his boat and we went to the island for the meeting. Edna Graves met us at the dock in her ox cart, looking far younger than her seventy years. Her eyes were afire when she saw us. As I walked up the dock, she shouted, 'We gonna strike the school. We gonna strike the school.'

It was an odd meeting that day. The Yamacraw people were not a political people. They tended to be passive during crises and concurred with the unwritten law that the bad times would pass after a while. Throughout their history, they had found it easier and safer to ride the waves no matter how savage or dangerous it became to do so. The white man made the decisions and enforced the rules; the black man paid lip service to these rules then lived according to his own tradition. The purpose of the meeting was to let the islanders know what exactly happened and why it happened. I wanted them to know that white men sometimes played dirty with white men, too.

About fifty people had assembled in the community house. All my students were there looking puzzled and disquieted by the recent chain of events. I began talking rapidly and angrily. It was not a speech I gave that day, but a harangue. Conrack discovered that afternoon, much to his dismay, that he had a bit of demagogue in him. I told them exactly what I thought about the administration, the island school, and the education their children were receiving. In the middle of my delivery, one lady shouted, 'Let's get a petition.'

'Petitions were fine this summer, but they ain't worth a damn now,' I answered. 'The time for petitions is over.'

Then Edna the Beautiful said majestically, 'Only one thing to do. We gonna strike the school. Ain't no chillun gonna go to that schoolhouse door.'

Then all the mothers were shouting, 'We gonna strike the school. Strike it startin' tomorrow.'

I issued a warning about the danger of a boycott. 'If you strike the school, you are going to have men coming out here threatening to put you in jail. Bennington's gonna come to your doors with a carful of white men and say you've gotta get your kids back in school. The sheriff will come out here and say it's against the law. It is gonna take more guts to strike the school than anything you've ever done.'

'Man, that ol' empty school bus gonna look so sweet ridin' by my house with no chillun in it,' said Cindy Lou's grandmother.

'Anybody send their chillun to school, they git beat up bad by the other parents,' Edna said.

'Beat 'em with sticks,' cried another voice.

I turned to my students right before they left the room. Richard and Saul were crying. The other kids still looked puzzled.

'I will try like hell to get back to teaching you,' I said. 'I promise I will try like hell.' And it was ironic to note that one of my most voluble supporters at the meeting was Iris Glover, the alleged root doctor and mistress of darkness whom I once had identified as the greatest threat to my survival on the island. It seemed like a good omen.

The next morning the yellow school bus drove the long dirt road that ran the length of the island without a single child in it. The Yamacraw Island boycott had begun.

* * *

But the people and I knew nothing of power and

331

how it works. We were to have several swift and unforgettable lessons. The day after the boycott began a man appeared on the island and went from door to door delivering a stern message. If the children were not in school by Monday, the parents would face a thirty-day jail sentence and a fine of fifty dollars per day, in violation of the compulsory-attendance law. This plunged the island into a mild panic and many of the mothers feared that the man was the harbinger of the law. On Monday four children were back in school. It was interesting to note that the children who broke the boycott had parents who worked in the school and whose only income was derived from the school being open. A rumor spread that these two mothers had been threatened with the loss of their jobs. When I heard about this intimidation, I returned to the island to tell the people that the compulsory-attendance law had never been enforced in the state of South Carolina. Edna Graves was one of the first people I talked to that day.

'Did a man come to see you, Edna?' I asked.

'Yeh, he come to say some stuff.'

'What did he say?'

'He tell Edna that she go to jail if she don't send no chillun back to that school. He tell me that I owe fifty dollar for ev'ry day my chillun not in no schoolhouse. I tell him to get his ass out my yard. I tell him he can put Edna under the jail for ninety-nine years. Her chillun ain't goin' to no schoolhouse.'

A group of mothers had gathered in Edna's yard. I told them that they were going to have to play it tough from now on. They nodded their heads in solemn agreement. Lois, Ethel's mother, said that another man had come to her house and said that her welfare checks would be cut off if she didn't send her children back to school. I tried to calm her down and explain that some white people would say anything to get them to return their children to school. Then I asked the six mothers why they had all gathered at Edna's house. This was the largest congregation of mothers I had ever seen at a private home.

'We waitin',' one of the ladies said.

'Waitin' for Lizzie,' the lady replied. Lizzie was Mary's mother.

'Why?'

'We gonna beat her up,' was the answer.

'Why are you gonna beat her up?'

'She break the strike. We say we beat up anyone who break the strike. She break it. So we beat her good.'

'Oh, that's great. That is just great. Man, you cannot just go around beating up people who don't agree with the strike. If Lizzie doesn't want to keep her children out of school, then that's her business.'

'We jes' gonna hurt 'er a little bit.'

'No, I don't want that to happen. Lizzie is probably worried she's gonna lose her job. Don't hold that against her.'

'You keep her girl, Mary, in your house, don't you?' Edna said.

'Yes, Edna, you know I do.'

'The whites don't like those colored chillun stayin' wit' you, do they? That's why they tell you to leave Yamacraw. You got colored chillun in your house. They don't want nobody who helps the colored. Nobody, I tell you. If I were you, I'd go home and t'row Mary into the street. If her mama cain't keep her chillun out a no school, I wouldn't keep her gull in my house in Beaufort.'

'Lizzie is just afraid, Edna. She isn't doing this because she is against us. She is just afraid.'

'Edna ain't afraid of nuttin'.'

'I know that, Edna. But you can't beat up another person because they are.' Lizzie was not cudgeled that afternoon, though someone must have exerted a certain amount of pressure on her. For on the next day the boycott was total again. The next day was significant for another reason, for it marked the very first time that Henry Piedmont felt the compulsion to set foot on Yamacraw Island.

He came with Bennington and the truant officer. It was to be the classic show of force, the moving of the big guns into strategic position. They called for a meeting at the schoolhouse to begin at one o'clock. No one showed up. Bennington then went around the island, rounding people up, and telling them they were required to attend the meeting with the superintendent of schools. I watched the action around the school from the edge of the woods. Sidney and Samuel had led me from Edna's house through the swamp and across the pond to a spot that gave us a commanding view of the entire scene. Six people eventually arrived for the meeting. Edna was one of them. I could hear her shouting for the rest of the afternoon.

Piedmont told the parents some interesting things. He told them I had not paid my rent when I lived on the island. He told them I had not paid my electric bills. He told them that many times I had left the landing at Bluffton and had never arrived on Yamacraw. It had also been reported that I spent a

334

large amount of my time in the nightclub on Yamacraw. This Conrack was not an honorable lad. He was not worth following. Piedmont reiterated the threat of jail and fines, then left. I never found out how he liked his first trip to the island.

A reporter for a local Beaufort paper had come with me to the island. He was not allowed inside but listened at the door. By the time the meeting was over, he was ready to break the story to Beaufort. I had said nothing to the press prior to this day since I wanted to give Piedmont, the board, and the politicians time to reconsider their decision. After this, I was going to sing like a canary to anyone who would listen. But when I got home that day I heard that the draft board was reclassifying me 1-A. I was being outflanked again.

On Friday I called off the boycott completely. Too many of the women were frightened by the economic and legal threats against them. When I talked to them, some of them would almost weep out of fear. The threats, spoken and unspoken, about reprisals against those who supported me increased each day. I finally decided that the boycott was more of a prop for my deflated ego than something that was doing the island and my students any good. It was not worth the suffering etched in the faces of these parents who were trying so hard and succeeding at being brave. Edna, however, would not send her grandchildren back to school. I pleaded with her and she shook her head firmly. Nor would Cindy Lou's mother send her children back. Their personal boycott lasted a week longer than anyone else's. Curiously enough, Edna did not receive her Social Security check for five months after the boycott.

The next act in the circus was my appeal before the board of education. I had enlisted the help of George Trask, a young Beaufort lawyer, to present my case before the board. George was astonished at the ferocity of the charges levied against me by Piedmont. He also told me that the law gave great powers to school boards and that all they needed to impale me was 'good and sufficient cause.' In the parlance of lawyers, I could urinate on the wrong part of a commode and if the board of education decided that this was 'good and sufficient' reason for dismissal, then the courts would automatically side with them. It looked rather bleak, but I had decided to fight it anyway.

When I walked into the board room on a tension-filled Tuesday night, I knew instantly that I would lose this phase of the appeal. The board members wore immovable, intransigent expressions, the unblinking faces of soldiers in a Greek tragedy. The dentist on the board sneered when he saw me. The doctor felt much too self-righteous to sneer. The entire board had all the more cheerful characteristics of a lynch mob. My friends had assembled again, a far more somber, truculent group than before. They had come to watch an execution and they saw no way to prevent it. The members of the board had already closed their minds to arguments on my behalf and all the laws of the world could not prevent them from rendering a decision against me. Yet the meeting brought out some emotional responses from the administrators that I will always treasure. Piedmont responded to a question from George Trask at the beginning of the meeting by saying, 'I run the most democratic school system in the country. If a teacher doesn't like something his principal does, then he can come to me with his complaint. If I do not give him a satisfactory answer, he can appeal to the board of education. Pat should know this better than anybody. He's the only teacher I know of that has followed this chain to the top. Of course, Pat feels that teachers are afraid of me. I told him that no one should be afraid of me.' Nor did he sense the irony in his words as he addressed the assembled crowd. And Bennington later answered a question from a board member by saying, 'Mr. Conroy does not communicate well with his elders. Communication is his major problem.'

After it had been proven that Mrs. Brown left the island for ten days without telling anyone, George Trask said to the board, 'You've got a principal at your school who doesn't inform anybody when she is absent on school days and doesn't make any provisions for substitutes. You don't do anything to her. You've got a teacher at your school who sends the authorized substitute with lesson plans and you fire him. As I say, the whole thing is absurd.'

My stomach crawled throughout the entire meeting; it felt ulcerous and dangerously acidic. The people who rose to defend me did so out of desperation. All of us knew what the final result would be. The talking was simply a showy preliminary to the final banishment. Eventually, however, George motioned for me to rise and give my farewell address.

The speech was not exactly my forte. I would have preferred to tell the board members to kiss my baby-pink behind. But the only chance I had was to crawl before the nine judges who stared at me. I traced my teaching career in the county. I told them

337

how I had been offered the job of assistant principal at the high school but turned it down because I wanted to remain in the classroom. Then I told them that when I found out that school was a place of timeclocks and rules, of teachers more concerned with attendance reports than with students, and students praying for the day of graduation when their reprieve from the stale grip of public education would be granted, I tried to make my classes a stimulating experience for my students . . . life experiences, creative experiences. I tried to get them to drop prejudices and conditioned responses from their thinking. In essence, I tried to teach them to embrace life openly, to reflect upon its mysteries, rejoice in its surprises, and to reject its cruelties. Like other teachers, I failed. Teaching is a record of failures. But the glory of teaching is in the attempt. I dislike poor teachers. They are criminals to me. I've seen so much cruelty toward children. I've seen so many children not given the opportunity to live up to their potential as human beings. Before you fire me, ask yourselves these questions that I feel are most critical and essential in the analysis of any teacher who comes before you. Did he love his kids? Did he love the act of teaching? Did his kids love him? If you answer negatively to any of these question, I deserve to be fired.

*   *   *

After this saccharine presentation, the doctor glared at me and asked, 'Why are you trying to intimidate us?' George finally ended my defense by suggesting that the members of the board read a book that seemed to apply to the case, *Catch-22*.

The board voted to sustain my dismissal. But because they were exemplary men, they offered me the chance to resign with honor and without a blot on my record, if I did not take the case to court.

Two months later Judge Street ambled heavily into his courtroom. Everyone rose according to custom. Dr. Piedmont rose, as did Bennington, Mrs. Brown, Ted Stone, and several board members summoned to testify against me. All the major protagonists of the year stood reverently as Judge Street cleared his throat, shuffled a few papers, then brought the court to order. It would be convenient to report that Judge Street was a gum-chewing illiterate ex-Klansman elevated to the judgeship by decadent politicians who wished to preserve the status quo. On the contrary, he was a magnificent man with a stentorian voice and a gray, leonine head who gave the appearance that justice was a frail maiden whom he served with unswerving fidelity. He treated all the witnesses with paramount consideration, though I thought he treated all the lawyers in the court with a visible contempt.

The trial was interesting. Most of my witnesses were from the island. The O.E.O. boat was making a special trip at seven o'clock in the morning to bring the seven parents who were testifying in my behalf. When the captain tried to start the engine, he discovered that the ignition system, which had worked perfectly the night before, did not even turn the engine over. At precisely the same time, the people saw Ted Stone's boat pass their stranded boat on the way to the trial. The people later told me that a part was missing from the engine. I did not have any witnesses from the island, but I learned still another lesson in the exercise of power.

The trial was a necessary, but masochistic, ritual. People from my past paraded to the witness stand to prove that I was really Jack Armstrong and not Godzilla. The administration paraded witnesses to the stand to show that I was a lousy teacher, a liar, an impudent troublemaker, and a discredit to the hallowed profession of teaching. I also had tried to politicize my students by letting them draw black power posters on the bulletin board. During the trial Piedmont did discover that Bennington and Sedgwick had authorized the use of the gas. His arguments that I did not follow the chain of command were a bit tepid after that. The judge discovered that the only punishment that existed in Piedmont's democratic kingdom was instant dismissal.

'Doctor Piedmont, what other punishment could you have levied against this young man besides firing him?'

'We have no other punishment, Your Honor.'

'You have no lesser punishment than dismissal? You mean if he is late to school a couple of times, you have no punishment like docking his pay or reducing his leave time?'

'Our teachers all obey the rules. We never have to discipline them.'

'You have certainly disciplined this young man, Doctor Piedmont. You fired him. That is a form of discipline, isn't it?'

Dr. Piedmont came down from the witness stand nervous and shaking. He was the final witness in the two-day trial. I walked up and shook his hand, and told him that I hoped the ordeal had not been

340

too painful. He responded by saying that I must always do what I thought was right, no matter what the consequences might be. After all the crap, Piedmont and I still grudgingly liked each other. Of course, I have to admit of a momentary desire to milk his rat as we stood there talking.

The lawyers, my friends, and I thought we had won the trial. The rest of that week was a celebration; the smoke had finally cleared and the villains had been exposed. Naturally we lost. When the judge delivered his opinion, he stated that the board of education was invested with the power to fire any teacher it considered undesirable. That was the law. It was very, very simple.

CHAPTER TWELVE

So Conrack, defrocked and slightly dishonored, retired to his room to write about his year on Yamacraw. It was a strange year, a kind of seasoning among the marshes, the migrating fowl, and the people of the island. I had to write this book to explain what happened and how it affected me. When I was severed from the school, I knew I had lost a relationship of infinite and timeless value, and one that I would never know again. For no matter how many accusations or charges the administration could summon up, it did not alter the fact that the kids and I really liked each other. In fact, it did not alter anything.

At first there was the time of great bitterness when I prowled about my room trying to fathom why I represented such a threat to Piedmont and

Bennington and why they felt compelled to extricate me from the island school. During this period they appeared, in my eyes, as evil incarnate. That they would fire me so insensitively was one thing, but that they would try to destroy my personal reputation was another. What they did was not simply a removal from office, it was a blood vendetta and for many months I could not talk about either man without becoming enraged.

But just as time heals the marsh grasses that wither and perish in the winter cold, so does it quell the storms that often threaten the human soul. And as time passed, so did my anger. When the anger subsided, I could see the message in the chaotic flow of events that had conquered me. The eye could focus clearly when it was not clouded with personal indignation. And eventually I gained a distance and could look back at people and places of the past year, frozen in event and memory, calcified and motionless in a grand chronology that began and ended in the month of September. When I finally reached the summit of this metaphorical hill, it was then and only then that I could come to some truce or understanding about myself and the people of Yamacraw Island.

I saw the necessity of living and accepting bullcrap in my midst. It was everywhere. In teachers' manuals, in the platitudes muttered by educators, in school boards, in the community, and most significantly, in myself. I could be so self-righteous, so inflexible when I thought that I was right or that the children had been wronged. I lacked diplomacy and would not compromise. To survive in the future I would have to learn the complex art of ass-kissing, that honorable American

342

custom that makes the world go 'round. Survival is the most important thing. As a bona fide ass-kisser, I might lose a measure of self-respect, but I could be teaching and helping kids. As it is, I have enough self-respect to fertilize Yankee Stadium, but I am not doing a thing for anybody. I could probably still be with the Yamacraw kids had I conquered my ego.

I also saw that Piedmont and Bennington were not evil men. They were just predictably mediocre. Their dreams and aspirations had the grandeur, scope, and breadth of postage stamps. They had rule books and Bibles and gold clubs and nice homes on rivers. They were deacons in their churches, had read to their congregations from the Good Book, and had delivered the message of Jesus in Sunday school. They quoted the Bible liberally and authoritatively and felt the presence of the Savior in their lives. They did not feel the need for redemption, because they had already been redeemed. The only thing they could not control was their fear.

It was so easy before. Segregation was such an easy thing. The dichotomy of color in the schools made administration so pleasant. The black schools were reservations where the sons and daughters of cotton pickers were herded together for the sake of form and convenience. Piedmont and Bennington, in turn, presided over student-council elections at the white schools, sat in a place of honor at football games, chaperoned school dances, and kissed the comely blonde elected homecoming queen. No more. That era of history had ended and will not come again. Now the homecoming queen might be named Ruby, Rosa Lee, or Jemima. There are very

343

few school dances because of that omnipresent southern fear that a sinister black male with an elongated, elephantine gland might approach a honey-vaginaed white maiden with a twinkle in his eye. Even the football games and elections seem different and potentially explosive.

It was once so much nicer. They controlled black principals who shuffled properly, who played the role of downcast eyes and easy niggers, and who sold their own children and brothers on the trading block of their own security. These men helped grease the path of the South's Benningtons and Piedmonts as they slid through the years. The important things were order, control, obedience, and smooth sailing. As long as a school looked good and children behaved properly and troublemakers were rooted out, the system held up and perpetuated itself. As long as blacks and whites remained apart—with the whites singing 'Dixie' and the blacks singing 'Lift Every Voice and Sing,' with the whites getting scholarships and the blacks getting jobs picking cotton and tomatoes, with the whites going to college and the blacks eating moon pies and drinking Doctor Pepper—the Piedmonts and the Benningtons could weather any storm or surmount any threat. All of this ended with the coming of integration to the South.

During the entire period of my banishment and trial, I wanted to tell Piedmont and Bennington that what was happening between us was not confined to Beaufort, South Carolina. I wanted to tell them about the river that was rising quickly, flooding the marshes and threatening the dry land. I wanted them to know that their day was ending. When I saw them at the trial, I knew that they were soldiers

344

of the rear guard, captains of a doomed army retreating through the snow and praying that the shadows of the quick, dark wolves, waiting in the cold, would come no closer. They were old men and would not accept the new sun rising out of the strange waters. The world was very different now.

Mrs. Brown was perhaps the most tragic of all the protagonists in the masque of Yamacraw. She was a woman victimized by her own insecurity. She wanted so badly to be accepted by whites. She luxuriated in the praise freely heaped upon her by Ezra Bennington. She emphasized over and over the fact that she was part Cherokee Indian, educated in a private school, and in no way related to the blacks who inhabited Yamacraw Island. She learned to hate me because I did not agree with her opinion of the island people. I imagine it was a liberating and purifying experience for her to be able to hate a white man. Mrs. Brown, I discovered, had nothing to do with my being fired. In fact she was not told of this action until after it happened. She was used as a pawn at the trial. The whole affair frightened and confused her. She once had talked to me about moving to Columbia and opening a pie shop behind her house there. I hope she does it and I hope she sells a million pies. I do not hope that she continues to teach children, but I do hope that she is happy the rest of her life.

Ted and Lou Stone will remain on Yamacraw until they die. They are permanently rooted in the island's history and soil. Though their attitudes would fit more comfortably in an earlier period of American history, their relationship to the people is a symbiotic one. Despite their paternalism, they help the people who need help and are the most stable institution on the island. I was the troublemaker they always feared and they exulted when I was permanently exiled, yet they were often kind to me and did me many favors that were unsolicited and spontaneous. They see a terrible world about to storm the fortress of their island and they cannot quite understand why it must come so soon. They are just people trying to fend off the apocalypse from their shores.

The town of Beaufort continues to undergo change, not revolutionary change, but gradual and slow change, like the erosion of a high bluff during spring tides. A kind of brotherhood hides beneath the shadows of columns and the mute verandahs—unspoken, inchoate, but present nevertheless. There is no widespread denunciation of the old values, but the erosion of these same values is already irreparable. For ten years I have been part of the town and have seen her grow more human and her people grow more tolerant as the past has crumbled and the old dreams burned out in a final paroxysm of sputtering paralysis and rage. The South of humanity and goodness is slowly rising out of the fallen temple of hatred and white man's nationalism. The town retains her die-hards and nigger-haters and always will. Yet they grow older and crankier with each passing day. When Beaufort digs another four hundred holes in her plentiful graveyards, deposits there the rouged and elderly corpses, and covers them with the sandy, lowcountry soil, then another whole army of the Old South will be silenced and not heard from again. The religion of the Confederacy and apartheid will one day be subdued by the passage of years. The land will be the final arbiter of human conflict; no matter how intense the conflict, the victory of earth and grave will be undeniable and complete. The eyes of the town are turning with excruciating reluctance toward the new flow and the new era. The eyes seem a bit brighter and less clouded with hate.

Of the Yamacraw children I can say little. I don't think I changed the quality of their lives significantly or altered the inexorable fact that they were imprisoned by the very circumstance of their birth. I felt much beauty in my year with them. It hurt very badly to leave them. For them I leave a single prayer: that the river is good to them in the crossing.